1-2-3® FOR WINDOWS™ HYPERGUIDE

Michael P. Griffin and
Jennifer Flynn

alpha
books

A Division of Prentice Hall Computer Publishing
201 W. 103rd Street, Indianapolis, Indiana 46290 USA

International Standard Book Number:1-56761-271-7
Library of Congress Catalog Card Number: 93-71675

96 95 94 93   9 8 7 6 5 4 3 2 1

Interpretation of the printing code: the rightmost number of the first series of numbers is the year of the book's printing; the rightmost number of the second series of numbers is the number of the book's printing. For example, a printing code of 93-1 shows that the first printing of the book occurred in 1993.

Screen reproductions in this book were created by means of the program Collage Plus from Inner Media, Inc., Hollis, NH.

Printed in the United States of America

Publisher
Marie Butler-Knight

Associate Publisher
Lisa A. Bucki

Managing Editor
Elizabeth Keaffaber

Acquisitions Manager
Stephen R. Poland

Production Editor
Linda Hawkins

Copy Editor
San Dee Phillips

Cover Designer
Jean Bisesi

Designer
Roger Morgan

Indexer
Craig Small

Production Team
Diana Bigham, Katy Bodenmiller, Brad Chinn, Scott Cook, Tim Cox, Meshell Dinn, Mark Enochs, Howard Jones, Beth Rago, Carrie Roth, Greg Simsic, Marc Shecter

Special thanks to Kelly Oliver for ensuring the technical accuracy of this book.

TABLE OF CONTENTS

PART II   BAM! IT'S A WORKSHEET

PART III   TUNE UP, TURN ON, PRINT OUT

V

PART V   GETTING GRAPHIC

PART VI   DIGITAL DATA DOMINATION

PART VII ELECTRIC ECLECTICA

CONTENTS

PART VIII PROJECTS

A Hip Introduction to 1-2-3 for Windows

If you're too cool to spend all your time at your computer, if you're too sexy for a normal book that explains formulas in boring lingo, if you're too terminally curious to let a mere spreadsheet intimidate you, then check out this book.

The *1-2-3 for Windows HyperGuide* explains the program in clear, concise terms that any chucklehead can understand. It explains how to harness the power of Lotus 1-2-3 Release 4.0 with 34 compact and graphical lessons and 21 projects. You get the steps you need, with a generous heap of screen pictures to show you what's going on. Each brief lesson runs through a critical 1-2-3 for Windows feature, so you can conquer it with no muss and no fuss. You won't get bogged down in a lot of words. Each lesson is snappy and brief but hip, sometimes humorous, and always informative. But wait, that's not all!

 Take a bold step into the world of 1-2-3 for Windows. You'll notice that we've made the first sentence of each numbered step bold. That bold text gives you the basic action you have to take with 1-2-3. You can get the job done by just reading the bold stuff. But, if you want to learn more about why you're taking that action, or want more specifics on making it happen—such as when to use the mouse or the keyboard—read the regular text that supplements the first bold sentence.

When you need to know more about a certain term, you've got it. When you see words that are big and funky **LIKE THIS**, look in the page margin for a HyperTip box that contains those same funky words. The HyperTip will give you the additional information you crave; or when you're in a hurry, you can skip it altogether.

When you see a word treated in *this way,* you can jump to the end of the lesson. The HyperLinks waiting for you there cross-reference the page numbers of other lessons that cover the topic that's treated *this way* in the text—makes it easy to learn more, or jump ahead if you want.

That's enough about the nitty-gritty. Strap yourself in, and party on!

What's the Big Deal with 1-2-3 Release 4.0 for Windows?

Lotus 1-2-3 Release 4.0 for Windows is a major upgrade from the previous release of 1-2-3 for Windows. New features have been added to help you work smarter and faster. New SmartIcons, Quick menus, and the "new and improved" status bar let you point and click to carry out tasks. The functionality of editing data and charts, copying and moving data, working with multiple worksheets, and working with database tables has been greatly improved. New high-power features include the Version Manager—a what-if analyzer for individuals and work groups—and the intelligent charting capability, which allows you to select the data to chart and turn 1-2-3 loose to automatically create a chart complete with titles, legends, and labels.

BLOW-BY-BLOW COVERAGE

This book, with its miserly use of words, its generous use of graphics, and its bumper crop of HyperTips and HyperLinks, makes learning 1-2-3 easy and the information very accessible. The HyperGuide groups lessons about related 1-2-3 for Windows features. Each group forms a part of the book. If you're a rookie, you can begin learning 1-2-3 by starting at the very beginning of the book. If you've already been clued in on spreadsheet basics, you can jump to the part that focuses on a feature you want to learn more about. Here's what you'll learn in each part:

◇ **Part I, 1-2-3 Boot Camp**—Gives you the information you need to get started.

◇ **Part II, Bam! It's a Worksheet**—Helps you to put together a worksheet.

◇ **Part III, Tune Up, Turn On, Print Out**—Shows you how to put the finishing touches on your work and how to print it out.

◇ **Part IV, Local and Global Questions**—A group of lessons that demonstrate how to manage your files, work with multiple worksheets, and control the default settings of 1-2-3.

◇ **Part V, Getting Graphic**—Demonstrates how you can draw objects and chart data.

◇ **Part VI, Digital Data Domination**—Three lessons that cover how to use the 1-2-3 database capabilities and the Version Manager.

◇ **Part VII, Electric Eclectica**—Shows you some more advanced stuff you might want to get into, such as how to customize SmartIcons and automate tasks with macros, and how to protect your work.

◇ **Part VIII, Projects**—Offers 21 projects that tell you about the goodies on the disk and how to use them. With these projects and the disk, you can practice using your new 1-2-3 skills and quickly become a 1-2-3 hot shot!

◇ **Appendix A** gives installation instructions. **Appendix B** offers a complete display and description of each of those "clickable," timesaving pictures called SmartIcons.

TRADEMARKS

All terms mentioned in this book that are known to be trademarks or service marks are listed below. In addition, terms suspected of being trademarks or service marks have been appropriately capitalized. Alpha Books cannot attest to the accuracy of this information. Use of a term in this book should not be regarded as affecting the validity of any trademark or service mark.

1-2-3 and Lotus are registered trademarks of Lotus Development Corporation.

Microsoft and MS-DOS are registered trademarks and Windows is a trademark of Microsoft Corporation.

Part I

1-2-3 BOOT CAMP

The lessons in this part of the book give you a jump start with 1-2-3 for Windows so that you can do your thing—start building worksheets. 1-2-3 Boot Camp shows you how to start up 1-2-3, choose commands, manage files, get help, and use those "clickable" little pictures called SmartIcons.

TUNING IN TO 1-2-3 FOR WINDOWS

Because 1-2-3 for Windows is a Windows-based program (as if you couldn't figure THAT out), before you can start 1-2-3, you must **START WINDOWS** and be familiar with a couple of Windows basics. The most mission-critical basic—using the mouse—is covered next. If you haven't installed 1-2-3, flip now to Appendix A of this book, or whip out the *Lotus 1-2-3 Release 4.0 for Windows User Guide*, which is included with the software, and follow Chapter 1 instructions for installing 1-2-3.

A RODENT-INFESTED ENVIRONMENT

If you're good with the mouse (and I know you are), then you'll find starting 1-2-3 and moving around the worksheet and the worksheet window a piece of cake. If you're mouse-aphobic, you may want to practice with one because the mouse (or some other type of pointing device) is the fastest and most intuitive way to use 1-2-3 for Windows. 1-2-3, like other Windows-based applications, offers a graphical user interface (GUI) that provides visual cues (such as on-screen windows and pictures called icons) for using mouse shortcuts to command your programs. In a GUI, you move the on-screen **MOUSE POINTER** and click a button to choose and select items, such as menus commands, icons, cells, and charts, and to carry out tasks.

The bottom line is: You're not going to survive Windows unless you master four basic mouse actions. Know them. Love them. Live them.

HYPERTIP

When you **START WINDOWS**, your system loads the Windows program into memory and opens the Windows Program Manager, the main brain that lets you run all other applications. Program Manager is like a desktop on which windows and icons lay around in order (or disarray, if you're like me). If Windows doesn't appear when you start your system, get to the prompt (**C:>** or a reasonable facsimile), type win, and press **Enter**.

HYPERTIP

The on-screen arrow is called the **MOUSE POINTER**, which you can use to move around the worksheet, to select items, and to execute commands.

Action	How to Do It
Point	Move the mouse, positioning the mouse pointer on an item of choice.
Click	Point to an on-screen item, and then press and release the left mouse button.
Double-click	Point to an on-screen item, and then quickly press the left mouse button twice.
Drag	Point to an item, and then press and hold the left mouse button as you move the mouse. The item follows the pointer around your screen. When finished dragging, release the mouse button.

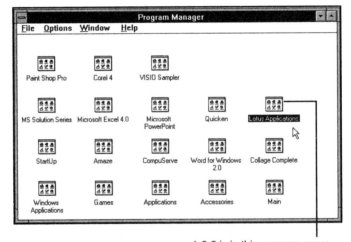

1-2-3 is in this program group.

The Windows Program Manager and the program group icon where you'll find 1-2-3 for Windows.

INITIATE SEQUENCE: STARTING 1-2-3 FOR WINDOWS

After you start Windows, the first thing you will see is the Program Manager. The Program Manager keeps programs in line by organizing them into groups pictured on-screen as program group icons, which are funky, little pictures on the screen. When you move the mouse pointer to one of these icons and press the left mouse button twice (a.k.a. double-click), a group window appears, containing still more icons for the programs contained in the group. You can also open a program group icon by selecting its name from the Window menu—see "2. By Your Command" for more info.

The program item icon that starts 1-2-3

The program group window

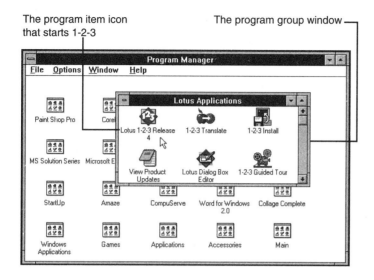

The program group window showing the program item icons for 1-2-3.

Installing 1-2-3 sets up a Lotus Group window holding the 1-2-3 programs and files. Double-click on the Lotus Group icon to open it into a window. Start up 1-2-3 by double-clicking the 1-2-3 program icon or by using the arrow keys to move the highlight to the 1-2-3 icon and then pressing **Enter**.

TOURING YOUR DIGITAL WORKSHEET

So you've started 1-2-3 and a grid and even more icons appear. This work of art is the worksheet window, which contains mysteriously named parts like the control panel, work area, and status bar.

Understanding the parts, purpose, and features of each element of the worksheet window will help you absorb (and remember) the high-speed shortcuts Lotus has wired into this release of 1-2-3 for Windows, so Achtung, Baby!

Control panel

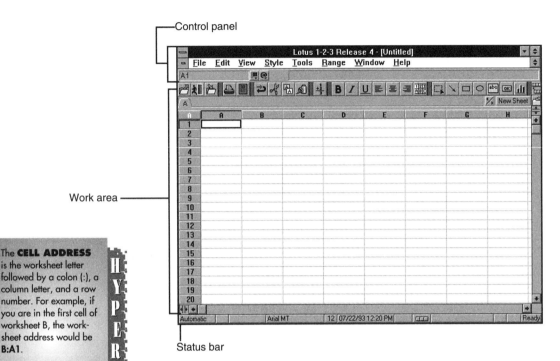

Work area

Status bar

Major regions of the 1-2-3 worksheet.

YOUR CONTROL PANEL

The control panel at the top of the 1-2-3 window displays information about 1-2-3 and the worksheet you're working in. It contains three parts: the title bar, menu bar, and *edit line*. Here you'll find key features to make you a more efficient 1-2-3 user—possibly a 1-2-3 hotshot.

◇ The **menu bar** (or main menu) contains the commands you use to get the job done with 1-2-3. Lesson 2 provides detailed instructions on how to choose menu commands.

◇ The **edit line** consists of the selection indicator, the navigator, the @function selector, and the contents box. See Lesson 6 for details on using the edit line.

◇ The **selection indicator** displays the **CELL ADDRESS** of the worksheet parts you are working with, such as a cell, a **RANGE** of cells, a chart, or an object.

◇ When you click on the **navigator**, it spits back a list of *range* names used in the file you are working with. Click on a range name; leap to it pronto. Range names are groups of cells which you've given a noncryptic (hopefully) name for snappy reference.

⬦ The @function selector gives you a quick way to enter *@functions* (special calculations) into your worksheet; just click and choose one from the list.

⬦ The contents box displays entries you are typing or editing. Lesson 6 gives much more detail on how to use the different elements of the edit line.

⬦ The title bar shows the name of the file you are working on. When you initially start up 1-2-3, the title bar shows that you are working on a worksheet without a name [**Untitled**].

The menu bar contains commands that let you get busy.

The name of your file appears here in the title bar.

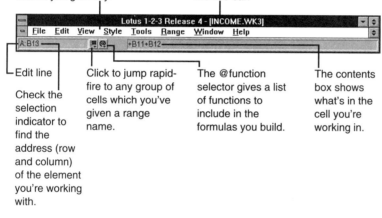

Edit line

Check the selection indicator to find the address (row and column) of the element you're working with.

Click to jump rapid-fire to any group of cells which you've given a range name.

The @function selector gives a list of functions to include in the formulas you build.

The contents box shows what's in the cell you're working in.

Dominate your worksheets: The control panel.

A CALCULATOR ON STEROIDS: THE WORK AREA

Spreadsheet programs let you hash and rehash data until it proves or disproves any point you want it to. Few limits exist in the kinds of formulas (calculations) you can create. Calculate the data. Sort it. Move it around, chart it, or annotate it with text and arrows. All this action happens in the work area: the section of the 1-2-3 window between the control panel and the status bar. The work area contains **SMARTICONS**, worksheet tabs, the tab scroll, new sheet buttons, and the file windows that you are working within.

SMARTICONS, the square buttons in the 1-2-3 window, let you skip the tedium of finding the command or macro you want to choose. To execute the task represented by a SmartIcon, just click on it. Use the **Tools SmartIcons** command to change the set of SmartIcons displayed in the work area and to create new SmartIcons for macros.

You can click on *SmartIcons* to access shortcuts. Worksheet tabs look like the tabs on file folders. They appear just above the worksheet that you are working on to let you name the worksheet. Files in 1-2-3 for Windows can contain more than one worksheet so you can work with multiple sets of data. When you start up 1-2-3, the file that appears ([**Untitled**]) displays a single worksheet tab labeled as **A**—the default name given to the first worksheet. You can add more worksheets to the file as you need them and customize the name on any tab by double-clicking on it and typing a new name. Tabs also allow you to move easily between worksheets by clicking a particular worksheet's tab to move to it.

Worksheet tabs let you name worksheets. Double-click on a tab and type a new name. Click on a tab to move to a particular worksheet.

Tab scroll buttons. Click to scroll the tabs left or right without changing worksheets.

Click to turn off worksheet tabs and view only one worksheet.

New Sheet button. Click to insert a new worksheet after the current worksheet.

SmartIcons

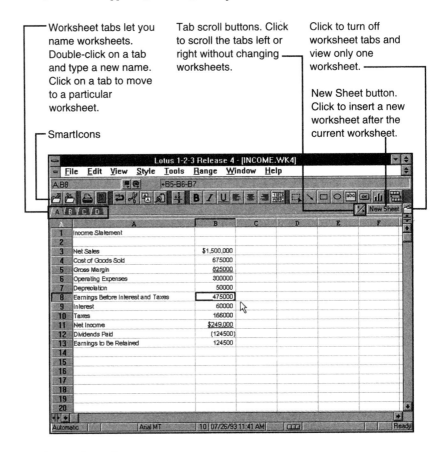

Get busy in the work area.

CHECKING OUT YOUR SITUATION ON THE STATUS BAR

The status bar hangs at the bottom of the 1-2-3 window. It displays information about the current selection (the highlighted cells or other object) and the current file. It also holds the status and mode indicators for 1-2-3, which not only display statuses and modes but let you change statuses and modes. Clicking on a status or mode indicator will either display a list of choices or instantly toggle (change) 1-2-3 to a new setting.

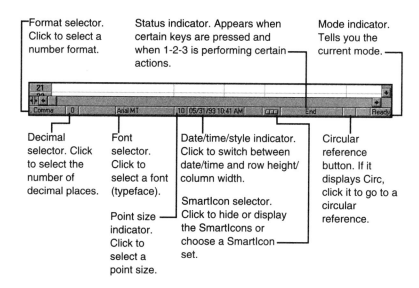

Status reporting from the status bar.

The oh-so-cryptic status indicators appear on the status bar only when you press certain keys or when 1-2-3 performs actions it wants to give you a "heads up" about (whether you wanna know or not). Table 1.1 runs down the status indicator lineup so you can ID them when you need to.

TABLE 1.1 *The Cypherpunk Guide to 1-2-3 for Windows Status Indicators on the Status Bar*

Status Indicator	Appears When . . .
Calc	You need to recalculate formulas by pressing **F9** (CALC), or whenever 1-2-3 is performing a background formula recalculation.
Circ	You enter a formula that contains a circular reference (refers to itself).
Cmd	A macro is running.
End	You press the **End** key to use it with a pointer-movement key.
Group	The current file is in Group mode.
RO	The current file has read-only status. Read-only status means you cannot save changes to the file unless you get the file reservation.
Step	You press **Alt+F2** (Step) and select Step to run a macro in Step mode.
Zoom	You press **Alt+F6** (Zoom Pane) for a full-window view of the current pane or worksheet.

To find out what's happening with 1-2-3, look to the mode indicator. You can find the mode indicator at the right end of the status bar—it tells you what mode (or state) 1-2-3 is currently in. Table 1.2 decrypts 1-2-3 modes.

TABLE 1.2 *The Altered States (Modes) of 1-2-3 for Windows*

Mode Indicator	What the Bleep It Means
Edit	1-2-3 is waiting for you to edit an entry because you pressed **F2** (Edit), are currently entering or editing text in a text box, or you made an incorrect entry.
Error	Some action has caused 1-2-3 to display an error message.
Files	You're using the 1-2-3 Classic menu command to display a list of file names.
Label	You're entering a label. A label is any cell entry you begin with a letter or label-prefix character, such as an ' (apostrophe), " (quotation mark), or ^ (caret).

Mode Indicator	What the Bleep It Means
Menu	You activated the main menu by clicking the menu bar, or pressing **Alt** or **F10** (Menu).
Point	You specified a range before choosing a command.
Ready	1-2-3 is ready for you to enter data or choose a command.
Value	You entered a value. A value is an entry that is a number, a formula, or an @function.
Wait	1-2-3 is completing a command or process.

WHERE ARE YOU?

You know where you are and you determine where to go by the cell address. The cell address consists of a worksheet letter followed by a colon (:), a column letter, and a row number. For example, if your cell pointer (rectangular highlight in the worksheet) is in the first cell of worksheet B, the worksheet address would be **B:A1**.

A block of cells is called a range. It can be as small as one cell or as large as all the worksheets in a file. You identify ranges by the addresses of the first and last cell.

For example, the range for a three by four cell area in the very top left corner of the B worksheet is **B:A1..B:C4**. You also can give names to ranges; the range names make more sense and are easier to remember than the letters and numbers in a cell address. For example, if a range contains projected sales, you could name it **SALES** using the **R**ange Name command. You can learn more about how to name blocks of cells and how to work with ranges by reading "7. It's the Range (Not the Frequency)."

JAMMIN' AROUND THE WORKSHEET

To do your thing in 1-2-3, you first need to select the cell or range you want to work on. To select a cell with the mouse, you click it and the cell pointer (rectangular highlight) moves to that cell, making it the current cell. You can also use the arrow keys to move around the worksheet. For you to do anything to a cell or range, such as enter data in it or format it in anyway, you must make the cell current. To select a range, you:

 Point to the cell in one corner of the range, and press and hold the left mouse button.

2 Highlight the range by dragging across the worksheet until the range is highlighted.

3 Release the mouse button.

"7. It's the Range (Not the Frequency)" gives more detail about how to select what you want to work on.

DO NOT PASS GO: GO DIRECTLY TO THE CELL YOU WANT

By pressing **F5** (GOTO), you can do the equivalent of the **Edit Go** To command. That is, you can quickly move the cell pointer to a specified cell, a named range, another worksheet, another active file, a drawn object, a chart, or a query table.

If you know exactly where you want to move to, the quickest method might be the **Edit Go** To command or **F5** shortcut. With this command, you can jump to specific cells, ranges, charts, drawn objects, and databases. If you don't know how to issue commands using the 1-2-3 menu bar, see "2. By Your Command."

1 Click on Edit in the menu bar, and then click on Go To. This displays the Go To dialog box.

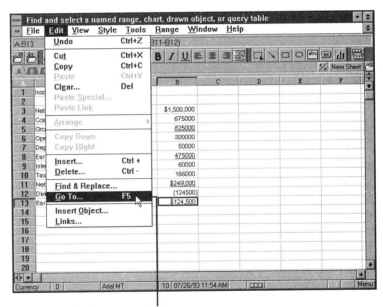

Choose Edit Go To or press F5 to display the Go To dialog box.

In the Type of item drop-down box, select the item type by clicking on the arrow to drop down the list of items, and then click on an item. The item types include things, such as ranges that you've assigned a name to (more on this later in the book), charts, and drawn objects.

┌Enter range name or select the name from the list box.

Select the type of item you want to go to.

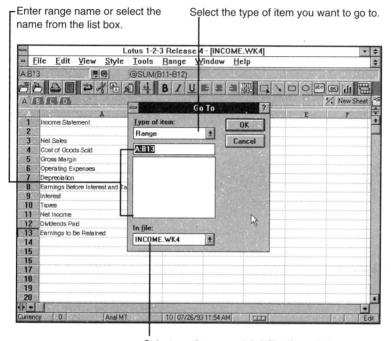

Select another open 1-2-3 file, if needed.

 To go to an item in another open 1-2-3 file, select the file in the In file drop-down box.

 Enter the name of an item in the text box, or select the item in the list box by clicking it.

 Click OK or press Enter.

RODENT FEAR AND LOATHING . . . MOVING AROUND WITH THE KEYS

If you really *have* to (ambitious soul, aren't you?), you can move around the 1-2-3 worksheet by using the keyboard keys. 1-2-3 offers key combinations that move the cell pointer around the worksheet when 1-2-3 is in Ready mode.

Really large and probably obvious hint: when this book tells you to press something like **Alt+F**, it means you should press and hold the **Alt** key, and press **F**. But don't forget to release those keys. Table 1.3 provides the key to these shortcuts.

TABLE 1.3 *Getting There in a Key or Two*

Key Combination	Gets to This Point
Ctrl+Home	Moves the cell pointer to cell **A:A1** in the current file.
Ctrl+← or Shift+Tab	Moves the cell pointer left the number of columns currently visible in the window.
Ctrl+→ or Tab	Moves the cell pointer right the number of columns currently visible in the window.
End+Home	Moves the cell pointer to the lower right corner of the worksheet's active area.
End+→ or End+←	Moves the cell pointer right or left to a cell that contains data and is next to a blank cell.
End+Up or End+Down	Moves the cell pointer up or down to a cell that contains data and is next to a blank cell.
Home	Moves the cell pointer to cell **A1** in the current worksheet.
Pg Up or Pg Dn	Moves the cell pointer up or down the number of rows currently visible in the window.
→ or ←	Moves the cell pointer right or left one column.
↑ or ↓	Moves the cell pointer up or down one row.

H Y P E R L I N K S

BY YOUR COMMAND

My fun, faithful dog is called Bo. Say "speak," and that dog barks its head off. Ask him to lay down, and he drops like a rock. Tell him to "come" when he's making a beeline for some fluffy girl dog, and . . . well, he's still working on that one.

In addition to being useful for basic dog management, commands let you tame the raw power of 1-2-3 for Windows (which tends to behave a little more reliably than Bo does). You choose commands from menus listed in the menu bar. The menu bar menus are only the beginning—sort of gateways to specific actions or tasks. When you choose a menu name from the menu bar,

a pull-down menu appears, showing a list of options—a group of related commands. For example, when you choose **V**iew from the menu bar, it displays a list containing these possible selections: **Z**oom In, Zoom **O**ut, **C**ustom, Freeze **T**itles, **S**plit, and Set View **P**references— all commands that in some way control the display settings of your 1-2-3 worksheets.

When you kickstart 1-2-3 for Windows, the menu bar (also called the main menu) appears directly below the title bar in the 1-2-3 window. The menu bar smorgasbord offers these menus (and commands):

File	Commands that create, maintain, and print worksheets and charts.
Edit	Commands that rearrange data and objects, manage links, and undo commands and actions.
View	Commands that control the worksheet display settings.
Style	Commands that control the appearance of data on the screen and in printed documents.

Tools   Commands that allow you to draw objects, query a database, audit formulas and data in a worksheet, use macros and add-ins, and change defaults.

Range   Commands that manipulate and analyze ranges of data in your worksheets.

Window   Commands that control the display of the Worksheet and Transcript windows.

Help   Commands that allow you to get on-line help.

The underlined letter in a menu name is its selection letter.

| ⊟ | File | Edit | View | Style | Tools | Range | Window | Help | | ▲▼ |

A close-up and personal look at the menu bar.

There are (count 'em) two ways to choose menus from the menu bar:

◇   *Click* on a menu name. (I'd use this method. The next ways slow you down.)

◇   Press the **Alt** key, or press **F10** (MENU) to activate the menu bar, and then press the **SELECTION LETTER** in the menu name.

The menus on the menu bar change depending on the deed you're doing on the worksheet. For example, if you click on a *chart* in your worksheet, the **R**ange menu is replaced by the **C**hart menu in the menu bar.

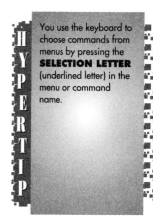

You use the keyboard to choose commands from menus by pressing the **SELECTION LETTER** (underlined letter) in the menu or command name.

POINT, CLICK, AND GET OUT OF THE WAY: CHOOSING COMMANDS WITH THE MOUSE

Rolling down a menu doesn't get you where you want to go, though. You're obligated to pick a command from the list that appears. Choose the **COMMAND** and Bam! 1-2-3 does

something—presumably what you wanted it to do. Using the mouse is the fastest way to choose a command, and here's how it goes:

Any **COMMAND** with a triangle beside it in the menu displays a submenu when selected. Click on one of the options in the submenu to select it.

Point to the name of the menu you want in the menu bar and click the left mouse button. 1-2-3 drops down the menu.

17

⌐Click on a menu name . . .   If you point to a command and hold down the left
mouse button, the title bar flashes the lowdown on
that command.

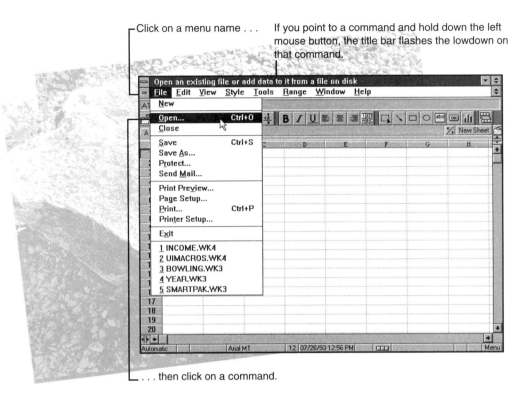

L . . . then click on a command.

 Point to the command you want and click the mouse button. 1-2-3 executes
the command or displays a dialog box into which you must enter or choose
additional information.

GOING KEYBOARD COMMANDO

If you prefer to rough it and use the **KEYBOARD** to choose commands, you can. (You can also drive from coast to coast instead of hopping on a plane if you don't mind spending days instead of hours to get to the same place.) Here's how to select a command with the keyboard:

 Press ALT or F10 (MENU). 1-2-3 highlights the menu bar.

 Press the selection letter in the name of the menu you want to pull-down.
The menu drops down below the menu bar.

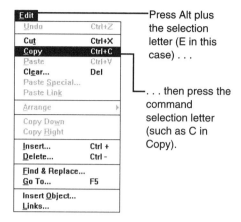

Press Alt plus the selection letter (E in this case) . . .

. . . then press the command selection letter (such as C in Copy).

 Press the selection letter in the name of the command you want.

CONDUCTING A MEANINGFUL DIALOG WITH 1-2-3

As if choosing a menu and a command isn't enough work, selecting a command with an ellipsis (...) beside it displays a dialog box where you have to make even more selections. Sheesh! The dialog box, which is a small window, contains options you can select, or you can enter text to tell 1-2-3 how you want a particular command carried out. After selecting options and/or entering text in a dialog box, you confirm and complete the command by choosing (clicking on) the **OK** button. If you want to back out of the command, you can select the **Cancel** button or press **Esc**.

Dialog boxes are easy to use once you've got some navigational experience in one. Mouse your way around a dialog box as much as you can for speed and convenience. Simply click on the option you want. (You can also press **Alt** plus the **option selection letter** to choose or jump to one of the options.) Option buttons, check boxes, and list boxes are the key dialog box elements, and here's a plain English description of each of them:

◇ **Option buttons** are round selection buttons. You can select only one option button in a group of related options by clicking on it. A selected option button contains a black dot.

◇ You select **check boxes** to turn an option on or off. When an **X** appears in the check box, the option is on, and conversely, when the box is blank, the option is off.

◇ Some dialog boxes also contain **command buttons** (they're the rectangular ones like the **OK** button) that you click on to execute a command or display another dialog box for even more command control. For example, the Print dialog box contains the Preview button, which you can click to see on the screen what your worksheet will look like when you print it.

◇ A **list box** is a list of choices. Click on the box to move to it. Some of the choices in a **LIST BOX** may not be visible without using the scroll bar

(click on the arrow at either scroll bar end to move the list) or the arrow keys to bring the other choices into view.

◇ A **text box** is a rectangular area into which you enter and edit text after you click to select it.

◇ A **drop-down box** shows a single option until you click the scroll arrow to the right of the option; then a list of options appears in a **DROP-DOWN BOX**. Some drop-down boxes give you the option of typing text while others require you to select an option.

When a dialog box appears, here's how to deal with it:

 Click each option you want to select. Click a text box to select it, and type the text. When working with a drop-down box, click the arrow to display the list, and click the **ITEM**.

 After making all your selections, click on OK or press Enter. 1-2-3 executes the command.

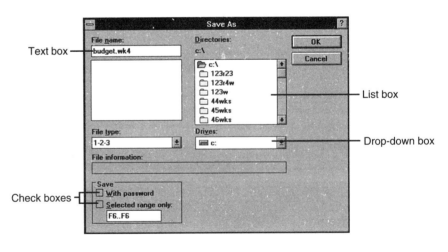

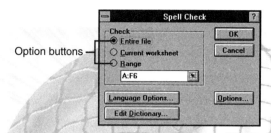

Option buttons ⟶

1-2-3 also enables you to navigate dialog boxes via the keyboard. In some cases, the following keystrokes may actually *be* shortcuts:

Alt+selection letter   Selects the option or command.

Alt+F4   Closes the dialog box without completing the command. This is equivalent to choosing the **Cancel** button.

Alt+Spacebar   Opens the Control menu for the dialog box. The Control menu contains commands to move and close the dialog box.

Alt+↑ or **Alt+↓**   Opens or closes a drop-down list.

End   Selects the last item in a drop-down list or list box.

Enter   Completes the command and closes the dialog box.

Esc   Closes the dialog box without completing the command. This is equivalent to choosing the Cancel button.

Home   Selects the first item in a drop-down box or list box.

Pg Up or **Pg Dn**   Moves to the top or bottom item in the list of items currently visible in a drop-down box or list box, and selects the item.

Shift+Tab   Moves backward to the previous option, from bottom to top and right to left.

Tab   Moves forward to the next option, from left to right and top to bottom.

↑, ↓, ←, or →   Moves within a group of options.

GETTING A RAPID RESPONSE: THE 1-2-3 QUICK MENUS

Even though mousing is pretty fast, it can still bog down a bonzo user. (How many times can you move your pointer up to the menu bar in one minute?) This new version of 1-2-3 has a cure: quick menus. A quick menu lists all the commands you can use with the **CURRENT SELEC-TION**. The commands available on a quick menu depend on what the current selection is; 1-2-3 compiles a quick menu of commands that you probably need with that selection. So, the list of

HYPERTIP

When you use the mouse and keyboard to select (highlight) areas of your worksheet, the element that's selected becomes the **CURRENT SELECTION**. It can be a cell, a range of cells, multiple ranges, a 3D range (which includes more than one work-sheet), a column or row, a worksheet, a drawn object, or a chart. See "7. It's the Range (Not the Frequency)" for details on how to select ranges. When you select a drawn object, chart, or chart element, handles (the small boxes on the edges of the selection) appear around it.

commands available in a quick menu when a range of cells is selected is different from the list available when a chart is selected. 1-2-3 anticipates certain tools that you will need to perform the task at hand and adds those tools to a handy tool box (the quick menu).

Quick menus improve your work speed (it is a contest, after all) by letting you make menu *selections* without having to activate the menu bar. By selecting a range or chart, or whatever, and then clicking the right mouse button, you display the quick menu commands at the location in your worksheet where you are currently working. You click right there

to issue further commands from the menu.

For example, with a cell or range selected, clicking the right mouse button displays a quick menu (with the commands you might need) positioned near the selection. The quick menu for a selected cell or range would contain Cut, Copy, Paste, Clear, Copy Down, Copy Right, Fill by Example, Number Format, Font & Attributes, Lines & Color, Alignment, and Name—commands that usually reside in the **E**dit, **S**tyle, **R**ange menus. Quick menu commands have no selection letters because you can only use a mouse to display quick menus. Here's how to make commanding 1-2-3 quick:

Make a selection.

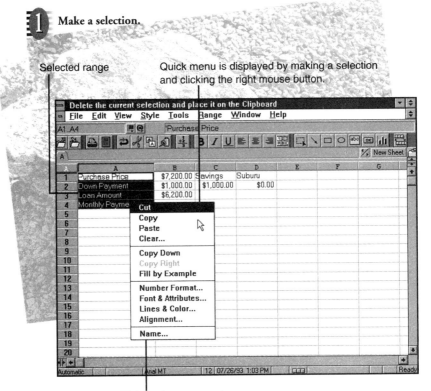

Selected range

Quick menu is displayed by making a selection and clicking the right mouse button.

Click on the command you want from the quick menu.

Click the right mouse button to display the quick menu.

 Point to the command you want and click the left mouse button. 1-2-3 executes the command or displays a dialog box into which you must enter or choose additional information.

JUST UN-DO IT

1-2-3 for Windows generously allows you to bail yourself out when you've boned up and executed the wrong command. 1-2-3 "remembers" what you just did (even if you don't) and has the ability to work backwards to undo your action. For example, if you delete a row from your worksheet and then suddenly realize that you deleted the wrong row—no problem! You can use **Edit Undo** or press **Ctrl+Z** to undelete the row. You can also use **Edit Undo** to reverse the effect of a **MACRO**. Choosing **Edit Undo** after executing a macro reverses the entire *macro*.

The **Undo** feature can pull you out of some minor and major disasters, but there are some actions it can't reverse:

A previous use of **Edit Undo**.

Any type of printer activity.

Cell pointer movement caused by pressing a pointer-movement key or by clicking a cell.

Actions taken by pressing the **F5** (GOTO) function key.

Actions taken by pressing the **F6** (PANE) function key.

Formula recalculations caused by pressing **F9** (CALC) or by updating links.

Changes made to data and settings in inactive worksheets.

Changes made to files on disk.

Changes made to Clipboard contents.

In case you haven't figured it out by now, here's how to use the **Undo** feature:

 Screw up in a major way (in 1-2-3). Do something you wish you hadn't done. Make a mistake. Live a little.

 Choose Edit Undo, or press Ctrl+Z. 1-2-3 will reverse the previous command or action. (If only life had an Undo feature. . . .)

A **MACRO** is a set of instructions, called macro commands, that automate 1-2-3 commands or tasks. The commands are stored like a miniprogram that you can play back with a few simple mouse clicks or a keyboard shortcut. Just about anything you can do with your keyboard or mouse can be automated with a macro.

The **F5** (GOTO) function key moves the cell pointer to a specified cell or range, another worksheet, another active file, a drawn object, a chart, or a query table. After you create panes, which divide a 1-2-3 window like window panes in the windows in your house, pressing **F6** (PANE) moves the cell pointer between panes. Depending on the mode 1-2-3 is in, **F9** (CALC) recalculates formulas (Ready mode) or F9+Enter converts a cell formula to its displayed value (Edit or Value mode). See "1. Tuning In to 1-2-3 for Windows" for more on *modes*.

The Edit menu contains the Undo command,
which reverses the effect of what you did last.

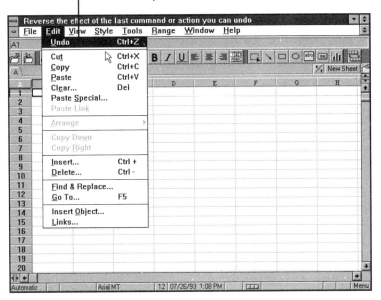

WHEN YOU'D RATHER JUST DO IT

Because the **U**ndo feature of 1-2-3 keeps
information related to your last action in
your computer's memory until you take
another action, you can turn off **U**ndo if
you are trying to conserve memory. You
turn **U**ndo on or off through the **T**ools
User Setup command.

 Choose Tools User Setup.

 Under Options, select Undo to turn Edit Undo on or off.

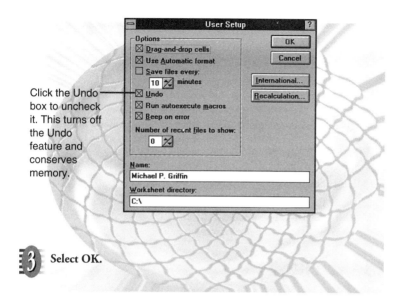

Click the Undo box to uncheck it. This turns off the Undo feature and conserves memory.

 Select OK.

CLASSIC COKE, CLASSIC MENU

If you have worked with DOS versions of 1-2-3 and fear change, you can still use the 1-2-3 commands that you learned using 1-2-3 for DOS. 1-2-3 for Windows offers the 1-2-3 Classic menu—the command menu of 1-2-3 for DOS Releases 2.x and 3.x. For the most part, you can work with 1-2-3 Classic commands just as you worked when you used 1-2-3 for DOS Releases 2.x and 3.x. However, some Releases 2.x and 3.x commands do not operate in 1-2-3 Release 4—they are obsolete. When you highlight an obsolete 1-2-3 Classic

command, the following message appears below the 1-2-3 Classic menu: **Obsolete menu option—has no effect in 1-2-3 Release 4**. 1-2-3 Classic menu commands cannot be executed by using the mouse, so of course using them is usually slower goin'.

If you are becoming a mouse lover, you should jump on the learning curve, forget about the 1-2-3 Classic menu, and start pointing and clicking at the menu bar. But, if you still feel the need to use the Classic menu (you're probably a Classic Coke fiend), here are the steps:

Press / (slash) or < (less-than symbol) to display the 1-2-3 Classic menu, or press : (colon) to use WYSIWYG (What You See Is What You Get) commands. For this step to work, 1-2-3 must be in Ready mode, and the active window must be the worksheet window.

1-2-3 Classic main menu: Better love your keyboard.

1-2-3 Classic WYSIWYG menu: Variation on a familiar theme.

 Select a command by pressing the first letter of the command name or by using the arrow keys to highlight a command, and then press Enter. Some commands display submenus; therefore, you may have to repeat this step to move through the submenus of commands. When you complete a command, 1-2-3 Classic disappears.

To close the 1-2-3 Classic window without completing a command, press **Esc** until you reach the main menu, and then press **Esc** again.

CLASSIC HELP

You can use the 1-2-3 Classic help facility by pressing **F1** (HELP) while you've got 1-2-3 in Classic mode. (Yes, because the Classic commands are different, Classic menu users need a different *help* system than those who choose the new improved flavor.) The Help window flashes open, showing a list of 1-2-3 Classic commands. Click on any one of the commands to display a table showing 1-2-3 Classic commands and how to complete each command in 1-2-3 Release 4.

Click here for Help about performing the equivalent of the Classic command /Worksheet Column in Release 4.0.

The 1-2-3 Release 4.0 equivalent of the 1-2-3 Classic command /Worksheet Erase

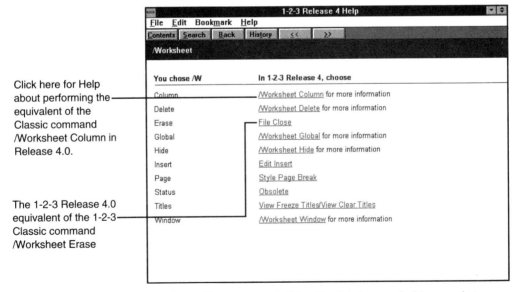

1-2-3 Help for Classic commands. It's a dirty job, but somebody's got to do it.

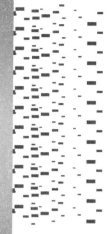

HYPERLINKS

CHART—See "26. The Chart of the Matter," p. 251, and "27. Ch-Ch-Ch-Ch-Changes (to Charts)," p. 266.

CLICK—See "1. Tuning In to 1-2-3 for Windows," p. 3.

HELP—See "4. Frantic Panic, and Where to Get Help," p. 37.

MODES—See "1. Tuning In to 1-2-3 for Windows," p. 3.

MACROS—See "32. MacroMania," p. 308.

SELECTIONS—See "7. It's the Range (Not the Frequency)," p. 66, "25. The Amazing Line and Shape Maker," p. 237, and "26. The Chart of the Matter," p. 251.

IT'S A FILE THING

BIRTH OF A FILE

When you start up 1-2-3, it automatically opens a file for you so you can start filling it with whatever kind of junk you want. Each file can contain many worksheets—up to 256 worksheets per file. Within the file, each worksheet is a single grid of rows and columns. Worksheets are stacked on top of one another, like papers on a desk or in a file folder. Worksheet tabs at the top of the window let you label the individual worksheets in a file. That first file is [Untitled], so before you quit your 1-2-3 session, you must assign it a name and **SAVE** it on a floppy disk or your hard drive. "But hey," you ask, "what if I need to open another new file to share info between two or more new files—how do I do that, hotshot authors?" Authors' snappy comeback: File New. The File

New command creates a new file and places that file in the 1-2-3 window as the current file (with the cell pointer in the new file ready to go, positioned in cell A1). The file that was already open stays open . . . behind the new file.

When you open a new file, 1-2-3 supplies a temporary default file name. The first default file name is **FILE0001.WK4**, the next default file name is **FILE0002.WK4**, and so on; 1-2-3 increases the number in the file name by one for each new file you open (duh!). Unless you don't mind hunting for a file for hours or you've got a photographic memory, you will want to save your new files with descriptive names. For example, if you create a budget worksheet, it would make sense to name it **BUDGET.WK4**.

To open a new file:

1 **Choose File New.** 1-2-3 places that file in the window as the current file. The cell pointer is positioned in cell A1. The first new file you open is named **FILE0001.WK4**.

Default file name is FILE0001.WK4.

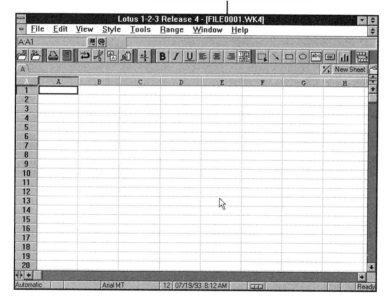

Sch-wing! Here's your new worksheet with the default file name.

I SAVE, THEREFORE I OPEN

Unless you live in an altered reality with more than 24 hours in each day, you will save many of your 1-2-3 files so that you can recycle them later: adding more data, revising formulas, or playing **WHAT-IF**. You also may have 1-2-3 files that were developed by others or actually want to use the 1-2-3 templates (preprogrammed 1-2-3 files that you plug

numbers into) that came with this book for the Projects part. You can open any and all of these files with the **File Open** command. When you open an existing file, 1-2-3 reads the file into memory, makes it the current file, and moves the cell pointer to the cell it was in when the file was last saved.

HYPERTIP

WHAT will net income be **IF** sales increase by 10%? What will our sales be if we capture 15% of the market? What will I have to pay in income taxes if my raise is $3,500? These are questions that you can answer using what-if analysis. There's no end to the business and personal finance scenarios you can dream up and examine by plugging different sets of data into 1-2-3. The 1-2-3 worksheet is a great basic "What if" tool, while the Version Manager, Solver, and Backsolver (see Lessons 30, 32, and 33) are better for more advanced analysis of assumptions and possibilities.

To open an existing file:

 Choose File Open. The Open File dialog box appears.

 Specify the name of the file to open in the File name box. You can do this several ways:

◇ Enter the name in the File name text box if the file you want to open is in the current directory.

OR

◇ Select the file name from the File **n**ame list box by clicking it.

◇ Use the **D**irectories list box and the Drives drop-down box to select a new current directory; then either enter the file name in the File **n**ame text box or choose it from the File **n**ame list box. To "climb back up" a level in the **D**irectories list, double-click on the directory above the one that's currently selected. For example, to back out of the directory **c:\budgets** and return to **c:**, you would double-click on **c:** in the **D**irectories list.

If you know the name of the file and it is in the current directory, you can type it in here.

File name list shows the files in the current directory. Click on a file name to select it.

Change the current directory by clicking on the one you want in the Directories list box.

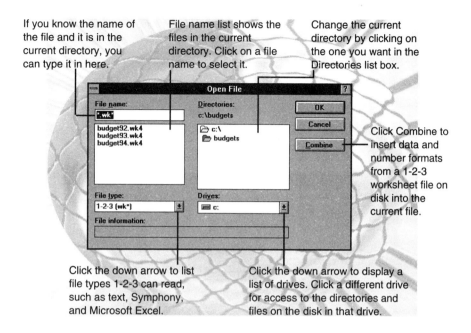

Click Combine to insert data and number formats from a 1-2-3 worksheet file on disk into the current file.

Click the down arrow to list file types 1-2-3 can read, such as text, Symphony, and Microsoft Excel.

Click the down arrow to display a list of drives. Click a different drive for access to the directories and files on the disk in that drive.

 **Choose OK.**

SAVE IT, OR YOU'LL LOSE IT

Before you shut down 1-2-3 for the day, you have to save your file so that you can pick up where you left off the next time you need it. The File Save command saves the current worksheet file on the hard or floppy disk of your choice. If the file you want to save is a new file (that is, you haven't saved it before), then 1-2-3 lets you enter a file name before confirming the save. If you've saved the file before, then the File Save command simply updates the contents of the file on disk, using the existing file name.

When you name a file, 1-2-3 automatically adds the extension **.WK4**. A file extension, found at the end of a **FILE NAME**, consists of a . (period) followed by up to three characters. You can specify an extension different from the 1-2-3 default extension by typing the extension you want when you enter the file name during a save. So, if you wanted all the 1-2-3 files that track your budget for CD purchases to have the same extension, you could save those files with the extension **.BUD**, or some other extension that you would associate with budgeting worksheets.

The **FILE NAME** can be up to only eight characters long (DOS can't handle any more than eight). Any combination of letters, numbers, _ (underscores), and - (hyphens) is okay.

31

To save your 1-2-3 file, begin by *selecting the file* (positioning the cell pointer in) you want to save, and then:

 Choose File Save. If the file is an existing file, you can jump to step 4. If the file is new, the Save As dialog box will appear.

 To name the file, enter a name in the File name text box. If you want to save the file in a different drive or directory, select from the **D**irectories *list box* and/ or the Dri**v**es *drop-down box*.

Name the file by typing a name in the File name text box.

Click here to select a different directory.

Click here to assign a password to the file.

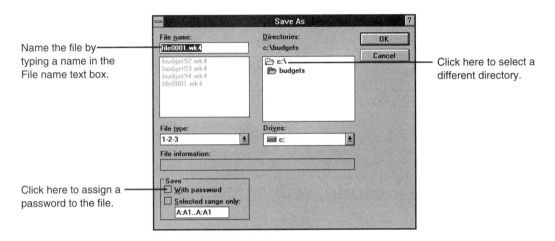

 (Optional) To assign a password to the file, select the With password check box.

 Choose OK. If you selected the **W**ith password check box, 1-2-3 displays the Set Password dialog box, which prompts you for the password. Enter the password in each text box, and then click on **OK**. You are returned to your file.

FILE FINALE

Although you've probably outgrown the stage where you even listen when someone tells you to clean up after yourself, clean up after yourself! When you're done working with a particular 1-2-3 for Windows file, you should save and put it away. Closing a file removes it from your PC's working memory (but does not remove it from disk), freeing up memory that may improve the speed at which 1-2-3 rattles and hums. You close your 1-2-3 files by using the **F**ile **C**lose command. If you have other 1-2-3 files that are open, the **F**ile **C**lose command closes the current file (the one the cell pointer is in) and then moves the cell pointer to the next open file.

Make sure that the cell pointer is in the file you want to close and that you save the changes you made to the file. Then, close it up as follows:

 Choose File Close. If you just saved the file, it will close. Zap. If you haven't saved the file since you last modified it, the Close dialog box will appear. It will ask you if you want to save the file before closing.

 If you see the Close dialog box, select Yes. If the file has already been saved with a name, it will automatically be saved under the same name. If the file has never been saved, the Save As dialog box will appear, allowing you to specify a new file name.

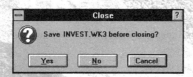

 If the Save As dialog box appears, give the file a name, and click on OK. See "Save It or You'll Lose It" earlier in this lesson if you need a quick refresher course on saving files.

SALIDAS! SORTIE! EXIT!

If you're at all tuned in to the computer world, you probably know that Windows lets you work with several programs at the same time. You can share data between applications (apps) and switch back and forth between apps with a simple mouse click or two. If you're temporarily finished with 1-2-3 but probably will go back to it in a few minutes, you don't need to exit the program. You can simply switch to another open app, such as your word processing program, and then switch back to 1-2-3. For more information on how to switch out of 1-2-3 for Windows, see "Application Surfing" in this lesson.

If you don't think you'll need to switch back to 1-2-3 during the current session, then you should bag it altogether— **EXIT** 1-2-3. By exiting (closing) 1-2-3, you may improve the speed of your other Windows apps by freeing up memory.

You can also **EXIT** 1-2-3 by double-clicking on the Control menu box in the upper-left corner of the 1-2-3 window. The box looks like a square with a minus sign in it. The Control menu displays commands for moving, sizing, and closing the window, and for switching to another Windows application.

When you end a session, the 1-2-3 window closes and you return to the Windows Program Manager. To exit 1-2-3:

 Choose File Exit. If all changes to open files have been saved, 1-2-3 simply closes at this point. Otherwise, follow the rest of the steps for this procedure.

Select Yes in the Exit dialog box. If open 1-2-3 files have changed since the last time you saved then, 1-2-3 displays the Exit dialog box. It asks whether you want to save the changes.

Select Yes to save. If any file isn't named, the Save As dialog box appears.

Select Cancel if you do not want to exit.

Select No to exit without saving.

Select Save All to save all open files. If any file isn't named, the Save As dialog box appears.

If the file already exists on disk, you have to tell 1-2-3 whether you want to:

◇ Replace data already in the file with the changed data (choose **Yes**).

◇ Create a backup of the file before replacing data in it (choose **No**).

◇ **Cancel**, ending the session.

◇ **S**ave All open files.

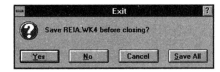

If the file is new, the Exit dialog box appears asking if you want to save the file before exiting. If you do want to save it, click on the Yes button. The Save As dialog box appears, allowing you to specify a new file name. You'll need to enter a file name and click **OK**.

Enter a file name. —

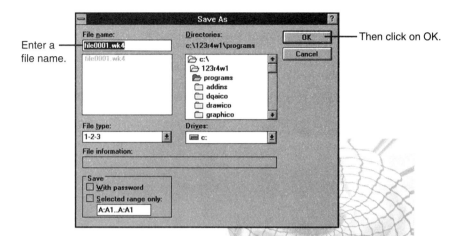

Then click on OK.

APPLICATION SURFING

If you can operate a TV remote, you can switch between open apps in Windows. **SWITCHING** allows you to share data and move quickly from one task to another. For example, you may be using a word processing application to compose a letter and have a need to crunch some numbers. You can quickly switch to Lotus 1-2-3, bang out the numbers, then switch back to the letter. You can switch by using the Control menu box, which is located in the left corner of a title bar.

To switch to another Windows application from Lotus 1-2-3:

 Click on the Control menu box to display the Control menu. It's in the upper-left corner of the window—at the left end of the title bar.

Control menu box—Click to display the Control menu.

Click to display the Task List showing open applications.

SWITCHING may be faster using the **Alt+Tab** key combination to cycle through the open applications. Try it!

 Click on Switch To. The Task List, a dialog box showing open applications you can switch to, appears.

 Double-click on the name of the application you want to switch to.

Double-click on the application's name, and Windows will immediately switch to it.

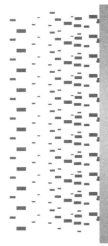

DROP-DOWN BOX, LIST BOX—See "2. By Your Command," p. 16.

SELECTING A FILE—See "20. Border Disputes: Arranging Windows," p. 195.

HYPERLINKS

FRANTIC PANIC, AND WHERE TO GET HELP

Yeah, you've shelled out your hard-earned, cold, hard cash for this book, and it's so help-a-liscious that it's all you'll ever need to get your money's worth out of 1-2-3. However, we authors are under a moral obligation to tell our readers about an application's on-line help facility—which offers answers to 1-2-3 questions at the speed of electricity. On-line help is much more helpful if you've had help learning to use it.

When you need help with such tasks as locating the appropriate command, working a dialog box, or creating macros, you can display a Help window that will give you additional information. The Help feature is context-sensitive, which means that pressing **F1** (HELP) opens the Help window and gives you help on what you're doing in 1-2-3 at that moment. Like, if you're about to select some options in the Set View Preferences

dialog box, while in that dialog box, you can press **F1** (HELP) and display a Help window that describes the dialog box options and how to choose those options.

You also can access Help from the **Help** menu, and use Help as a 1-2-3 on-line reference manual. You can do this in two basic ways. First, you can display a list of Help topics in the 1-2-3 Release 4 Help Contents window by choosing **Help** Contents. Secondly, you can choose **Help** **Search** to use keywords to search for Help topics and definitions of unfamiliar terms and phrases.

Note that there are several "layers" in Help. Almost every screen shows some text in green. The green text indicates you can get further information on the green topic by choosing it. To get help on any green topic, point to it until you see the hand icon, and then click.

Use this button to search for a term.   Returns to previous Help screen

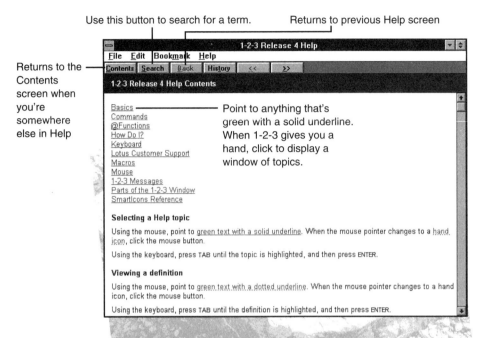

Returns to the Contents screen when you're somewhere else in Help

Point to anything that's green with a solid underline. When 1-2-3 gives you a hand, click to display a window of topics.

Getting a handle on Help . . . 1-2-3 Help Contents window.

Here's a lowdown on each of the categories on the Help Contents screen:

The **Basics** category includes these topics: Entering Data, Copying, Moving, and Pasting Data, Selecting the Data You Want to Work On, Enhancing the Appearance of a Worksheet, Creating a Chart, Creating Drawn Objects, Keeping Records in a 1-2-3 Database Table, Setting Up 1-2-3 to Look and Act the Way You Want, Writing a Formula, and Printing Data.

Commands gives you information on each 1-2-3 command menu.

The **@Functions** category answers the question What Are @Functions?, provides descriptions of individual @Functions, lists @Function categories, and describes the @Function selector.

How Do I? provides information on such important topics as becoming familiar with 1-2-3, creating a worksheet, making the worksheet look the way you want it to look, printing your worksheets, creating charts, analyzing data, and using macros.

Keyboard gives you information on ways that you can use the keyboard to do a variety of 1-2-3 tasks.

Lotus Customer Support tells you how to contact Lotus Customer Support.

Macros tells you what macros can do for you and describes individual macro commands.

Mouse tells you how to use both the left and right mouse buttons.

1-2-3 Messages provides an alphabetical listing and an explanation of all 1-2-3 messages.

Parts of the 1-2-3 Window tells you the names and purposes of each part of the 1-2-3 Window and allows you to take a guided tour of the window.

SmartIcons Reference explains SmartIcons and provides a reference of SmartIcons by menu command.

You also can use keywords to search Help to view a **DEFINITION** of a technical term or to display a window of helpful information about a command or feature of 1-2-3. Stay tuned—searching is covered later in this lesson.

> **HYPERTIP**
>
> You can use Help to view a **DEFINITION** of a technical term. In Help, these terms appear in green with a dotted underline. You know the drill for viewing the definition. . . . Point to green text with a dotted underline, then click when the mouse pointer changes to a hand.

TOGETHER AGAIN ON THE BIG SCREEN

Help just isn't as helpful when you can't see what in the help it's talking about in your 1-2-3 window. If you're new to 1-2-3 or you plan on using some advanced features that you are a bit unsure about, you may be accessing Help often. To make it easier to work, you may want to try *arranging the windows* (1-2-3 and Help) so that both windows remain fully visible as you work like a

banshee. There isn't one specific command or any automatic way of arranging the Help window and 1-2-3 window so that they are both visible on the screen. It's a bit tricky at first—you have to play with it to get the hang of it. To display Help and 1-2-3 together so both are visible on the screen, follow these steps:

 If the Help window fills the whole screen, click the Restore button. You also can click on the **Control menu** box to display the Control menu and click on Restore. You'll know you can restore the window if there's no border around it. After you restore it, the border reappears.

Click on the Restore button if the Window fills the entire screen . . .

. . . or display the Control
menu and click on Restore.

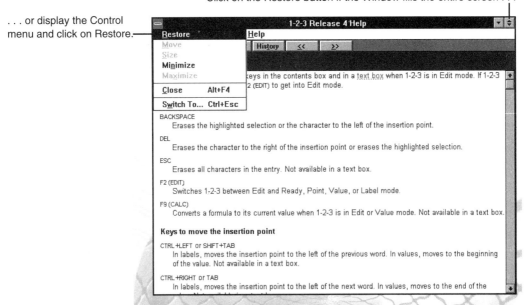

2 **Point to the Help window title bar, hold down the left mouse button, and drag it left.** Release the mouse button when the left border rests along the left edge of the screen.

Point to the title bar, and drag
it to the left side of the screen.

Release the mouse button
when the left border is flush
with the left edge of the screen.

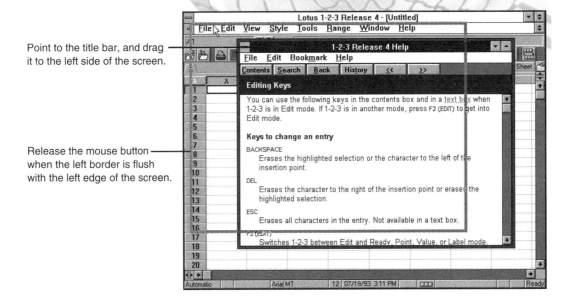

Resize the Help window to fill the left 1/3 to 1/2 of the screen by dragging a top, bottom, or side border. The mouse pointer changes to a white, two-headed arrow when you are pointing to a **BORDER**.

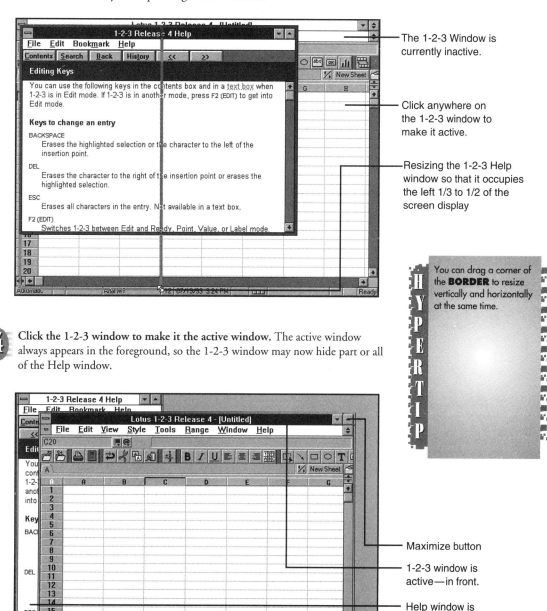

The 1-2-3 Window is currently inactive.

Click anywhere on the 1-2-3 window to make it active.

Resizing the 1-2-3 Help window so that it occupies the left 1/3 to 1/2 of the screen display

You can drag a corner of the **BORDER** to resize vertically and horizontally at the same time.

Click the 1-2-3 window to make it the active window. The active window always appears in the foreground, so the 1-2-3 window may now hide part or all of the Help window.

Maximize button

1-2-3 window is active—in front.

Help window is inactive—in back.

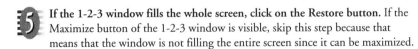

If the 1-2-3 window fills the whole screen, click on the Restore button. If the Maximize button of the 1-2-3 window is visible, skip this step because that means that the window is not filling the entire screen since it can be maximized.

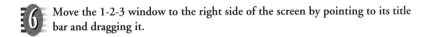

Move the 1-2-3 window to the right side of the screen by pointing to its title bar and dragging it.

Move the 1-2-3 window to
the right side of the screen
by dragging its title bar.

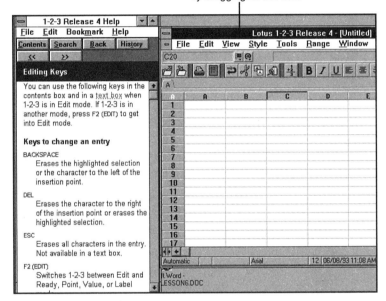

Resize the 1-2-3 window to fill the right side of the screen by dragging a top, bottom, or side border. The Help window retains its position, appearing in the same position the next time you start 1-2-3 and access Help.

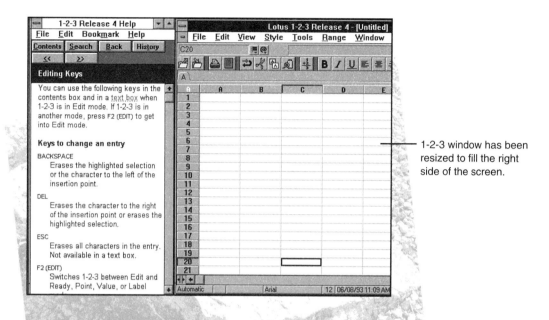

1-2-3 window has been resized to fill the right side of the screen.

IN SEARCH OF . . . HELP

If you've searched all your life for a practical application for even one iota of the geometry junk you had to learn in the tenth grade, here it is. In using Help, the shortest distance between two points is a straight line. That is, searching can be a lot faster than dealing with the green words and the hand icon. With so much information about 1-2-3 in the Help files, you can use the power of your PC to search for Help topics and quickly and efficiently find the information you need.

When using Search, the challenge is to locate a topic by coming up with a keyword or phrase associated with the topic. For example, you know you can press a function key to jump to another area of the worksheet (you're not crazy, you've done it before), but you can't remember the key. You could enter the keyword **Go** and the Help search would show four related topics, one of which is *F5 (GOTO)*—the key you can press to jump to another worksheet location. Isn't that easier than fumbling through the index or table of contents of a reference manual?

With the Help window displayed, you can search for a Help topic, just like this:

 Click on the Search button. 1-2-3 displays the Search dialog box.

Click to start your search.

Type a keyword or phrase in the search text box or select one by clicking on it in the list box. If you type your search keyword or phrase in the text box, the list box scrolls to the keyword that most closely matches what you are typing.

Type a keyword or phrase in the text box.

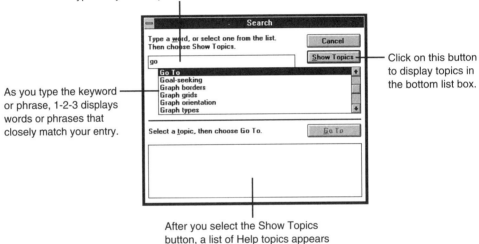

As you type the keyword or phrase, 1-2-3 displays words or phrases that closely match your entry.

Click on this button to display topics in the bottom list box.

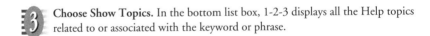

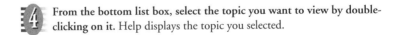

After you select the Show Topics button, a list of Help topics appears here.

Choose Show Topics. In the bottom list box, 1-2-3 displays all the Help topics related to or associated with the keyword or phrase.

From the bottom list box, select the topic you want to view by double-clicking on it. Help displays the topic you selected.

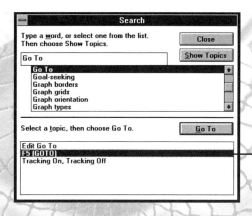

View the topic by double-clicking on it or by highlighting it (clicking on it) and selecting the Go To button.

COPYING FROM YOUR NEIGHBOR . . . YOU'RE NOT IN SCHOOL ANYMORE

For you dinosaurs out there who prefer having everything on paper (and nicely formatted, mind you), or for those of you who live for your own computer crib sheets, there's yet another way you can use Help. You can copy a Help topic to the **WINDOWS CLIPBOARD**. From there, you can paste the Help topic into another application (such as your word processing program), reformat it (even adding graphics if you want), and print it out at a later time.

Here's how to copy Help info onto the Clipboard:

 Go to the Help screen you want to copy. You should know how to get there by clicking or searching by now. If not, go back to the beginning of the lesson. Do not pass Go. Do not collect $200.

 Pull down the Edit menu, and choose Copy.

The **WINDOWS CLIPBOARD** is a temporary storage area Windows uses to store data when you use **Edit Cut** or **Edit Copy**.

45

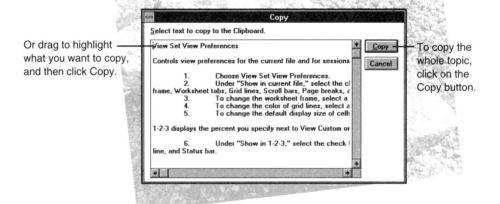

Click on the Copy button. This copies the whole topic to the Clipboard. If you want to copy only a part of the topic, drag (with the left mouse button held down) to highlight the part that you want to copy, and then select the Copy button.

Or drag to highlight what you want to copy, and then click Copy.

To copy the whole topic, click on the Copy button.

Switch to the application you want to paste the Help info into. To *switch to an application*, it has to be running under Windows.

Position the cursor in the document, and then choose Edit Paste. If your application doesn't offer this exact command, you'll have to poke around for one that's similar.

 Format for fun and pleasure, and then print.

LOW-BUDGET HARD COPIES

If you don't have time for the rigmarole of copying Help info to a word processor to *print* it, you can print a down-and-dirty copy from the Help window. In some cases, this may be a more practical alternative to viewing the topic on-screen.

With the hard copy of the Help topic in hand, you can perform the 1-2-3 task without having to resize and reposition the Help window and without having to jump back and forth between Help and 1-2-3.

To print a Help topic from Help, you've got to:

 Go to the Help screen you want to copy.

 Choose File Print Topic. The Print Topic dialog box is displayed to inform you that the topic is being printed.

MORE HELP THAN HUMANS SHOULD BE ALLOWED TO HAVE: ADDING YOUR NOTES TO HELP

You, too, can add your own useful tips or reminders to a Help topic, with the handy-dandy Edit Annotate command

found in the Help window menu system. Just follow these steps, and voilà!

 Go to the Help screen you want to add a note to.

 Pull down the Edit menu and choose Annotate.

 Type the text you want to add in the Annotation text box.

To take a look at **ANNOTATIONS** that you have added, go to the topic that contains the note, and click on the **paper clip** icon. To close the note, choose **Cancel**. To remove an annotation, click on the **paper clip** icon, and choose **Delete**.

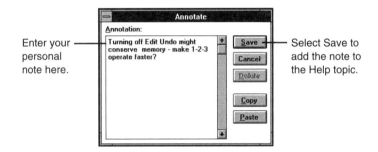

Enter your personal note here.

Select Save to add the note to the Help topic.

 Choose Save. ANNOTATIONS (notes you add to a Help topic) are marked in the text of the topic with a paper clip icon.

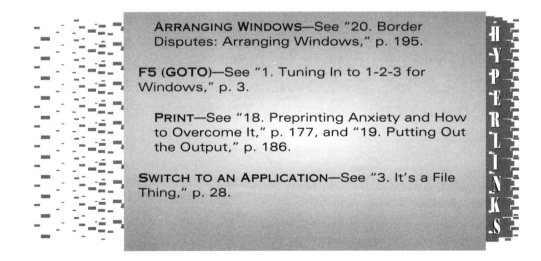

ARRANGING WINDOWS—See "20. Border Disputes: Arranging Windows," p. 195.

F5 (GOTO)—See "1. Tuning In to 1-2-3 for Windows," p. 3.

PRINT—See "18. Preprinting Anxiety and How to Overcome It," p. 177, and "19. Putting Out the Output," p. 186.

SWITCH TO AN APPLICATION—See "3. It's a File Thing," p. 28.

SMARTICONS: PICTURES ON SMARTDRUGS

Software creators are always looking for ways to idiot-proof their programs. One of 1-2-3 for Windows' best "Yo! Stupid" features is the SmartIcons.

SmartIcons appear as the row of small square pictures along the top of the 1-2-3 window. You can click on one of these suckers to bypass the menus. Click and zap! 1-2-3 performs the command or *macro* represented by the SmartIcon without you having to choose menus and select commands. You can't choose SmartIcons with the keyboard, so if you want to, you're simply S.O.L.

You can display only one **SET** (pre-defined group) of SmartIcons at a time. The set of icons that appears in the work area changes depending on what is currently selected. For example, the set of icons that appears when a range of cells is selected is different from the set that appears when a chart is selected.

A **SET** is a named group of icons that you use for the same purpose, like formatting.

CYPHERPUNK SPECIAL

Because most of us need more than a little hieroglyphic to figure out a SmartIcon's purpose, 1-2-3 lets you display a description of each icon without having to risk clicking on it and doing something heinous like deleting your data. (There's always *Undo*.) To learn what the special purpose of a particular SmartIcon is, do this:

 Position the mouse pointer on the icon.

 Press and hold down the right mouse button. The description of the selected SmartIcon appears in the title bar. Amazing!

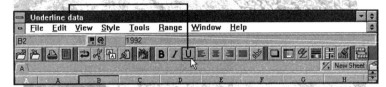

A description of a SmartIcon appears in the title bar when you point to it and press the right mouse button.

CLICKING RIGHT ALONG

Nothing in 1-2-3 is as easy as using a SmartIcon to perform a task or execute a command, like this:

 Position the mouse pointer on the SmartIcon.

 Click the left mouse button. 1-2-3 performs the task or executes the command.

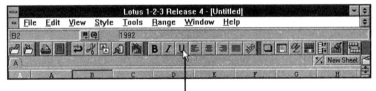

To use a SmartIcon, position the mouse pointer on the icon and click the left mouse button.

CREATING AN ORDERLY CHAOS

You can juggle around the SmartIcon set so that the icons are in an order that is best for you. For example, you may have some favorite SmartIcons that you use the most. It makes sense to position your faves together in the set. Or if you're a southpaw, it may speed you up to move critical icons to the left side of the set where it's more comfortable for you to click on them. (You'll learn even more ways to *customize SmartIcon sets* later in this book.) To move icons in the SmartIcon set that's currently displayed, just:

Hold down Ctrl.

 Drag the icon to its new position. That is, point to the icon, hold down the left mouse button, and move it! If you drag an icon off the set, 1-2-3 will place that icon at the end of the set.

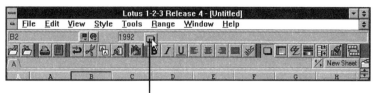

By holding down Ctrl, you can drag an icon
to a new location in the SmartIcon set.

GOIN' MOBILE

When you start up 1-2-3, the SmartIcon set appears at the top of the 1-2-3 window. That is the initial default position. Bor-ing! You don't have to settle for conformity—you can move the SmartIcon set to virtually any on-screen location you want:

 Choose Tools SmartIcons.

 Select one of the options from the Position drop-down box. (Clicking the down arrow beside the list displays your options.)

When you create a **FLOATING SMARTICON SET**, it appears in a window that has all the characteristics of other windows. In addition to dragging this window around by its title bar, you can point to any of its borders and drag to resize it or use its Control menu. This option lets you position your SI set for max efficiency.

Floating creates a **FLOATING SMARTICON SET** that you can move (drag) to any place in the 1-2-3 window.

Left displays the SmartIcon set on the left side of the 1-2-3 window.

Top displays the SmartIcon set at the top of the 1-2-3 window.

Right displays the SmartIcon set on the right side of the 1-2-3 window.

Bottom displays the SmartIcon set at the bottom of the 1-2-3 window.

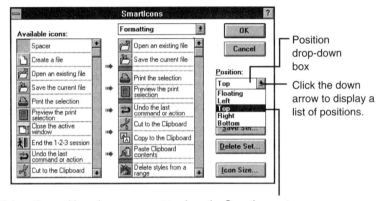

Click on the position where you want to place the SmartIcon set.

 Click on OK.

PICK A SET, ANY SET

For the low, low price of 1-2-3 for Windows, you get the complete, amazing set of default SmartIcons. But wait, there's more! You also get several other **SMARTICON SETS** specialized for operations like formatting. For example, if you are planning to create macros, you can display the Macro Building

SmartIcon set, which includes SmartIcon shortcuts for writing, running, and debugging macros. The quick-and-easy way of switching between SmartIcon sets is to click the **SmartIcons** button on the status bar. To choose a different SmartIcon set:

1-2-3 offers eight **SMARTICON SETS** for your fun and pleasure, but you can create your own sets of SmartIcons, and you can create custom SmartIcons that run macros. To learn how to create your own SmartIcon sets and customized icons, see Lesson 31, "Even Smarter SmartIcons."

Click on the SmartIcons button on the status bar at the bottom of the 1-2-3 window. A list of SmartIcon sets appears above the bar.

Click on the name of the set you want to display.

| 15 |
| 16 |
| 17 |
| 18 |
| 19 |
| 20 |
| 21 |

Default Sheet
Editing
Formatting
Goodies
Macro Building
Printing
Sheet Auditing
Working Together
Hide SmartIcons

Automatic | Arial | 12 | 06/09/93 12:10 PM | Ready

Status bar

SmartIcons button. Click on it
for a list of SmartIcon sets.

 Click on the name of a SmartIcon set.

Default Sheet   The initial set to appear when you start 1-2-3, offering the most-used icons.

Editing   Icons that help you clean up your worksheet, delete items, paste contents and styles, transpose ranges, and insert columns and rows.

Formatting   Icons that help you format your worksheet, add color and borders, select style templates, and change fonts.

Goodies   A group of miscellaneous icons that are not found in the other sets.

Macro Building   Icons that help you create, run, and debug macros.

Printing   Icons that help set up a page, select data to print, set page orientation (landscape vs. portrait), and set print titles.

Sheet Auditing   Icons that let you track what your worksheet is doing; find formulas, cell dependents, and file links; and navigate through the worksheet.

Working Together   Icons that start other Lotus Windows applications, such as Ami Pro, Freelance Graphics, Lotus Organizer, Improv, Lotus Notes, and cc:Mail.

Hide SmartIcons   Select this if you don't want to display a SmartIcon set.

At the far right side of every SmartIcon set (unless it's one that you've changed yourself), you'll see a handy little icon that looks like two rows of icons connected by arrows. Clicking on this SmartIcon displays the next available set. If you know the set you want by sight, just click this icon until that set appears.

This SmartIcon lets you display other SmartIcon sets.

The ubiquitous SmartIcon.

MONSTER SMARTICONS

The initial default size of the icons is medium (there is no small). But you may have an easier time clicking when the SmartIcons are a bit larger. You can increase the display size of the SmartIcons. Here's how:

 Choose Tools SmartIcons.

 Select the Icon Size button.

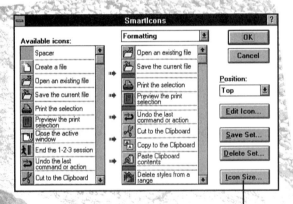

Click here to resize the icons.

Select the Large option button to maximize the size of the icons. If you have already increased to Large, select Medium to shrink the icons back to the initial default size.

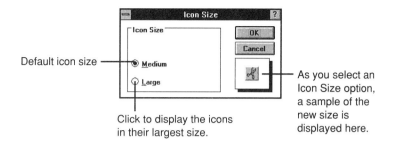

Default icon size —

Click to display the icons in their largest size.

As you select an Icon Size option, a sample of the new size is displayed here.

 Choose OK.

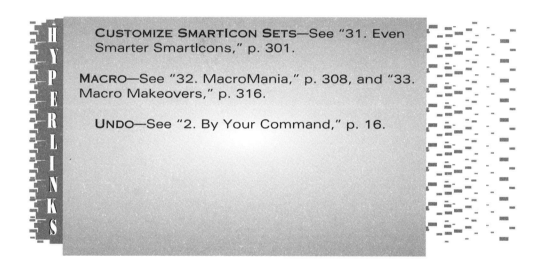

CUSTOMIZE SMARTICON SETS—See "31. Even Smarter SmartIcons," p. 301.

MACRO—See "32. MacroMania," p. 308, and "33. Macro Makeovers," p. 316.

UNDO—See "2. By Your Command," p. 16.

Part II

BAM! IT'S A WORKSHEET

Building a worksheet is a lot like building a house. You begin by laying its foundation and putting up its rough frame. Then you move on to the finish work. With Lotus 1-2-3, your worksheets can be "do-it-yourself projects." You lay the foundation of a worksheet by entering data, formulas, and @functions. In this part, you will learn how to enter data into your worksheets, work with ranges of cells and worksheets, and construct formulas and @functions so you can crunch numbers. And like any do-it-yourself project, you will have to correct mistakes—so Lesson 10 shows how to edit, erase, fix, and replace.

TYPIN' DATA

1-2-3's not going to help you very much until you type some stuff in (it's good, but it's not that good). You begin building your worksheets by first **ENTERING DATA**—labels, values, and formulas. After you start up 1-2-3, you can begin entering data in the worksheet when you see the **Ready** mode indicator in the lower right corner of the 1-2-3 window.

To enter data:

So you think you're pretty smart, and typing data in may seem self-explanatory. You're right, it is fairly easy. Okay, you are pretty smart. But if you take the time to read through this lesson, you may pick up some ideas about how to improve your technique.

> **HYPERTIP**
>
> After **ENTERING DATA** (typing the data) that you want to appear in a cell, you can press one of the pointer-movement keys to complete the entry. For example, if you are entering data in the cells of a row, you can type the data and press the right pointer movement key to complete the entry and move to the next cell.

 Move the mouse pointer to the cell into which you want to enter the data. Click on the cell. If you want to use only the keyboard, use the pointer-movement keys (arrow keys) to move the cell pointer to the cell into which you want to enter the data.

 Type the data. As you type, your data appears in the cell and in the contents box, and the Cancel and Confirm buttons appear to the left of the contents box.

Cancel button. Click if you
change your mind and don't want
to enter data into the cell.

Confirm button. Click or press
Enter to enter data into the cell.

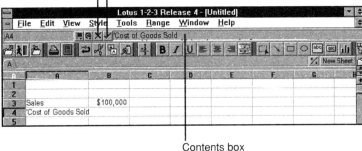

Contents box

 Click on the Confirm button to complete the entry, or press Enter. Your data
appears in the cell. If you click on the **Cancel** button, the contents box is
cleared, and nothing appears in the cell. If, when you click on the **Confirm**
button, you hear a beep, you made an error. Edit your entry, or press **Esc**, or
click on the **Cancel** button to clear your entry and start over.

BETTER VALUES

1-2-3 automatically classifies the data you
enter as either a label or a **VALUE** based
on the first character that you type. That
way, 1-2-3 will not use a label when

calculating a range. In other words, 1-2-3
recognizes a label as having no value. A
value can be a number, *formula*, or
@functions.

 Move the mouse pointer to the cell where you want to enter the number.
Click on the cell. The cell pointer moves to the cell you selected. If you want to
use only the keyboard, use the pointer-movement keys (arrow keys) to move the
cell pointer to the cell where you want to enter the number.

 Type the number. Begin with a number from 0 to 9, or start with a decimal
point. If the number you want to enter is negative, begin with a minus (–) sign.
As you type, your number appears in the cell and in the contents box, and the
Cancel and Confirm buttons appear to the left of the contents box.

Value entries have to start with a number.

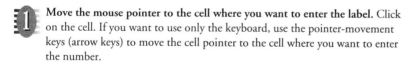

Click on the **Confirm button to complete the entry, or press Enter.** If you click on the **Cancel** button, 1-2-3 clears the contents box and leaves the cell empty.

STICKING ON SOME LABELS

Labels are text entries that can include letters and numbers. For example, an address such as 808 Wood Street is a label. If the first character of your label is a letter, 1-2-3 will automatically precede the entry with a **LABEL-PREFIX CHARACTER**. If the label you are entering starts with a character other than a letter, you have to begin the entry with one of the label-prefix characters to tell 1-2-3 that the entry is to be a label and not a value. Here is a summary of the label-prefix characters:

'	For left alignment
"	For right alignment
^	For center alignment
\	For a repeating label

By default, labels are left-aligned. 1-2-3 precedes the text that you enter with '—the **LABEL-PREFIX CHARACTER** for left alignment.

To enter labels ASAP:

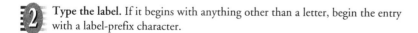

Move the mouse pointer to the cell where you want to enter the label. Click on the cell. If you want to use only the keyboard, use the pointer-movement keys (arrow keys) to move the cell pointer to the cell where you want to enter the number.

Type the label. If it begins with anything other than a letter, begin the entry with a label-prefix character.

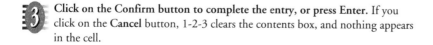

Click on the **Confirm button to complete the entry, or press Enter.** If you click on the **Cancel** button, 1-2-3 clears the contents box, and nothing appears in the cell.

MAKING AN EXAMPLE OF YOUR DATA

You can have 1-2-3 automatically enter data in a range if the range is to have a certain sequence to it. For example, if you want to enter the months of the year in a column, you can enter **January** and then **February**. Then, *selecting the range* of cells that you want to enter the months into, choose Range Fill By Example, and 1-2-3 will enter the month names for you. 1-2-3 can **FILL A RANGE BY EXAMPLE** for any range that will have a sequence to the data in it.

To fill in the blanks:

1. **Select the range to fill.** Be sure to include the data that you have already entered that contains a sequence that 1-2-3 can interpret. For example, if you want to create a sequence with an increment value of 1 (for example, 1 through 12), make sure the first cell in the range contains the value 1. If you want to create a sequence of months, make sure the first cell contains the first month.

    To create a sequence with an increment value other than 1 (for example, 10, 20, 30 and so on), make sure the first two cells in the range contain the data you want 1-2-3 to use to calculate the sequence. If 1-2-3 is unable to interpret a sequence in the data in the first and second cells in the range, it uses only the data in the first cell to fill the range.

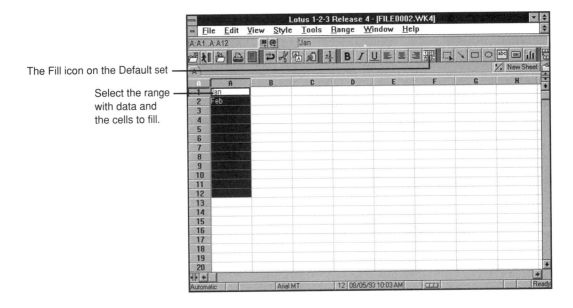

The Fill icon on the Default set

Select the range with data and the cells to fill.

 Choose Range Fill by Example.

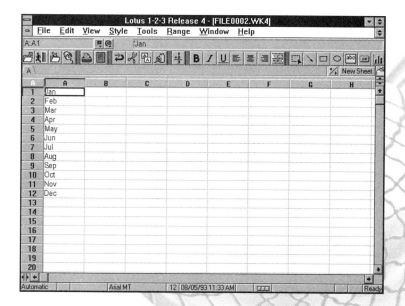

1-2-3 has filled in the months.

I Edit, Therefore I Am

In the third line of the control panel of the 1-2-3 window is a hip little tool called the *edit line*. You can use the edit line to display and edit data in a cell and to move around the worksheet. The edit line contains six parts: selection indicator, navigator, @function selector, Cancel button, Confirm button, and contents box. Table 6.1 describes what you can do with each of these little items.

TABLE 6.1   *Some of the Critters You Use to Edit*

Thang	Thang's Function
Selection indicator	Indicates the address or name of the current selection.
Navigator	A drop-down box that lets you go to and select an item on the worksheet. When you click on the navigator, 1-2-3 displays a list of named ranges in the current file.
@function selector	A drop-down box that lets you insert an @function in a formula.
Cancel button	Allows you to cancel a cell entry.
Confirm button	Allows you to confirm a cell entry.
Contents box	Displays entries you are typing or editing.

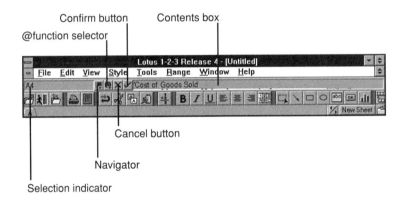

Getting a line on editing.

When you edit data, you either replace an existing cell entry, clear a cell, or correct an error. When you need to replace the entire contents of a cell, you can select the cell and type a new entry. When you are finished typing, simply press **Enter** to replace the previous entry. Retyping an entry is a crude way of editing data. There are better and more efficient ways of doing worksheet editing.

But what if you want to edit part of a lengthy cell entry without retyping the whole entry? No problem. You can edit only those parts of the entry that need changes. Select the cell to edit, and press **F2** (EDIT), or select the cell and click on the contents box in the edit line. Or double-click on the cell to put 1-2-3 into Edit mode.

Probably the quickest of the three editing methods is to double-click the cell and then edit the entry right in its cell. This is a feature new to 1-2-3. Or you do it the old-fashioned way and edit in the contents box. Either way, you can correct errors without having to completely retype the entry.

 Double-click on the cell you want to edit, select the cell you want to edit, and press F2. Or select the cell, and click on the contents box in the edit line. Each one of these actions puts 1-2-3 into Edit mode. When you edit a cell, the insertion point appears to the right of the last character.

Edit the entry. Use the right and left arrow keys to move the insertion point. Press **Del** to delete characters to the right of the insertion point or to erase the **HIGHLIGHTED SELECTION**. Use **Backspace** to delete characters to the left of the insertion point or the highlighted selection. To insert characters, move the insertion point to the appropriate location, and start typing.

When the entry is the way you want it, press Enter, or click on the Confirm button.

You can make a **HIGHLIGHTED SELECTION** within a cell you want to edit by holding down the left mouse button and dragging the insertion point across the characters. For example, if you have characters that you want to delete, highlight them by dragging on them, and then press **Delete**.

@FUNCTIONS—See "9. Forming @Functions," p. 87.

FORMULA—See "8. Calculate This!" p. 77.

SELECTING THE RANGE —See "7. It's the Range (Not the Frequency)," p. 66.

IT'S THE RANGE (NOT THE FREQUENCY)

Okay, so you've typed some things in and you're cruising on this worksheet now. In fact, let's say that you're cataloging all 8,192 of your CDs (which is coincidentally exactly the number of rows available in a 1-2-3 for Windows worksheet), entering the Name, Artist, Date Purchased, Where Purchased, and Purchase Price. You decide the list would look better if the name of each CD was bold. If you're currently between employment gigs and have plenty of time on your hands, you could move the cell pointer one at a time to each name and make it bold. Or you could select all the names and change your worksheet in a single, bold stroke.

To work on data, charts, databases, and other items in your worksheets, you have to select those items first. For example, if you want a group of cells to be formatted as percentages (%), you need to select those cells, and then select the format. Often, the quickest way to work on data is to select a range of cells so that you only need to perform the command once.

A range is a rectangular block of cells of any size—even an entire worksheet or multiple worksheets in a file. A range is identified by its address, which consists of the addresses of the top left and bottom right cells in the range (including the worksheet letter, if any), separated by two periods. For example, A:A7..A:C12 is a **RANGE ADDRESS**. If your file had only one worksheet, the range address wouldn't contain the worksheet letter and would look something like A7..C12. When you select a range, 1-2-3 displays the range address in the selection indicator of the edit line. You also should know that clicking outside of a selected range or pressing an arrow key deselects that range.

The selection indicator shows the address of the selected range.

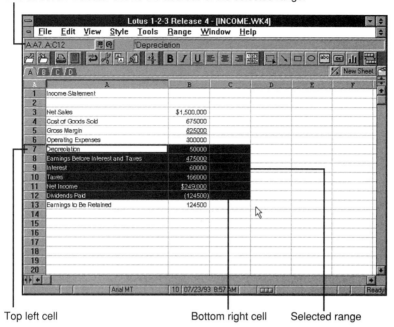

Top left cell   Bottom right cell   Selected range

A range by any other name . . . would be a different range.

YOUR BASIC EVERYDAY RANGE SELECTION

If you've used a spreadsheet program before, you probably have experience in **SELECTING RANGES**, such as an entire **ROW** or **COLUMN**, before you execute a command. For those who prefer to stick with this routine, here's how to do it in 1-2-3:

 Move the mouse pointer to a cell in one corner of the desired range.

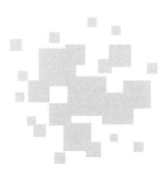

An alternative for **SELECTING RANGES** is to click on the top left cell of the range, and then move the mouse pointer to the bottom right cell of the range, completing the selection by pressing **Shift** and clicking on the right mouse button.

To select an entire **ROW** or **COLUMN**, click on the column letter or on the row number.

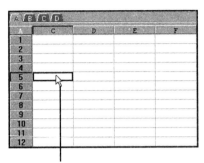

Point to a corner cell, and then
hold down the left mouse button.

2 Anchor the cell pointer in the cell by pressing and holding down the left mouse button.

3 While still holding down the mouse button, drag to highlight the desired range. Notice that as you *drag,* the cell pointer changes shapes.

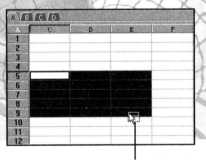

When you drag to select a range, the cell
pointer changes. Release the mouse button
when you've highlighted all the cells you want.

4 Release the mouse button when the range you want is highlighted.

BASS-ACKWARDS RANGE SELECTION

If you're one of those people who tucks in your shirt after you've buttoned up your pants (admit it), you'll appreciate the new feature in 1-2-3 for Windows, called the range selector, which lets you select a range for a command after you select the command. Dialog boxes let you select a range from the dialog box, as follows:

 Choose the command you want. For example, you might choose Style Number Format. A dialog box appears.

 Click on the range selector located at the right end of the Range text box. When you click on the range selector, 1-2-3 removes the dialog box so you can see the worksheet. The address of the current cell appears in the contents box.

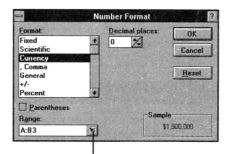

Range selector—click it to select a range in the worksheet.

Point to a cell in one corner of the desired range.

Anchor the cell pointer in the cell by pressing and holding down the left mouse button.

Drag to highlight the desired range.

Release the mouse button when the range you want is highlighted. Now that you have selected the range, the dialog box reappears, and the address of the range you selected appears in the text box.

STARTING YOUR OWN COLLECTION

A group of ranges is called a *collection*. Collections let you perform commands on two or more ranges at once. For example, if you want the numbers in cells A1 through A10 and B10 through D15 to be formatted as dollars, you can select that collection of ranges and format all those cells by issuing one command.

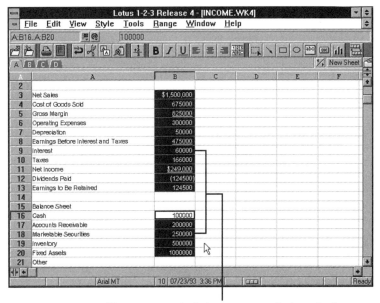

Two or more selected ranges are called a collection.

Bonzo range selection.

A collection can include ranges in *multiple worksheets* of the same file but cannot contain items of different types, such as both ranges and charts. You also can **REMOVE A RANGE** from a selected collection at any time. To select a collection:

 Select a range.

 Press and hold down Ctrl and select the next range you want to add to the collection.

 Repeat step 2 until you select the entire collection.

GOING 3-D

You've already learned that each 1-2-3 file can hold more worksheets than you can shake a stick at. Adding worksheets to a file is like adding graph paper to a three-ring binder . . . you get layers and layers of identical, identically aligned boxes. (If you want to jump ahead for more dirt on multiple worksheets, see Lesson 21.)

In building your *multiple worksheet* spreadsheets, you may need to select ranges of cells that run through several worksheets. For example, you may have 10 retail locations. You could create a budget worksheet for each location, including all 10 worksheets in a single file. Then, to calculate total sales for July, you would need to sum a range that includes the same cell (let's say cell C20 contains July sales for each location) in 10 consecutive worksheets (cell C20 on worksheet A, cell C20 on worksheet B, and so on). That's a 3-D (three-dimensional) range. Any range that includes the same cells in two or more consecutive worksheets is a 3-D range.

The address of a 3-D range includes the worksheet letters in the cell addresses. For example, the address **A:A1..D:F10** tells you that the range A1..F10 is selected in worksheets A through D. To select a 3-D range:

 Select the range in the first worksheet of the 3-D range.

 Hold down the Shift key, and click the worksheet tab of the last worksheet you want in the range. In the example shown here, the range **B3..B13** is selected on worksheets A through D.

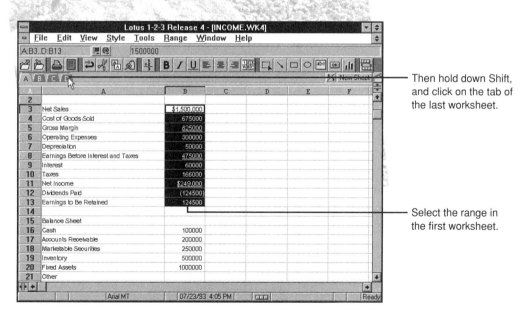

Then hold down Shift, and click on the tab of the last worksheet.

Select the range in the first worksheet.

SELECTING THE WHOLE ENCHILADA

You can select an entire worksheet by clicking on the worksheet letter, which is located in the top left corner of the worksheet at the intersection of the column headings and the row numbers. To select a group of worksheets, click on the worksheet letter of the first worksheet in the range, and then hold down **Shift**. Click on the worksheet tab of the last worksheet you want to include in the range.

Select the entire worksheet by clicking on the worksheet letter.

To select a group of worksheets, click on the worksheet letter of the first worksheet, hold down Shift, and click on the worksheet tab of the last worksheet.

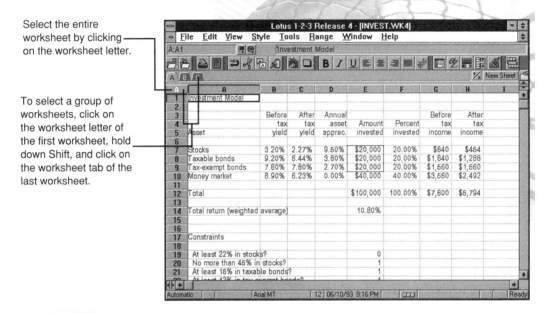

You can also **GO TO A RANGE** by using the navigator in the edit line of the 1-2-3 Window. Click on the navigator to see the list of range names. Click on the name of the range you want to go to, and 1-2-3 selects that range.

HYPERTIP

NAME YOUR POISON

Range addresses, though pretty much a normal convention of spreadsheet applications these days, are still about as useful as pig Latin. You can babble all day long, but you really miss the significance of some of the words. To make your 1-2-3 worksheet *formulas* look a little less like pig Latin and to speed up operations with some commands (like *Edit Go To*), you can assign a name to a range, and then you can use the range name in commands and formulas, instead of the range address. Range names even make it easier to specify an address when you want to **GO TO A RANGE** or select a range.

Using range names makes your formulas easy for anyone using your worksheets to decrypt. For example, the formula **+SALARY+INTEREST+DIVIDENDS** tells you more about what's happening than a formula that reads **+B1+B4+B7**.

A range name can be a word or a phrase that you assign to a range by using the Range Name command. There are a few rules you must follow when **NAMING RANGES**. A range name can be up to 15 characters long, but there are some character restrictions. You can't start a range name with ! (exclamation point), and don't even think about including any of the characters listed in Table 7.1 in the range name.

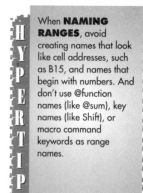

When **NAMING RANGES**, avoid creating names that look like cell addresses, such as B15, and names that begin with numbers. And don't use @function names (like @sum), key names (like Shift), or macro command keywords as range names.

TABLE 7.1 *Don't Even Think About Using One of These Characters in a Range Name*

, (comma)	+ (plus sign)	< (less than)
; (semicolon)	- (minus sign)	> (greater than)
. (period)	* (asterisk)	@ (at sign)
? (question mark)	/ (slash)	# (pound sign)
(space)	& (ampersand)	{ (left curly brace)

To name a range, simply:

 Select the range.

Selection indicator shows the selected range.

Click on the navigator for a list of range names.

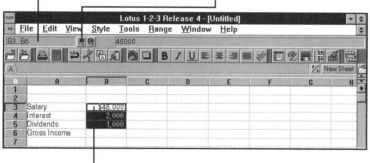

Selected range is highlighted.

 Choose Range Name.

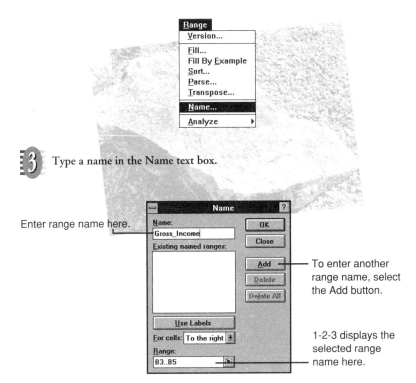

3 Type a name in the Name text box.

Enter range name here.

To enter another range name, select the Add button.

1-2-3 displays the selected range name here.

4 To create another range name, choose Add and repeat steps 1 and 3. When you click on the Add button, the current range name is added to the Existing named ranges list, and the Name text box is cleared, enabling you to type in a new name. Select the new range using the range selector.

5 Choose OK.

DITCHING OLD USED-UP RANGE NAMES

You can also use the Range Name command to delete range names in the current file. When you **DELETE A RANGE NAME**, you are just stripping the assigned name from the range; the data in the range remains unchanged. To delete a range name:

You can **DELETE A RANGE NAME** by clicking on any cell in the worksheet containing the name you want to delete. Then press the right mouse button to display the Quick menu. Click on **Name** to display the Name dialog box. Click on the name of the range to delete in the Existing names ranges list box. Select the **Delete** button, and choose **OK**.

Choose Range Name.

 Click on the name of the range to delete in the Existing names ranges list box. Or you can simply type the name of the range into the text box.

Or type the range name.

Select the range name to delete by clicking on it.

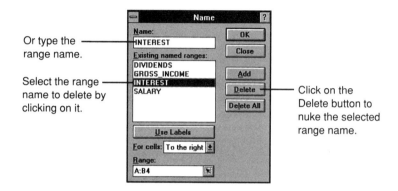

Click on the Delete button to nuke the selected range name.

 Select the Delete button.

 Choose OK.

NUKE 'EM ALL

To **DELETE ALL RANGE NAMES** from the current file, use almost the same procedure:

 Choose Range Name.

 Click on the Delete All button.

If you **DELETE ALL RANGE NAMES** and then change your mind, immediately choose Edit Undo to restore the names.

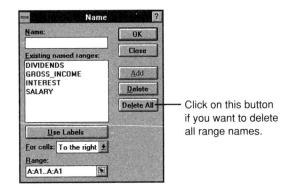

Click on this button
if you want to delete
all range names.

 Choose OK.

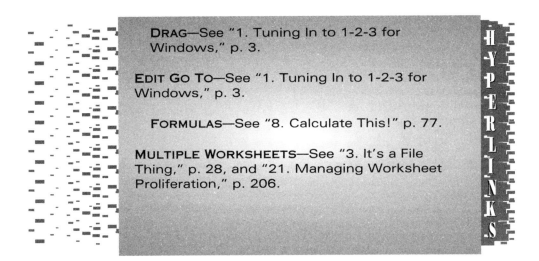

DRAG—See "1. Tuning In to 1-2-3 for Windows," p. 3.

EDIT GO TO—See "1. Tuning In to 1-2-3 for Windows," p. 3.

FORMULAS—See "8. Calculate This!" p. 77.

MULTIPLE WORKSHEETS—See "3. It's a File Thing," p. 28, and "21. Managing Worksheet Proliferation," p. 206.

HYPERLINKS

Now You're Cooking...
Building Formulas

Links to Reality

Take One Range Name,
Add in a Cell...

Everything's Relative
(or Absolute or Mixed)

CALCULATE THIS!

If you were one of those people who had nightmares about huge mathematical symbols chasing you around every time you had a high school math test, you can stop your therapy now. The purpose for spreadsheet programs like 1-2-3 for Windows is to add, subtract, divide, multiply, find averages, and perform more different kinds of calculations than you knew existed. 1-2-3's good, and it ought to be, since it runs on a machine several hundred times larger and more powerful than a calculator. Enter a formula (which is basically a math statement, including some rather small math symbols) into a worksheet, and 1-2-3 spits back an answer. Ahhh!

There are three types of formulas you can build into your 1-2-3 worksheets: text,

logical, and numeric. Because much of what you do with 1-2-3 involves number crunching, you'll work most often with numeric formulas, which (duh) calculate numbers. Text formulas let you manipulate text. The text formula +"Mr."&" Couture" combines the two words to display the label Mr. Couture in a worksheet cell.

If you have ever done any programming, you are probably familiar with logical formulas. 1-2-3 logical formulas evaluate a condition as true or false by using what are called *logical operators* or *logical @functions*. (Mr. Spock would be proud.) The logical operators are symbols in a formula that indicate a relationship between two values. Table 8.1 describes the logical operators used in 1-2-3.

TABLE 8.1   *A Little Logic Never Hurt Anyone . . .*

Logical Operators	Their Logical Meanings
=	equal to
<	less than
<=	less than or equal to
>	greater than
>=	greater than or equal to
<>	not equal to
#AND#	AND
#NOT#	NOT
#OR#	OR

> There are five **ARITHMETIC OPERATORS** you can use in numeric formulas:
>
> + Addition
> – Subtraction
> * Multiplication
> / Division
> ^ Exponentiation
>
> **HYPERTIP**

The result of a logical formula is the value 1 for a condition that is true, or 0 when a condition is false. For example, the formula **+SALARY>30000** displays 1 (true) when the value in the cell named SALARY is greater than 30000, and returns the value 0 (false) when SALARY is less than 30000.

Numeric formulas perform calculations using values. Often, a numeric formula uses one or more of the **ARITHMETIC OPERATORS**. For example, if you have ranges named Salary, Interest, and Dividends and you want to add them up using the addition operator, you could enter this formula:

+Salary+Interest+Dividends

When entering a numeric formula, you must tell 1-2-3 that you are building a numeric formula. 1-2-3 recognizes several characters as the beginning of a numeric formula, including:

◇   A number

◇   One of these characters: +, -, =, .(period), (, #, $ (or any currency symbol).

◇   An **@FUNCTION**. (*@functions* are covered in more detail in the next lesson.)

> An **@FUNCTION** is a formula that's pre-programmed into 1-2-3. So, by entering the @function name into a formula, you can ask 1-2-3 to perform certain calculations. For example, the @AVG function calculates the average of values you enter into the cells averaged by the formula.
>
> **HYPERTIP**

FORMULATION FRENZY

Instead of giving 1-2-3 actual numbers to work with in a formula, use the cell addresses and range names of numbers. Doing this leaves it up to 1-2-3 to find the numbers and calculate with them. Using cell addresses and range names makes your worksheet dynamic. A change in any of the values referenced in

a formula will result in an immediate and automatic change in the value displayed by the formula.

In English, this means that if you have a formula in cell B4 that adds the values in cells B2 and B3 (let's say you've typed 5 into B2 and 10 into B3), the total displayed in B4 would be 15. If you changed the value in cell B2 to 10, the result in cell B4 would change to 20.

There are two ways you can enter a cell address in a formula: by typing it as you create the formula or by selecting the cell address using the mouse. Selecting the cell address using the mouse is an easy and accurate way to enter a cell address. Instead of having to remember a cell address and then making sure you avoid a typo, you can just click on the cell that you want to reference (the cell, range address, or range name that you want to point to) in the formula. Just remember: As you're entering a formula, do not put any spaces in it. 1-2-3 recognizes spaces in formulas as errors.

Here are a few examples:

A formula that performs simple addition and subtraction using cell addresses:

> +A2+A3-A4

A formula that uses range name to calculate net income:

> +SALES-
> COST_GOODS_SOLD-
> EXPENSES+OTHER_INCOME

A formula that uses two @functions:

> @SUM(B9..B11)-
> @AVG(C9..C11)

You enter a formula in the cell where you want the result to be displayed. 1-2-3 displays the result in the cell and the actual formula (as opposed to its results) in the contents box. If you want to cancel an entry before entering it into the cell, click on the **Cancel** button (button with an X on it) in the edit line, or use **Backspace** to make changes if you mess up during formula entry.

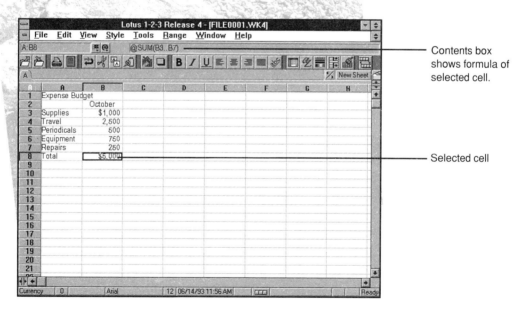

Check out the contents box to see the formula and the cell for the results.

To enter a formula, follow these steps:

 Select the cell where you want the results of the formula to be displayed.

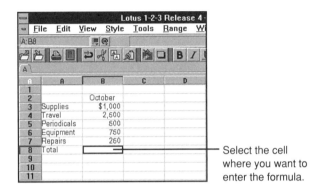

Select the cell where you want to enter the formula.

 Enter one of the characters to begin the formula. For example, you can enter + or an @function to tell 1-2-3 that you are beginning to build a formula.

Enter one of the accepted characters that tells 1-2-3 that you are beginning to enter a formula.

Enter the value, cell address, or range name (also known as operands).

Enter the value, text, cell address, or range name (operands) that you want 1-2-3 to operate upon. Or select the cell or range that you want the formula to refer to by clicking on it (in the case of one cell) or dragging over it (in the case of a range).

Enter the first operator. Operators are symbols you put into your formulas to tell 1-2-3 what math you want performed, what relationship you want examined between two values, or the type of operation to be performed. The three 1-2-3 operators are arithmetic, logical, and text operators. If you are beginning the formula with an @function, an operator is not needed.

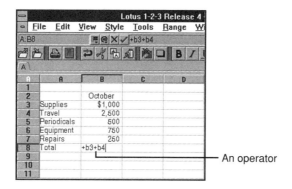

An operator

5 Enter the next value, text, cell address, or range name (operands) that you want 1-2-3 to operate upon.

6 Repeat steps 4 and 5 until you have entered the rest of your formula.

7 Click on the Confirm button, or press Enter. The Confirm button "forgives" by adding a final parenthesis when you leave it off an @function formula.

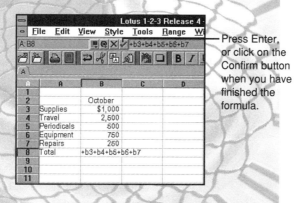

Press Enter, or click on the Confirm button when you have finished the formula.

The Standard SmartIcon set offers a shortcut for entering a formula that sums a group of contiguous cells in a column or row. Simply select the cell below or to the right of the group of cells you want to add up, and click the summing SmartIcon.

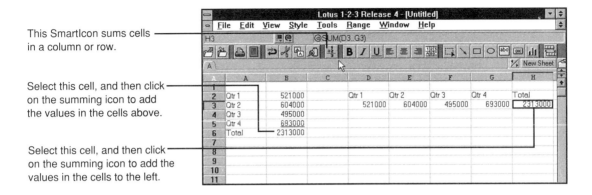

This SmartIcon sums cells in a column or row.

Select this cell, and then click on the summing icon to add the values in the cells above.

Select this cell, and then click on the summing icon to add the values in the cells to the left.

JOINING YOUR FILES AT THE HIP WITH FORMULAS

If 1-2-3 is set to automatically recalculate formulas (Tools User Setup Recalculation) and the file you open includes a formula with a **FILE LINK** to another active (open) file, 1-2-3 will automatically update the file link using the current data from the linked file. If the file you open is linked to a nonactive (unopened) file, you have to update the file link manually by using the Edit Links command, which allows you to update links to files that are not open but are on disk.

You're not at all limited to referencing cells in the current file in your 1-2-3 formulas; you can pull values from cells or ranges that are in other 1-2-3 files. Such a formula creates a **FILE LINK**. For example, if you are creating a master budget, you may have one file named SALES.WK4 that contains the sales forecasts—the foundation of the budget. When you need to include sales forecast numbers in your budget file, you can link the range (in a worksheet called FORECAST.WK4 that contains the sales forecast) to SALES.WK4. You would do this by entering a file reference to

FORECAST.WK4 in the formulas you create in SALES.WK4.

In a formula, the format for a file reference is

$$+<<filename.WK?>>range$$

where *filename*.WK? is the name of the file and *range* is the address or range name of the data from the file that you want to include in the formula. For example, if the cell you want to link to in the **BUDGET.WK4** file is **B10**, the file-link reference is this baby +<<**BUDGET.WK4**>>**B10**. If you want to create a linking formula, do this:

 Open both files.

 Enter the formula in the first file up to the point at which you want to enter the file reference.

 Press Ctrl+F6 to go to the other file, and then use the mouse to select the cell or range. If you don't want to switch to the other file and you remember the range you want, you can type the file reference into the formula using the file-link reference format discussed above (+<<*filename*.WK?>>*range*).

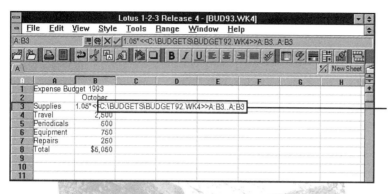

File reference provides a link to cell B3 of worksheet A of a file named BUDGET92.WK4.

 Complete the formula and then press Enter or click the Confirm button.

THROW AWAY YOUR SECRET FORMULA DECODER RING

Let's say you give a printout of a 1-2-3 worksheet that totals your company's paper clip expenditures for the previous year to a coworker so he can double-check the totals. Comparing your results to his, he says, "You bonehead! You're off by at least 2.1 million dollars. Are you sure you multiplied the total by the discount percentage?" You pull up your worksheet file to check it out, but your formulas are gobbledygook—like @sum(B14..B31) and +B32*.035. By the time you figure out what the formulas you created a week ago mean, you've eaten a whole bag of corn chips and a six-pack of cola. This is not good for your diet.

A **RANGE NAME** lets you make your worksheets user-friendly. You can assign a name to a range, then use the *range name* in commands and formulas instead of the range address. Range names make it easy to specify an address to **Go To**, to select a range, or to reference a range in a formula; all you have to remember is a simple name.

Use range names in your formulas so they'll be easier to understand. For example, the stunning formula **+SALARY+INTEREST+DIVIDENDS** tells you more about what's happening in that formula than **+B1+B4+B7**.

Before you can enter a **RANGE NAME** in a formula, you must name the range by using the Range Name command, which is covered in Lesson 7. Formulas can include a range name that hasn't been assigned to a cell or range. However, the formula will display **ERR** (error) until you assign the range name to a cell or range.

To enter a range name in a formula, follow these steps:

 Enter the formula up to the point at which you want to enter the range name.

Enter the formula up to the point where you want to enter the range name.

Click on the navigator to display a list of range names.

Select a range name from the list by clicking on it.

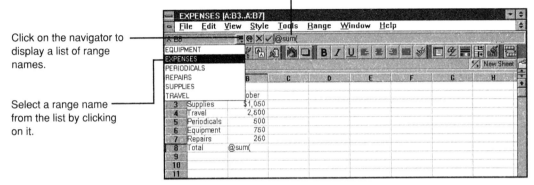

Enter the range name in the formula. You have your pick of three methods for doing so. Choose the one you prefer:

◇ Click the navigator to display the drop-down list of range names, and click on one of the names in the list.

◇ Press **F3** (NAME) to display the Range Names dialog box, and select a range name from the list.

◇ Type the range name.

Complete the formula, and then press Enter, or click on the Confirm button.

Click on the Confirm button, or press Enter once you have finished entering the formula.

Range name in the formula

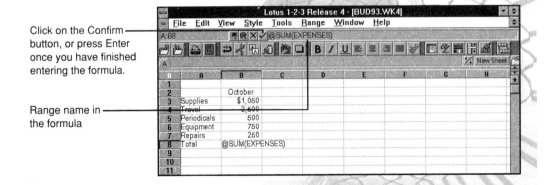

REUSE, RECYCLE, REHASH YOUR FORMULAS

While having a lot of old formulas lying around on your worksheets won't release toxins or anything, reusing some of that old stuff can save you significant amounts of time. If you have created a formula that you would like to use in other locations of the worksheet, select the cell that holds that formula, and then use one of the *Copy* commands: Edit Copy, Edit Copy Right, or Edit Copy Down. Select the cell or range to copy to, and then choose Edit Paste. Copying formulas works pretty much the same as copying other data, except you must determine whether you want the cell and range references used in the copied formula to adjust when you copy that formula.

Generally, when you copy a formula to a new location, its range addresses will automatically adjust to the new location in the worksheet unless you change the addresses to either **ABSOLUTE OR MIXED REFERENCES**. An address that adjusts to its new surroundings when copied is a relative reference. Here's how a relative reference works. If a formula in cell B15 is **+100+A10** and you copy it to B17 (down two rows), the new (copied) formula in B17 would read **+100+A12**. The cell reference in the copy of the formula has adjusted by two rows, from **A10** to **A12**.

HYPERTIP

If you don't want cell references to change when you copy a formula, use either an **ABSOLUTE OR MIXED REFERENCE** in the formula. An absolute reference does not change when you copy the formula—it always refers to the same cell or range. A mixed reference is written so that either the column or the row reference changes when the formula is copied. To create absolute or mixed references, include a dollar sign before the column letter or row number you want to remain fixed, as in A10 or B$32.

ABSOLUTELY MIXED-UP REFERENCES

You can build your formula using relative addresses and then change those addresses to either an absolute or mixed reference depending on what your needs are when copying the formulas. If you don't want addresses to adjust when you're copying, use an absolute reference, and if you want to freeze either the column letter or row number of the address, use a mixed reference.

If you want to make an address absolute by typing the address, you can type **$** (dollar sign) before each element of the reference. For example, if you want to reference cell B10 in a formula as an absolute, then type it as **B10**. The first dollar sign tells 1-2-3 that the column (B) reference should not change, and the second dollar sign freezes the row number

(row 10). No matter where you copy the formula, the reference **B10** never changes.

To make an address a mixed reference, type **$** before the part of the reference that you want frozen when you copy the formula. In other words, enter the **$** before the element you want to keep from adjusting. For example, if you want only the column letter of the cell reference B10 to adjust, type **B$10** as the cell reference. All elements of the reference **$B:A10** will adjust when copied except for the worksheet letter (B).

An even easier way to change cell or range references from relative to absolute or mixed is to use the **F4** key. When 1-2-3 is in Point, Value, or *Edit mode*, pressing **F4** changes the cell references in

a formula from relative to absolute to mixed back to relative. Each time you press **F4**, the type of reference changes from relative to absolute to mixed. To use F4, follow these steps when you are creating a formula:

 Select the cell you want and begin typing the formula.

 Press F4 when the insertion point is on or to the right of a reference.

With the insertion point on or to the right of the reference, you can press F4 to change the reference to an absolute, mixed, or relative reference.

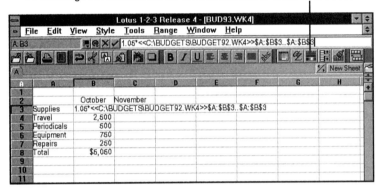

 Press F4 until you see the correct kind of reference. Each time you press F4, the reference changes from relative to absolute, to mixed, and then finally back to relative. 1-2-3 changes the references by entering a $ (dollar sign) in front of the worksheet letter, column letter, row number, or range name.

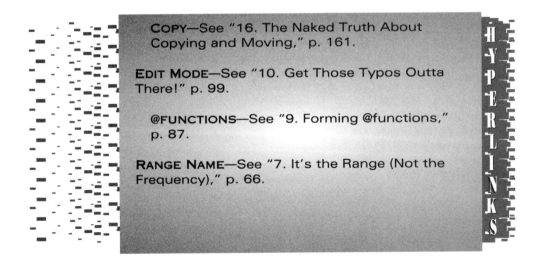

COPY—See "16. The Naked Truth About Copying and Moving," p. 161.

EDIT MODE—See "10. Get Those Typos Outta There!" p. 99.

@FUNCTIONS—See "9. Forming @functions," p. 87.

RANGE NAME—See "7. It's the Range (Not the Frequency)," p. 66.

FORMING @FUNCTIONS

Come out of the closet . . . reveal your math fetish to the world! This program offers enough calculation options to keep even the most obsessive number crunchers busy for hours on end. 1-2-3 has more than 300 @functions—built-in formulas that perform calculations quickly and accurately without your having to remember lengthy and complex formulas.

Lotus has organized the @functions into 10 categories. These categories group together @functions that perform similar or related tasks. For example, @functions that you can use to calculate rates of return and future dollar amounts are grouped under the category of Financial. Table 9.1 lists the @function categories and their purposes in life.

TABLE 9.1 *A Category for Everyone*

@function Category	Its Purpose in Life
Calendar	Calculates dates and time values.
Database	Statistical calculations and queries in database tables.
Engineering	Engineering calculations and advanced mathematical operations.
Financial	Calculations of time value of money, investments returns, annuities, periodic depreciation; and loan payments.
Information	Displays information about cells, ranges, the operating system, and other aspects of 1-2-3.
Logical	Calculates the results of conditional or logical formulas.
Lookup	Searches and finds the contents of a cell.
Mathematical	Mathematical operations.
Statistical	Basic statistical calculations.
Text	Displays information about text in cells and performs other operations on text.

For an alphabetical list of all **@FUNCTIONS**, click on the **@function** selector in the edit line, and then choose **List All**.

HYPERTIP

You can't possibly master all 300+ **@FUNCTIONS** (unless you're a genius . . . not!). Fortunately, 1-2-3 provides you with a lot of help so that you can find the @function that can best meet your number-crunching needs.

Choose **Help Contents**, and the window that appears includes @Functions as a topic. Click on that topic to learn the fundamentals of @functions. You can also use Help to examine the various categories of @functions and to review the specific @functions that are available in each category. Here's Help for the @functions that ail you:

 Choose Help Contents.

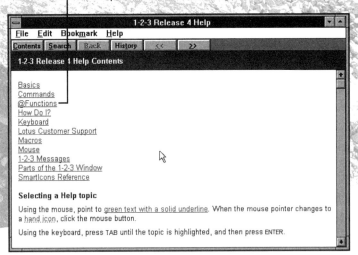

Select **@Functions** by clicking on that topic in the list of topics.

Click on this topic to learn more about @functions.

Select @Function Categories or Descriptions of Individual @Functions.
The first choice explains @functions that perform related calculations. The
second choice lets you search for helpful information on a specific @function. If
you want to search for help on a particular @function, choose the **S**earch
button, then enter the @function name in the text box (without the @), and
search for it as you would any other topic. For example, if you want to learn
more about the @SUM function, enter its name—**SUM**. For more information
on *searching Help*, see Lesson 4.

Click for a brief
introduction to
@functions.

Click for a description of a particular @function by
using the search capability of @function Help—a help
subsystem of the 1-2-3 Help facility.

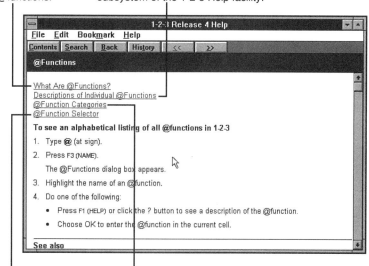

Click to learn how to
use the @function
selector to enter
@functions.

Click to track down a description of an @function by its
category. For example, to learn about @IRR (calculates an
internal rate of return on an investment), go to the list of
Financial @functions, and click on @IRR.

GETTING YOUR FIX OF @FUNCTIONS

@functions wouldn't help an iota if they
were complicated to use, so the format
for just about all @functions is the same.
There are three elements: the @ (at sign),
the name of the function, and one or
more arguments enclosed in parentheses.
Arguments are data you provide for 1-2-3
to perform the @function calculation on.

For example, to find the average of the
values in cells B3 through B9, you can
enter the @AVG function by following
this format: @AVG(List). The actual
formula would read **@AVG(B3..B9)**,
because List is the argument—a range of
cells you want to sum.

Some @functions require multiple arguments, separated by commas within the @function's parenthesis. Some arguments require cell or range addresses, while others require values. If you're not familiar with the specific argument requirements of an @function that you want to use, the easiest way to get the info you need is to use the **@FUNC-TION SELECTOR** to display the syntax and description of a selected @function. Also, if it is not apparent to you what the argument requirement is for a particular @function, you can get additional information by using the @function help subsystem of the Lotus 1-2-3 Help. For more information on how to get help with your @functions, go back to the beginning of the lesson, which gives you step-by-step help.

Here are some examples of @functions and their arguments:

@DATE(year,month,day)   The arguments are year,month,day with year being an integer from 0 (the year 1900) through 199 (the year 2099), month an integer from 1 through 12, and day an integer from 1 through 31.

@DATE(93,8,4) Results in the value 34,185, which is the date value for August 4, 1993.

@SUM(LIST)   The argument **LIST** is any combination of formulas, numbers, range addresses, or range names.

@SUM(EXPENSES)   Results in adding the sum of the values in the range that was named **EXPENSES**.

@SMALL(range, n)   The arguments are Range and n. **Range** is a range of cells while **n** is the nth smallest value in a range.

@SMALL(A1..A10,2)   Results in the 2nd smallest value in the range of cells A1 through A10.

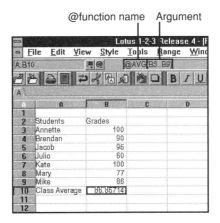

Anatomy of an @function.

When *building formulas*, you can combine numeric, logical, and text operations with @functions. For example, suppose you want to add up a column of numbers (B10 through B25), and then multiply the result by 1.05. You can enter the formula **@SUM(B10..B25)*1.05**—a formula that uses an @function and a numeric operator. Including an @function in a formula is as easy as drinking a latte:

 Select the cell where you want the results of the formula to be displayed.

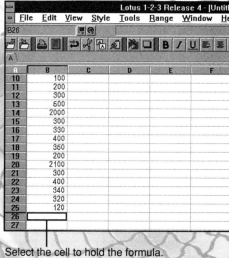

Select the cell to hold the formula.

 Enter one of the characters to begin the formula. There are several characters that 1-2-3 accepts as the beginning of a formula. A commonly used character for this is the **+** (plus sign). You can also start a formula with the @function because 1-2-3 recognizes the @ (at sign) as the beginning of a formula.

91

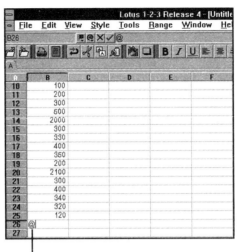

Type one of the characters that tells
1-2-3 you are entering a formula.

Enter the values, cell references, range names, @functions, and operators.
Operators are symbols you put into your formulas to tell 1-2-3 what math you
want performed, what relationship you want examined between two values, or
the type of operation to be performed. The three 1-2-3 operators are arithmetic, logical, and text operators.

Formula that contains an @function.

Click on the Confirm button, or press Enter.

@FUNCTIONS FOR THE MEMORY IMPAIRED

If you want to see an alphabetical listing of all @functions in 1-2-3 to get help on one, or so you can enter an @function into a formula, press **F3** after you've entered the @ sign.

This shortcut pastes the @function into the formula you're building, including argument **PLACEHOLDERS** and argument separators. Argument placeholders are words and brief phrases that 1-2-3 inserts into the @function so you can go back and replace them with

the specific arguments that you want 1-2-3 to operate on. For example, if you enter the @SUM function with the @function selector, 1-2-3 will paste @SUM(*List*) into the selected cell. The word *List* is the argument placeholder, which you can replace with a specific range of cells. Argument separators can be a **,** (comma), **;** (semicolon), or **.** (period), which are used to separate one argument from another in an @function.

> You don't have to immediately replace the **PLACEHOLDERS** of an @function that you have pasted into a formula. You can go back at a later time and replace the placeholders. The @function will display (and evaluate to) **ERR**, or error, until you replace the placeholders with appropriate values or cell references.

Here's how to use the F3 shortcut:

 Select a cell and then type @ (at sign) in a cell.

Select a cell and type @.

 Press F3 (NAME). The @Function List dialog box appears.

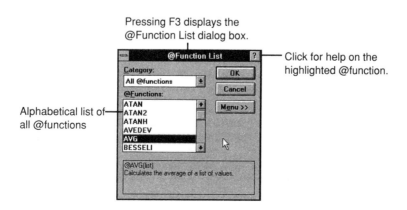
Pressing F3 displays the @Function List dialog box.

Click for help on the highlighted @function.

Alphabetical list of all @functions

 Highlight the name of an @function by clicking on it.

 Do one of the following:

◇ Press **F1** (HELP) or click on the **?** button to see a description of the @function.

◇ Choose **OK** to enter the @function in the current formula.

 Edit to replace the argument placeholders with real references and values. For more on editing, see Lesson 10.

 Finish the formula, and click on the Confirm button or press Enter.

EVEN BETTER, SLICK: THE @FUNCTION SELECTOR

The @Function List does give you a description of the function you're looking for, but it's for wimps. For the quickest @function entry, use the @function selector located in the edit line of the control panel.

Click on the @function selector to display a pull-down menu listing the most popular @functions. Click on the one you want, and 1-2-3 enters it (with argument placeholders and argument separators) into the formula you're building.

Here's the skinny on this operation:

Select the cell where you want to enter the @function.

Click on the @function selector. You'll see a drop-down list of @functions called the @function menu.

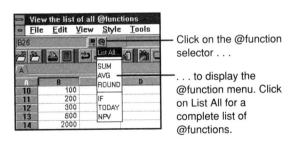

Click on the @function selector . . .

. . . to display the @function menu. Click on List All for a complete list of @functions.

3 **If you see the @function you want, click on it. If the @function you want is not on the @function menu, choose List All and continue to step 4.** The @Function List box appears.

4 **If you know the category of the @function, select the category from the Category drop-down box.** If you don't know the category of the @function that you want, select **All @functions** from the **C**ategory drop-down box to see an alphabetical list of all the @functions.

5 **Select the @function you want from the @Functions list box by clicking on it.**

6 **Click on OK.** 1-2-3 enters the @function name, placeholders for required and optional arguments, and argument separators in the formula so that you can go on to replace the placeholders with specific arguments.

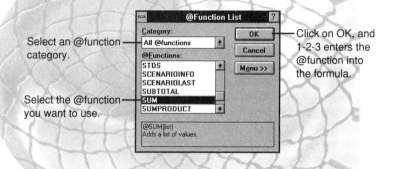

Select an @function category.

Select the @function you want to use.

Click on OK, and 1-2-3 enters the @function into the formula.

7 **Replace argument placeholders with the real live values and references.**

8 **Click on the Confirm button, or press Enter.**

@FUNCTION MENU IMPROVEMENTS

We're having fun now, but it gets even better than this. You can **CUSTOM-IZE** the @function menu for your own kinky purposes. Adding frequently used @functions to the pull-down saves time because you can choose and enter them without displaying the entire @Function list and the List dialog box. To add an @function to the @function menu, try this:

1 Click the @function selector.

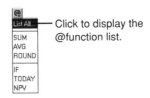

Click to display the @function list.

2 Click List All.

3 Choose Menu.

Click on the Menu button to add or remove @functions from the @function menu.

4 Click on the @function in the @Functions list box.

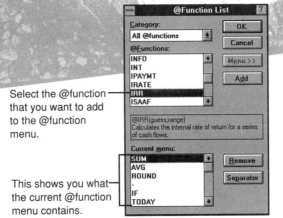

Select the @function that you want to add to the @function menu.

This shows you what the current @function menu contains.

Choose Add.

Choose OK.

@FUNCTION MENU REDUCING PROGRAM

My friend's mother always used this gentle reminder to straighten him out: "I brought you into this world, and I can take you out." Like an omnipotent parent, you can remove any @function from the @function menu. For example, you may have added date and time @functions to the menu while building a worksheet requiring a lot of work with dates and times. Your next worksheet might require other types of calculations, but none of which involve dates and times. In that case, you can remove the date and time @functions and add other @functions that you plan on using.

To remove an @function for the current menu, follow these steps:

 Click on the @function selector.

 Click on List All.

 Click on Menu.

 Click on the @function in the Current menu list box.

Click on the @function that you want to remove in the current @function menu.

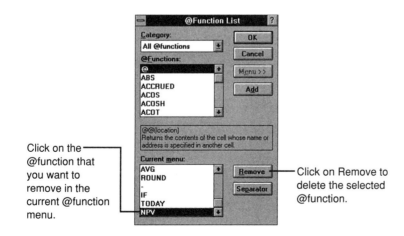

Click on Remove to delete the selected @function.

 Click on Remove.

 Click on OK.

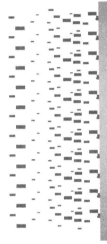

BUILDING FORMULAS—See "8. Calculate This!" p. 77.

EDITING—See "10. Get Those Typos Outta There!" p. 99.

SEARCHING HELP—See "4. Frantic Panic, and Where to Get Help," p. 37.

HYPERLINKS

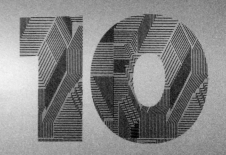
GET THOSE TYPOS OUTTA THERE!

If you're lucky (read: not working for a company that spies on their employees), no one's taking pictures of you when you build your worksheets. You can make mistakes all the way to oblivion and have an ERR result for every formula with very few consequences. But on those rare occasions when you have to hand over something coherent on paper to prove you're earning your paycheck, you may need to go back and edit some cell entries to correct mistakes.

When you edit data, you either replace an existing *cell entry*, clear a cell, or correct an error. When you need to replace the entire contents of a cell, you can select the cell and type a new entry. When you are finished typing, simply press **Enter** to replace the previous entry. Retyping an entry is a crude way of editing data. There are better and more efficient ways of doing worksheet editing.

For example, 1-2-3 has features that allow you to quickly check and correct the spelling of an entire file. 1-2-3 also has a feature that lets you find specified words, phrases, or characters and automatically replaces those items with items you specified. Spell checking and finding and replacing are covered in more detail later in this lesson.

But what if you want to edit part of a lengthy cell entry without retyping the whole quesadilla? No problem. You can edit only those parts of the entry that need changes. Select the cell to edit, and press **F2** (EDIT), or double-click on the cell. By either double-clicking on the cell or pressing **F2**, you put 1-2-3 into Edit *mode*, which simply means that you can edit an entry right in its cell or in the contents box without having to completely retype it, like this:

 Double-click on the cell you want to edit, or select the cell you want to edit and press F2. Either one of these actions puts 1-2-3 into Edit mode.

Double-clicking a cell or pressing F2 puts its contents in the Contents box.

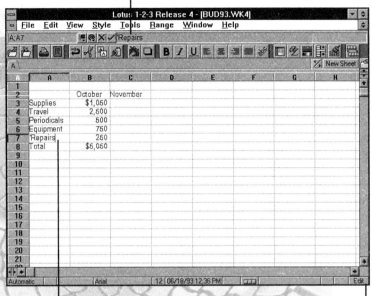

When you edit a cell, the insertion point appears to the right of the last character.

1-2-3 goes into Edit mode when you press F2 or double-click on a cell.

You can make a **HIGHLIGHTED SELECTION** within a cell you want to edit by holding down the left mouse button and dragging the insertion point across the characters. For example, if you have characters that you want to delete, highlight them by dragging on them, and then press **Delete**.

 Edit the entry. Use the right and left arrow keys to move the insertion point. Press **Del** to delete characters to the right of the insertion point or to erase the **HIGHLIGHTED SELECTION**. Use **Backspace** to delete characters to the left of the insertion point or the highlighted selection. To insert characters, move the insertion point to the appropriate location, and start typing.

When the entry is the way you want it, press Enter, or click on the Confirm button.

Soon after they started evaluating 1-2-3 for Windows, army efficiency experts found that there are special key combinations you can use to move the insertion point when editing cells:

Ctrl+¨ In labels, moves the insertion point to the left of the previous word. In values, moves to the beginning of the value.

Ctrl+→ In labels, moves the insertion point to the left of the next word. In values, moves to the end of the value.

End Moves the insertion point to the last character in the entry.

Home Moves the insertion point to the first character in the entry.

→ or ← Moves the insertion point one character to the right or left.

100

DATA BE GONE

When data has outlived its usefulness, you may want to erase the data from a cell or a range of cells. Two commands help you do this: Edit Clear and *Edit Cut*. Edit Clear erases the current selection without changing the contents of the *Windows Clipboard*. The Clipboard is the Windows application that acts as a temporary storage area for copied or cut data—like formulas, text,

or graphics. Using Edit **CUT** puts data on the Clipboard so you can paste (Edit Paste command) the contents of the Clipboard into 1-2-3 or into other Windows applications. With Edit Clear, the **DATA YOU CLEAR** does not get copied to the Clipboard—it just gets sent off into hyperspace, for ever and ever. To the naked eye, cutting and clearing appear the same.

If you need to bring back any **DATA YOU CLEAR**, immediately choose Edit Undo, or click on the **Undo** SmartIcon.

Most SmartIcon sets offer editing SmartIcons for your convenience. These can make you considerably more efficient at cleaning up around the worksheet.

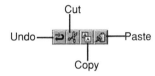

Quick cuts (and copies, and pastes).

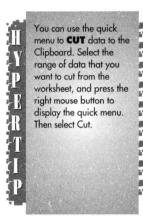

You can use the quick menu to **CUT** data to the Clipboard. Select the range of data that you want to cut from the worksheet, and press the right mouse button to display the quick menu. Then select Cut.

To use **E**dit Clear, follow these steps (whether you like it or not):

 Select the cell or range you want to clear.

 Choose Edit Clear. Rather than use **E**dit Cl**e**ar, you can select a cell or range and press the **DEL** key.

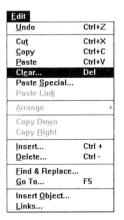

 Select Cell contents only, Styles only, or Both.

Clears data and formulas but leaves assigned styles intact

Clears only the formatting styles of
the selected range, such as the
number format, fonts, lines, and so
on—anything you can assign to a cell
or range via the Style menu

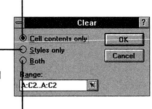

Clears data and formulas, and any styles that have been assigned

 Choose OK.

HELP FOR SORRY SPELLERS

Want to be embarrassed in 30 seconds or less? Then, the next time you have a large worksheet file you're going to show to others, don't check the spelling. Mistakes do creep in, especially when you're working with large, complicated files. To help you catch your misspelled words,

1-2-3 has a spell check feature that is similar to those found in word processing applications. With the Tools Spell Check command, you can check the spelling of words used in your worksheets, charts, and other file items. To put those misspellings in check:

 (Optional) Select a range to check. If you want to check the entire file, do not *select a range.*

 Choose Tools Spell Check.

 Select an option from the Check group.

Checks all worksheets, charts, query tables, and text blocks in the file. Select this option to check the spelling in charts.

Checks all cells, query tables, and text blocks in the current worksheet

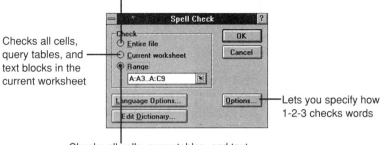

Lets you specify how 1-2-3 checks words

Checks all cells, query tables, and text blocks within the selected range

 (Optional) Choose Options, specify how 1-2-3 checks words, and click on OK. The Options dialog box appears. Select the check box of one or more options.

Turn on the check box for each option you want . . .

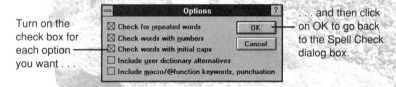

. . . and then click on OK to go back to the Spell Check dialog box.

 Choose OK.

SEEK, AND YE SHALL FIND

Being the creatures of habit that we humans are, you may use the same phrases over and over when building large worksheets. For once, your lack of creativity can work in your favor . . . like if you ever need to search for and replace certain data. For example, you may want to find a phrase that you used several times throughout a file, such as "Slave Labor," and replace that phrase with a more politically correct phrase: "Salaries." Sometimes, you may just search for a certain phrase as a quick way to jump to that section of the worksheet.

Searching for data in a large worksheet can be time consuming and cumbersome if you have to search cell-by-cell. Fortunately, 1-2-3 gives you the ability to find data quickly and, if you choose, to replace that data with new data. The Edit Find & Replace command finds or replaces specified characters in labels, formulas, or both. To find out how a simple find works, try it:

 (Optional) Select a range to search. If you want to search the entire file, do not select a range.

 Choose Edit Find & Replace.

 In the Search for text box, enter the characters you want to find.

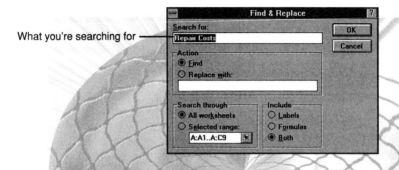

What you're searching for ⎯ (points to "Repair Costs" in the Search for box)

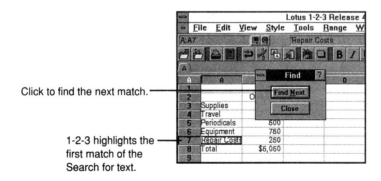

Under Action, select Find.

Under Include, select Labels, Formulas, or Both.

Under Search through, select All worksheets or Selected range.

Choose OK. 1-2-3 highlights the first occurrence of the search characters. The Find dialog box appears, and 1-2-3 highlights the cell containing the first occurrence of the search characters.

Choose Find Next to find the next instance of the text you're searching for.

Click to find the next match. ⎯ (points to "Find Next" button)

1-2-3 highlights the ⎯ (points to "Repair Costs" in cell)
first match of the
Search for text.

EVERYONE'S REPLACEABLE

Replacing gives you even more mileage from Edit Find & Replace. Replacing lets you type one correction to several cells, minimizing your chance of making a heinous error. To replace the characters you're searching for:

 (Optional) Select a range to search. If you want to search the entire file, do not select a range.

 Choose Edit Find & Replace.

 In the Search for text box, enter the characters you want to find.

 Under Action, select Replace with, and then enter the replacement characters in the Replace with text box. You can specify up to 512 characters.

 Under Include, select Labels, Formulas, or Both.

 Under Search through, select All worksheets or Selected range.

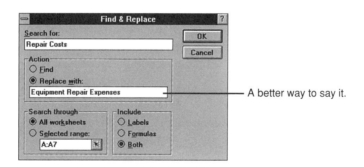

— A better way to say it.

 Choose OK. The Replace dialog box is displayed.

 Select one of the Replace dialog box buttons.

Replaces the highlighted characters with the replacement charac-
ters and searches for and highlights the next occurrence.

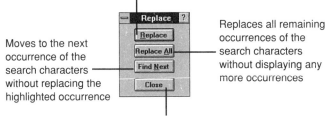

Moves to the next
occurrence of the
search characters
without replacing the
highlighted occurrence

Replaces all remaining
occurrences of the
search characters
without displaying any
more occurrences

Stops the search, and returns 1-2-3 to Ready mode

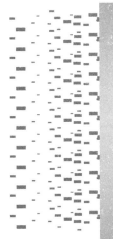

CELL ENTRY—See "6. Typin' Data," p. 59, "8.
Calculate This!" p. 77, and "9. Forming
@functions," p. 87.

EDIT CUT—See "16. The Naked Truth About
Copying and Moving," p. 161.

MODE—See "1. Tuning In to 1-2-3 for Windows,"
p. 3.

SELECT A RANGE—See "7. It's the Range (Not
the Frequency)," p. 66.

WINDOWS CLIPBOARD—See "16. The Naked Truth
About Copying and Moving," p. 161.

Part III

Tune Up, Turn On, Print Out

Entering data, formulas, and @functions into your worksheet is just the beginning. It lays the foundation and puts up the rough frame of your application. From there, you can move onto the finish work—hiding data, adjusting column and row widths, aligning data, formatting, and coloring your work so it looks just right when you display or print it. The lessons in this part help you to take your worksheets from the rough stages to a final product that effectively communicates your messages. Anything that looks better has more impact!

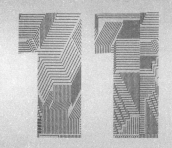

TECHNO-SUBVERSIVE ACTIVITIES: REMOVING AND HIDING DATA

There are basically two kinds of cooks in this world: those who leave the kitchen so clean you can do surgery in it, and those who proceed with reckless abandon so the kitchen looks like it sustained a Tomahawk-missile strike. If you're a neat cook, you'll be able to use the techniques in this lesson to maintain a precise, accurate worksheet as you go along. Missile-dodgers can use what they learn here to whip worksheet debris into shape.

Cutting data from your worksheets and placing it on the Windows Clipboard is one way to be neat. The command for this, Edit Cut, removes the data from its current location—much like the Edit Clear command but with one major difference. Edit Clear trashes the data without placing it on the Clipboard; Edit Cut cuts data and related styles and places them on the Clipboard so you can *paste* them in another part of your worksheet, in another worksheet file, or in another Windows application—such as a word processing program. The Edit Cut command is one of those fundamental commands that is available in just about all Windows applications. To cut data from your worksheet and place it on the Windows Clipboard:

 Select the range, drawn object(s), or other items that you want to cut.

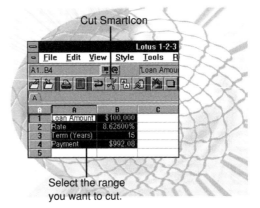

 Choose Edit Cut. The cut data remains on the Clipboard until you use Edit Copy or **EDIT CUT** again.

ERADICATING ERRANT ROWS AND COLUMNS

You can delete entire columns or rows in the **CURRENT WORKSHEET** while, at the same time, closing up the space left by the deletion, by taking these steps:

Select the columns or rows you want to delete. A quick way to do this is to click on the column letter or row number to highlight the entire column or row.

Select column or row by clicking its letter or number.

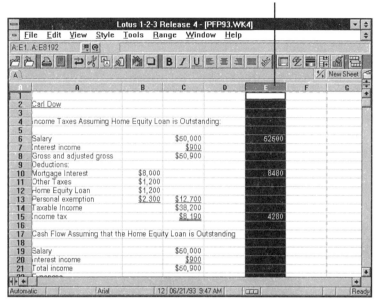

Choose Edit Delete. 1-2-3 **DELETES** the rows or columns and the data they contain and closes up the space.

There are SmartIcon shortcuts on the Editing SmartIcon set for deleting selected rows and columns. Click on one of them to delete the selection.

Caution: Be sure the cell pointer is positioned in the worksheet, row, or column you want to delete before using one of these icons.

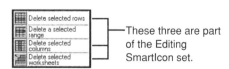

These three are part of the Editing SmartIcon set.

Click one of these oh-so-smart icons to delete the current selection.

For a shortcut that **DELETES** a selected row or column, press the key combination **CTRL+ -** (minus sign from the numeric keypad).

ELECTRONIC INVISIBLE INK

You can hide data in your worksheets so that it is invisible, even though the data still is in the cells. (Someone's been hangin' at the Pentagon again.) Use this little ruse if you are working on confidential data, like salaries, so no one can peek over your shoulder to see it on the screen. Hidden data does not appear on a *printout*. However, you should know that hidden data is not completely invisible. When the cell pointer is in a hidden cell and the cell is **UNPROTECTED**, the data appears in the edit line. If the cell containing hidden data is **PROTECTED**, the data does not appear in the edit line.

To hide ranges of data:

 Select the range.

Select the range you want to hide.

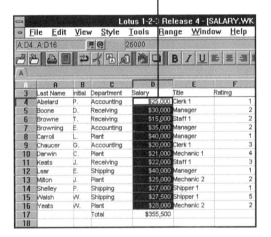

 Choose Style Number Format.

3 Click on the Hidden format in the Format list box.

Select the Hidden format to hide
the selected range of data.

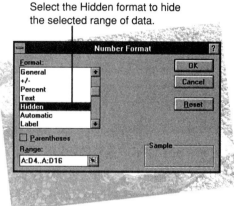

4 Choose OK.

The contents of the current cell are visible in the
contents box even though the cell is in the hidden range.

Current cell

The data in range
D4:D16 is hidden.

To make hidden data visible, select it, choose Style Number Format, and click on
Reset.

COLLAPSIBLE COLUMN (OR WORKSHEETS)

Instead of just making small ranges of data disappear, leaving blank cells intact on your screen, you can choose to remove columns or entire worksheets from view as if they'd been sucked into a black hole. Though your data's still there, the columns (or worksheet) are AWOL and inaccessible. Use this feature if you are working on confidential information "for your eyes only," or if you have a column of formulas that don't need to be seen on the printed copy.

Before you start hiding parts of your 1-2-3 files, you should know more about what you are getting yourself into:

⬦ You can't move the cell pointer to hidden columns or worksheets.

⬦ You can't enter data into hidden columns or worksheets.

⬦ Formulas in hidden columns or worksheets and formulas that refer to data in hidden columns and worksheets continue to work correctly. So, anyone who can look at the formula and solve for the hidden data (remember algebra, kids?) will soon know what you have to hide.

You can also **HIDE COLUMNS** by collapsing them. To do this, move the mouse pointer to the border that is to the right of the column letter of the rightmost column you want to hide. The mouse pointer changes to a black two-headed horizontal arrow. Then drag to the left until the mouse pointer is on the left column border of the leftmost column you want to hide.

H Y P E R T I P

To **HIDE COLUMNS** or worksheets:

1 **Select the range.** The range needs to include only one cell in each of the columns or worksheets you want to hide.

Drag with the left mouse button to select columns to hide.

 Choose Style Hide.

Select Column or Sheet. If you want to hide an entire worksheet select Sheet.

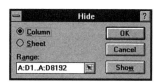

Choose OK.

Columns D and E are completely hidden.

	A	B	C	F	G	H
1	Last Name	Initial	Department	Rating		
2	Abelard	P.	Accounting	1		
3	Boone	D.	Receiving	2		
4	Browne	T.	Receiving	2		
5	Browning	E.	Accounting	2		
6	Carroll	L.	Plant	1		
7	Chaucer	G.	Accounting	3		
8	Darwin	C.	Plant	4		
9	Keats	J.	Receiving	3		
10	Lear	E.	Shipping	1		
11	Milton	J.	Plant	2		
12	Shelly	P.	Shipping	1		
13	Walsh	W.	Shipping	5		
14	Yeats	W.	Plant	2		
15			Total			
16						
17						
18						

THEY'RE BA-ACK!

Redisplaying hidden columns or worksheets is as easy:

Choose Style Hide.

Select Column or Sheet.

 In the Range text box, enter the cell address from the hidden column or worksheet. For example, if the hidden column is C, type **C1** in the range text box. Or click on the Range Selector, and select a cell range that spans across the column you want to display; you can select **B2..D2** to redisplay column C. If you've hidden a worksheet, such as worksheet B, you can type **B:B1**.

Enter a cell address from the
hidden range or worksheet here.

 Choose Show. The hidden column or worksheet reappears.

ZAPPING THOSE UNSIGHTLY ZEROS

There may be times when your worksheet displays many zeros, like when you've used lots of formulas and some of those formulas calculate out to zero. This zero overpopulation makes it hard to zero in on the interesting nonzero results you want to see. You can have 1-2-3 hide all cells in the current worksheet that contain the value zeros or evaluate to zero, or you can choose to have zeros display as a special character like *, N/A, or whatever you want in place of zeros, by following these steps:

 Choose Style Worksheet Defaults.

 Turn off the "Display zeros as" check box.

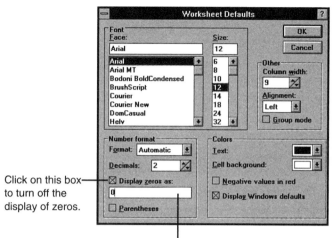

Click on this box to turn off the display of zeros.

To replace zeros with some other character(s) like * or N/A, turn on the check box, and enter the character(s) in this text box.

Click on OK.

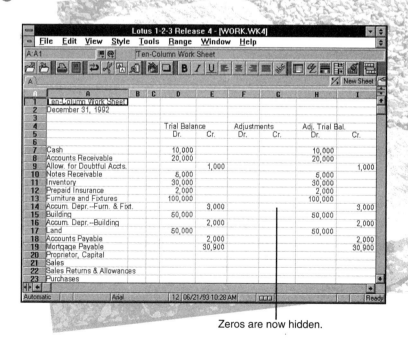

Zeros are now hidden.

PASTE— See "16. The Naked Truth About Copying and Moving," p. 161.

PRINTOUT—See "18. Preprinting Anxiety and How to Overcome It," p. 177, and "19. Putting Out the Output," p. 186.

PROTECT DATA—See "34. Protecting the Data You Love," p. 321.

HYPERLINKS

YOU LOOK MAHHVELOUS!

In the stone age, you didn't have much choice in how your data looked after you typed it in. Yeah, you could center an entry, change the font to one of the other three whopping choices you had, or maybe be real daring and show another decimal place. (Yawn.) But because control is a beautiful thing, 1-2-3 now gives you ultimate power over how your data looks. You can position data just about anywhere in a cell, adjust columns and rows with the flick of your wrist, and snazz up all your letters and numbers.

As part of 1-2-3 *worksheet defaults*, labels (text entries) are left-aligned and values (numbers) are right-aligned. You can change the alignment of either labels or values, and your options include much more than just left or right alignment.

Specifically, your other options include:

◇ Adjusting the cell contents' vertical alignment within a row, moving entries to the top or bottom row border, centering the entries, or running the text vertically (from top to bottom).

◇ Choosing a General alignment that eliminates the thousand separator and trailing zeros in values and uses a minus sign for negatives.

◇ Centering data, spacing it evenly across one cell, or centering it over a group of selected cells.

◇ Wrapping text in one cell, so that 1-2-3 displays the full cell entry in one or more lines in the cell.

The Formatting set offers SmartIcons that let you left-align, center, right-align, and evenly space selected data.

Alignment options even an artist can love.

You can also use label-prefix characters to change text **ALIGNMENT**. (Type in one of these at the start of your entry.)

'   Left alignment

"   Right alignment

^   Center alignment

\   Repeats text in the cell

You can also use the quick menu to align data. Select the range, and press the right mouse button to display the quick menu. Then choose Alignment.

To change the **ALIGNMENT** of text or numbers:

 Select the range containing the labels and/or values you want to align.

 Choose Style Alignment.

Under Horizontal, select an option.

Aligns labels to the left and values to the right.

Aligns data to the left.

Centers the data within individual cells.

Aligns data to the right.

Stretches data within the cell by expanding the space between words and letters.

For ranges only, aligns the data from the leftmost cell over the columns within the range.

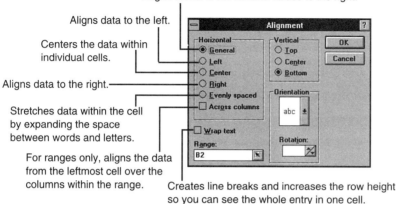

Creates line breaks and increases the row height so you can see the whole entry in one cell.

 (Optional) For ranges only, select the Across columns check box to align the data in the leftmost cell over the columns within the range, according to your selection under Horizontal.

 Choose OK.

COLUMN WIDTH MUTATION

The initial width for all the columns in a 1-2-3 file is nine characters. You can change the column width for the entire file by choosing Style Worksheet Defaults. However, you may be satisfied with the paltry nine-character default width and only need to change it once in a while when you're working with

LONG LABELS, **LARGE NUM-BERS**, or cell entries of only a few characters. In those cases, rather than change all the column widths, you can select only those columns that need to be changed and then adjust the width. You can try each method next.

If you enter a **LONG LABEL** (more characters than the width of the cell) and the cells to the right are blank, 1-2-3 displays the label across the blank cells. However, if the cells to the right contain data, 1-2-3 displays only the part of the label that fits in the cell where it is entered.

When a column is too narrow to display **LARGE NUMBERS**, 1-2-3 displays *** (asterisks) instead of the value. To fit the numbers, you may be able to use **Style Number Format** to change the *number format*. For example, if you are using the Currency format with two decimal places, you may be able to fit the numbers by changing the format to Currency with no decimal places. You can also try **Style Font & Attributes** to reduce the point size of the characters in the column.

STYLE COLUMN WIDTH AND YOU

Use this method when you need to size several columns, or know roughly how many characters wide you want the column(s) to be.

  Select the column or range of columns you want to adjust.

Select one or more columns.

This SmartIcon sizes the selected column(s) to fit the widest entry and can be found in the Formatting SmartIcon set.

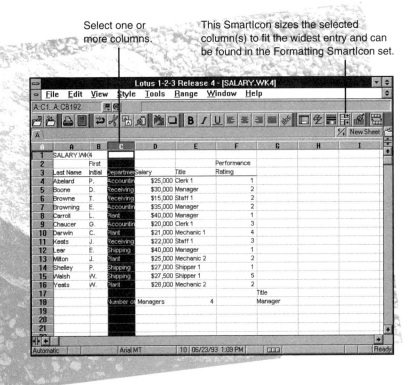

 Choose Style Column Width.

Select an option. If you select Set width to, then you must specify a number from 1 through 240 in the characters text box. If you select Fit widest entry, 1-2-3 adjusts a column to the width of the widest entry in that column. If you select **Reset to worksheet default**, 1-2-3 adjusts the columns to the default width defined with Style Worksheet Defaults.

Enter column width here, or click the up or down
arrows to increase or decrease the column width.

Choose this option to
adjust columns to
accommodate the widest
entry in the column.

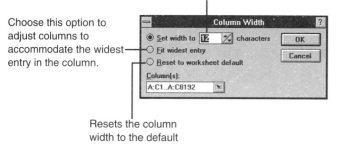

Resets the column
width to the default

 Choose OK.

MOUSE PATROL

Dragging is the fastest way to change the width of a **SINGLE COLUMN**. Here's
the evidence:

 **Move the mouse pointer to the border on the right of the column letter of the
column that you want to adjust.** The mouse pointer changes to a black two-
headed horizontal arrow.

Point to the right border of a column letter until the mouse pointer changes,
and then drag to resize the column.

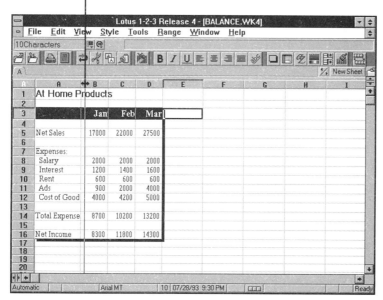

A shortcut way to resize
a **SINGLE COLUMN**
to the width of the data it
contains is to double-
click on the border to the
right of the column letter.

123

 Drag (right or left) until the column is the width you want.

I CAN CHANGE MY ROW HEIGHTS IF I REALLY HAVE TO

Usually, you have better things to do than think about row heights—1-2-3 makes automatic adjustments for you. However, when giving your worksheet its own style, you may want to create white space between rows of data. You can change row height using the direct approach of dragging with the mouse, or you can use Style Row Height to specify a specific row height, which is measured in **POINTS**. Both approaches are outlined below.

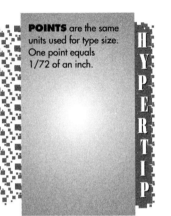
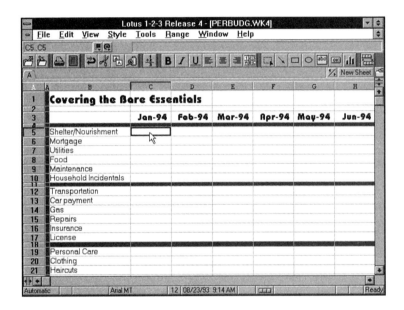

Resize blank rows and columns to separate data; add a color background for emphasis, too.

SIZING TO THE POINT

Use this method to do your thing on multiple rows.

 Select the range of rows you want to change by dragging on the row numbers.

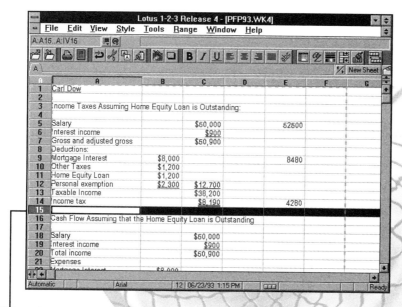

Click on the row number to select it.

 Choose Style Row Height.

 Select Set height to, which adjusts row height. Specify a height from 1 through 255 points in the points text box.

Select to specify the row height.

Type the row height you want in points (1 point = 1/72 of an inch), or click an arrow to increase or decrease the row height.

Select to adjust the row to accommodate the largest font used in the row.

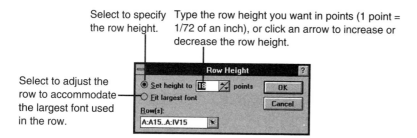

 Choose OK.

LESSON 12

RESIZING'S A DRAG

As for sizing a single column, changing the height of one row is fastest with a mouse. Voilà:

 Move the mouse pointer to the lower row border. The mouse pointer changes to a black, two-headed vertical arrow.

Point to the bottom border of a row number until the mouse pointer changes, and then drag to resize the row.

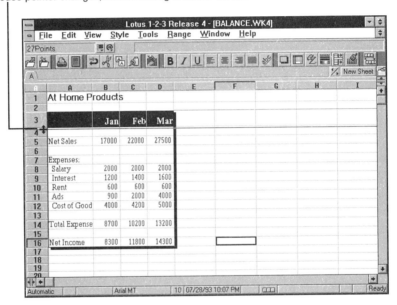

 Drag down or up until the row is the height you want.

THE FONT YA WANT

If you don't like something about yourself, or your worksheet, you're perfectly free to change it. The characters that you enter into your 1-2-3 worksheets are displayed with three highly changeable attributes: typeface, size, and style.

Typeface is the distinctive graphic design of letters and numbers. 1-2-3 allows you to choose from several **TYPEFACES**. The popular ones for business reports are Times New Roman, Arial, Courier, and Helv (Helvetica). The size of a typeface is

When you run 1-2-3 under version 3.1 of Windows, you can use TrueType **TYPEFACES**, which are scalable to any size and look exactly on-screen as they do when printed.

HYPERTIP

a measure of the height of a font and is measured in points. There are 72 points in an inch. Or put another way, if you wanted your type to be approximately 1 inch in height, then you would choose a size of 72. Type style refers to attributes, such as bold, underline, and italics.

To adjust the typeface and size of your data:

 Select the range of text you want to change.

 Choose Style Font & Attributes.

 Select a typeface from the Face list box.

 Select a point size from the Size list box.

Type in or click on a point size in the Size list.

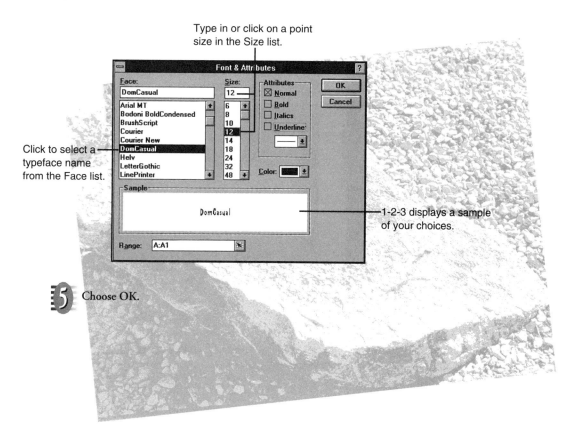

Click to select a typeface name from the Face list.

1-2-3 displays a sample of your choices.

Choose OK.

Being the cool program that it is, 1-2-3 offers status bar and SmartIcon shortcuts for choosing typefaces and character sizes.

Click to change a font, size, and more.

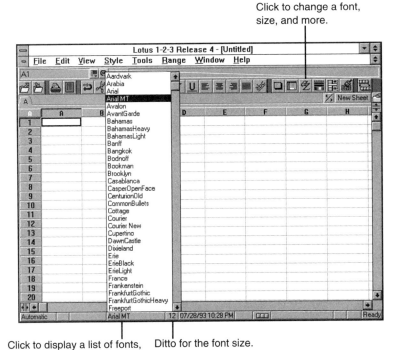

Click to display a list of fonts, and then click on a font.

Ditto for the font size.

Click for a change to typeface and size.

WHAT'S SO GREAT ABOUT LOOKING NORMAL, ANYWAY?

It's a bummer that you can't put big flashing lights on important data to make sure it's noticed. But, Mr. Obvious says you can make some of your data bold, italicized, or underlined to call attention to it. For example, using boldface type for the label "Totally Bogus Total" will give it special emphasis. Check out how to assign **ATTRIBUTES**:

If you don't like the **ATTRIBUTES** you've applied, you can reset them by selecting the range of text and using **Style Font & Attributes** to select the Normal check box to remove bold, italics, or underline.

HYPERTIP

Select the range you want to add attributes to.

 Choose Style Font & Attributes.

 Select the Bold, Italics, or Underline check box.

 If you select Underline, select a line style from the Underline drop-down box.

The choice for conformists

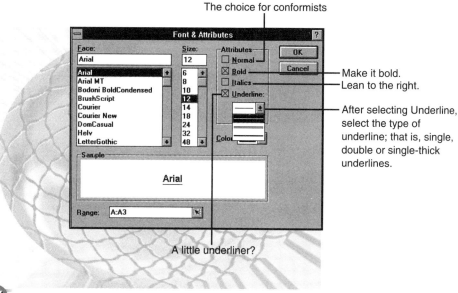

Make it bold.
Lean to the right.

After selecting Underline, select the type of underline; that is, single, double or single-thick underlines.

A little underliner?

 Choose OK.

Several SmartIcons help you make selected text bold (look for an icon with a bold **B**), italic (the *I* has it), underlined (<u>U</u>), and boring (N). Some or all of these *SmartIcons*, and others, appear on various SmartIcon sets. You can also use the quick menu to change the attributes of text. Select the range, and press the right mouse button to display the quick menu, then choose Font & Attributes.

HYPERLINKS

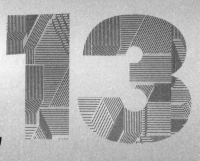

NUMBER FORMATS TO GO

Somewhere back in time, we humans all agreed to use some curly little symbols along with numbers so we could decode what numbers mean . . . dollar signs, percentage signs, and all that. If you neglect to use these symbols in your worksheet, it begins to look like that classic painting, "Polar Bear in a Blizzard." All the numbers kind of blend into one heaving mass of sameness.

Using those doodads (a.k.a. **NUMBER FORMATTING**) improves the readability of your worksheets. Formatting dollar amounts with leading dollar signs, percentages with trailing percent signs, and large numbers with thousands separators makes the meaning of worksheet values crystal clear. You have the option of setting up global number formatting (for the whole file), or you can just format selected cells.

You can have 1-2-3 display every value as currency ($). That's called setting the *default number format*, which you do with the Style Worksheet Defaults command. For example, with the default format set to **Comma** (which is a number format name), values greater than 999 will include thousands separators (commas). The number 2000 is displayed as **2,000**. That's just peachy, but the practice for many types of business reports is to use dollar signs for the first value in a column and for subtotals and totals. Even though you may have selected Comma as your default format, you can format selected ranges (such as those containing totals) in the Currency format, or for that matter, any format you want. In selected ranges you can override the **DEFAULT NUMBER FORMAT** by using Style Number Format or by using the format and decimal selectors on the status bar.

NUMBER FORMATTING sets how the values of your worksheet will look— only the display of values, not the values themselves are affected. For example, if you format the value 1500.51 as Currency with no decimal places, the value will be displayed as **$1,501**. But the real value, when used in calculations, is $1,500.51.

To reset the format of the current selection to the **DEFAULT NUMBER FORMAT** specified in Style Worksheet Defaults, choose Style Number Format, and click on the Reset button.

MAKING THAT POLAR BEAR BLACK (NUMBER FORMATTING A RANGE)

Even a totally inept spreadsheet-phobic loser can change the **NUMBER FORMAT** in a range. Do it just like this:

 Select the range to apply a new number format to.

Select the range of cells you want to format.

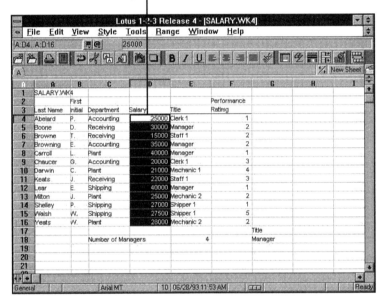

 Choose Style Number Format.

3 Select a format from the Format list box by clicking on your choice. As you click on a choice, 1-2-3 displays a sample of what your numbers will look like. The options include:

Fixed With this format, you'll have minus signs in front of negative numbers and decimal values will have zeros in front of them (leading zeros). You can also specify the number of decimal places you want to display.

Scientific Use this if your numbers need to be in scientific (exponential) notation. You can choose the amount of decimal places you want displayed.

Currency This format automatically inserts a currency symbol and thousands separators. You can also specify how many decimal places you want displayed.

, Comma This format is basically the same as Currency. The only difference is that it doesn't show the currency symbol. It's called "comma"

because of the commas that show up as thousands separators.

General With this format, negative numbers have minus signs in front of them. There are no commas to separate thousands and no trailing zeros to the right of the decimal point.

+/– This shows a row of plus signs or minus signs that are equal to whatever the integer value is of the number in the cell. For example, if you typed **4.3**, you would see ++++ in the cell. It's kind of hard to tell what the minus signs stand for because they run together and look like one big line. But if you highlight the cell and look in the contents box, you'll be able to see the real value. If your number is between -1 and 1, you'll see a period instead of a plus or minus sign.

133

Percent   This format converts numbers to percentages. You'll see the percent sign. You can also set the decimal point limit on this one.

Text   Use this format if you want to see your formulas exactly as you typed them instead of the value(s) they represent.

Hidden   This is just what it sounds like. The contents of the cell are invisible on the spreadsheet, but they still show up in the contents box.

Automatic   This format will try to intelligently convert whatever

you entered into the proper format. For example, if you typed $86.00, the cell will become formatted as Currency.

Label   Everything you enter in a cell with a Label format will have a label-prefix character inserted in it.

Date formats   There are several different ways to display dates. Just choose the one you want.

Time formats   There are also several different ways to display the time. Pick the one you want.

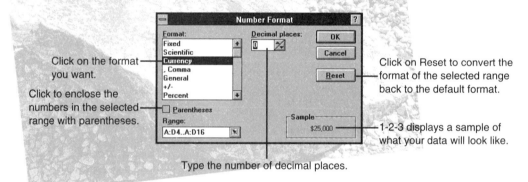

Click on the format you want.

Click to enclose the numbers in the selected range with parentheses.

Click on Reset to convert the format of the selected range back to the default format.

1-2-3 displays a sample of what your data will look like.

Type the number of decimal places.

 (Optional) If you select either Currency, Scientific, Percent, Comma, or Fixed in step 3, type the number of decimal places (0 through 15) in the Decimal places text box, or click the up or down arrows to increase or decrease the number of decimal places.

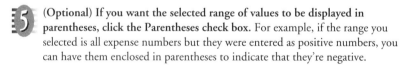 (Optional) If you want the selected range of values to be displayed in parentheses, click the Parentheses check box. For example, if the range you selected is all expense numbers but they were entered as positive numbers, you can have them enclosed in parentheses to indicate that they're negative.

Choose OK.

There are three SmartIcons for quickly formatting values. They apply Currency, Percentage, and Comma formats—all with two decimal places. You can *customize any SmartIcon set* by adding these icons.

Smart number formatting icons.

THE STATUS BAR TO THE RESCUE

Check your menus at the door and use this easier number-formatting technique. The status bar contains a format selector and a decimal selector—small bars you can click on to display a list of choices. Number formatting becomes a quick point-and-click task:

 Select the range to format.

 Click on the format selector on the status bar. A list of formats appears.

Click on a format to select it.   Select the range of cells to format.

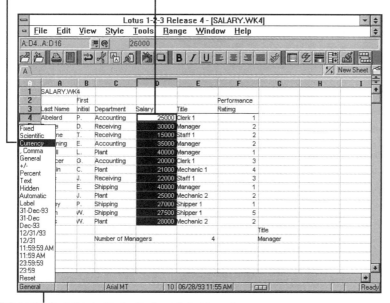

Click on the format selector to display a list of formats.

 Click one of the formats.

 Click on the decimal selector on the status bar. A list of decimal places is displayed.

Make a choice from the
list by clicking.

8	Carroll	L.	Plant	$40,000.00	Manager
9	Chaucer	G.	Accounting	$20,000.00	Clerk 1
10	Darw	C.	Plant	$21,000.00	Mechanic 1
11	Keats	J.	Receiving	$22,000.00	Staff 1
12	Lear	E.	Shipping	$40,000.00	Manager
13	Milton	J.	Plant	$25,000.00	Mechanic 2
14	Shelle	P.	Shipping	$27,000.00	Shipper 1
15	Walsh	W.	Shipping	$27,500.00	Shipper 1
16	Yeats	W.	Plant	$28,000.00	Mechanic 2
17					
18			Number of Managers		4
19					
20					
21					

| Currency | 2 | | Arial MT | | 10 | 06/28/93 11:5 |

Click on the decimal selector
to display the list.

 Click a choice.

MORPHING FORMULAS TO VALUES

You can copy and paste the results of a formula—not the formula, but just the result it calculates to. In other words, you can convert a formula to its value. You may want to do this if you have made several calculations in cells that are referenced in other calculations. To speed up the calculation of the worksheet, you can convert those calculations that you won't need to recalculate to values. Converting a selected range of formulas requires you to cruise through the *Windows Clipboard.* Or if you want to convert only one formula, there's a snappy mouse shortcut. Read on.

A SPECIAL KIND OF PASTE

To convert a selected range of formulas, use *Edit Copy* to put a **COPY** of the range formulas on the Clipboard, and

then paste only the values by using Edit Paste Special, like so:

 Select the cell or range that contains the formula you want to convert to values.

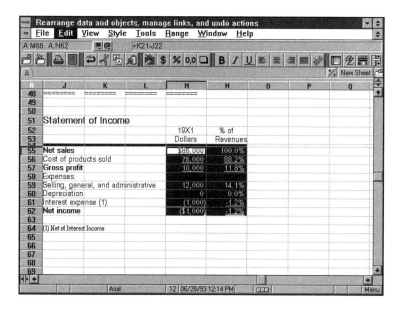

 Choose Edit Copy.

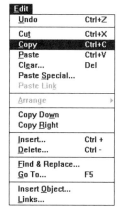

3 Select the entire range or the top left cell of the range in which you want to paste the data. If you want to convert the range you selected in step 1 to values, you don't need to select a range because it will still be selected from step 1.

4 Choose Edit Paste Special.

5 Under Paste, select Formulas as values.

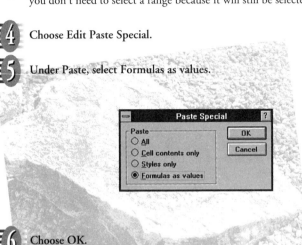

6 Choose OK.

THE DOUBLE-CLICK TRICK

If you have only one formula that you want to convert to its value, save yourself some time:

1 Double-click on the cell containing the formula.

Double-click on the cell to put the insertion point in the cell and the formula in the contents box.

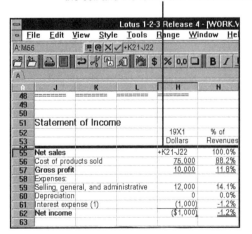

 Press F9 (CALC).

Press F9 (CALC) to convert the formula to its value, which appears in the cell and the contents box.

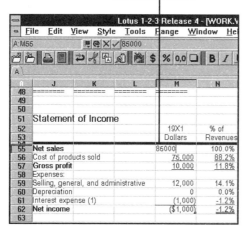

THE UGLY TRUTH: FORMATTING NEGATIVES IN RED

Another numeric tradition you'll have to conform to eventually is displaying negative numbers, such as net losses, unfavorable spending, and cash outflows in red. This makes number management simple: the more red you see, the more you should panic. (Just think of what your personal checking account register would look like. Ouch!)

Use the Style Lines & Color command to turn on this kind of formatting for the selected range or **WORKSHEET**. For example, if you want all spending variances calculated in cells B5..B20 to be in red, then select that range before choosing Style Lines & Colors.

If you think you can take all the bad news (a shot of tequila first might help), here's how to see red:

If you want all negative values in a **WORKSHEET** to be displayed in red, then select the whole worksheet by clicking on the worksheet letter in the worksheet frame located at the top left-hand part of the frame—above row 1 and next to column A, and then choose Style Lines & Color.

 Select the cell or range in which you want to display negative values in red.

 Choose Style Lines & Color.

 To display negative values in red, select the Negative values in red check box.

Click on this check box to see red.

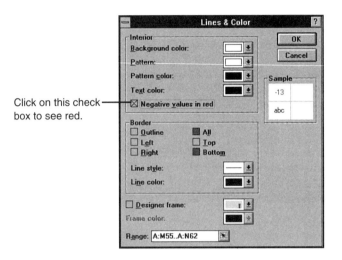

 Choose OK.

CUSTOMIZE ANY SMARTICON SET—See "31. Even Smarter SmartIcons," p. 301.

DEFAULT NUMBER FORMAT—See "24. Enhancing the Global Environment," p. 229.

EDIT COPY—See "16. The Naked Truth About Copying and Moving," p. 161.

INCREASE THE COLUMN WIDTH—See "12. You Look Mahhvelous!" p. 119.

WINDOWS CLIPBOARD—See "16. The Naked Truth About Copying and Moving," p.161.

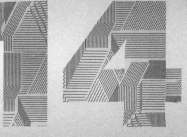
COLOR, SHADING, LINES, AND SHADOWS

This is your big opportunity to make your worksheet look really garish and to obscure your data with all kinds of pretty junk. 1-2-3 is willing and able to format cells with patterns, colors, borders, and even designer frames. But unless you don't give a flying fig whether anyone else can read your data, use this formatting sparingly to keep your worksheet legible. Also keep the capabilities of your printer in mind: If all you've got is a lame old dot-matrix boat anchor, formatting that looks fine on-screen can look like ca-ca on paper.

Tastefully done (you do have taste, don't you?), this kind of *formatting* can give certain ranges special emphasis by visually grouping certain cells, to give your work a polished, professional appearance. Patterns are particularly useful when you want to use 1-2-3 to produce an on-screen form. For example, if you use 1-2-3 to create a *trip expense report*, you can choose some type of dark or solid patterns to break up parts of the report, such as meals or transportation.

LET GO OF YOUR BORING OLD PATTERNS

Earlier versions of 1-2-3 only let you add shading to ranges of cells. But the obviously superior version 4.0 for Windows empowers you to add a variety of patterns, including diagonal lines, stripes, polka dots, checkerboards, and brick patterns. There are 64 different

patterns. (And a **PATTERN** can be colorized from a palette of 256 colors. If you have access to a color printer, your worksheets can really blow everyone else's out of the water.) To empattern your cells:

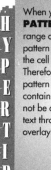

When you add a **PATTERN** to a cell or range of cells, the pattern is overlaid on the cell background. Therefore, if you add a pattern to a cell that contains text, you may not be able to see the text through the pattern overlay.

 Select the cell or range of cells to which you want to add a pattern.

 Choose Style Lines & Color.

Selected range the pattern will apply to

Click this SmartIcon in the Formatting set to display the Lines & Color dialog box.

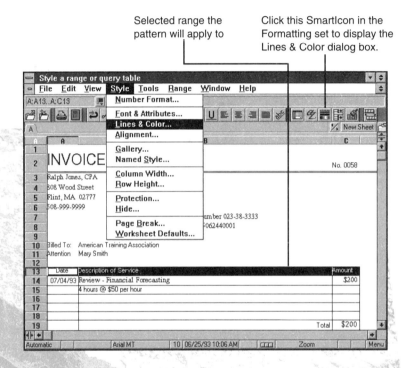

Select the pattern drop-down box arrow to display a matrix of patterns.

Select one of the patterns by clicking on it.

Click to show off pattern choices.

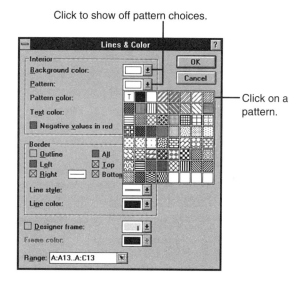

Click on a
pattern.

 (Optional) To change the color of the pattern, click on the Pattern color
drop-down box arrow, and select a color from the palette by clicking on it.

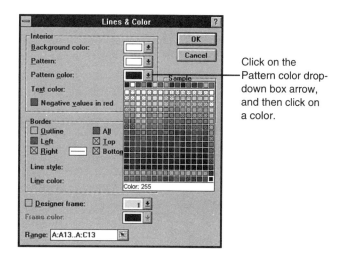

Click on the
Pattern color drop-
down box arrow,
and then click on
a color.

 Choose OK.

PSYCHEDELIC CELLS

You don't have to settle for black-and-white worksheet cells. Be the Ted Turner of 1-2-3 worksheets—colorize your worksheets by changing the colors of cell backgrounds and text. The default colors for your worksheets are white for the cell background and black for text. You can choose new colors for both background and text from a palette of 256 colors.

Here are examples of effective use of color:

⬦ Use a color for headings that describe different sections of your worksheet.

⬦ Use a bright color to highlight surprising, important, or significant information in a worksheet. For example, you could colorize the number of invoices that are more than 90 days old.

⬦ Use a color different from other colors in the worksheet to highlight action items. For example, use orange to colorize a spending variance that you want to research because it is surprisingly out of whack.

⬦ Use a color to signify that a particular range is a data entry area.

⬦ Use red (or some other color) to show changes that you have made to a worksheet that you are sharing with others.

To colorize your worksheets like a real media mogul:

 Select the cell or range you want to colorize.

 Choose Style Lines & Color.

Select the cell or range you want to color.

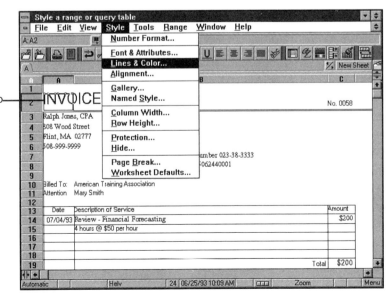

Select one or more drop-down boxes under Interior (Background color or Text color) by clicking on the down arrow.

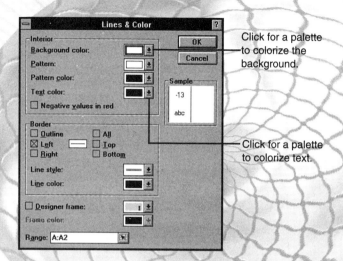

Click for a palette to colorize the background.

Click for a palette to colorize text.

Select a color from the palette by clicking on it.

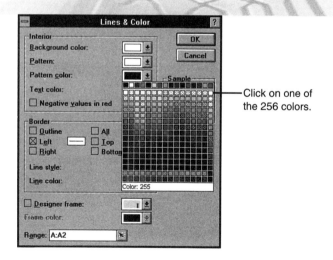

Click on one of the 256 colors.

Choose OK.

DIVIDE AND CONQUER

LINES AND BORDERS can enclose **SEVERAL RANGES** of the worksheet, dividing up the worksheet, marking subtotals and totals, and specifying data entry areas. Lines give structure to a worksheet *printout*, and if used properly, direct the reader's attention and make the worksheet more appealing. However, don't go crazy. I know it's tough, but be conservative in your use of lines—especially if you are preparing a business report. Too many borders and lines will make your worksheet look like a bunch of Tic Tac Toe games—detracting from the message you want to convey.

Line 'em up:

 Select the cell or range of cells that you want to draw lines around.

 Choose Style Lines & Color.

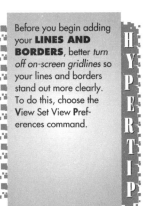

You can add borders to **SEVERAL RANGES** at once. Instead of selecting one range before using Style **Lines** & Color, select a collection of ranges by selecting the first range and holding down Ctrl, while selecting each additional range you want to format.

Before you begin adding your **LINES AND BORDERS**, better *turn off on-screen gridlines* so your lines and borders stand out more clearly. To do this, choose the **View** Set View **Pref**erences command.

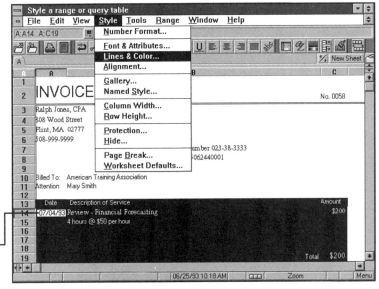

Select the cell or range.

Select one or more check boxes under Border.

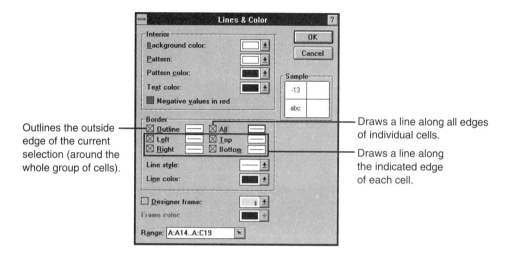

Outlines the outside edge of the current selection (around the whole group of cells).

Draws a line along all edges of individual cells.

Draws a line along the indicated edge of each cell.

 To apply a style to a line, click on the sample line next to one of the check boxes, and select a style from the Line style drop-down box.

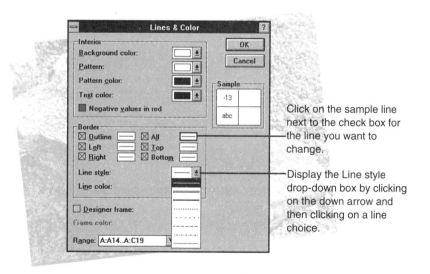

Click on the sample line next to the check box for the line you want to change.

Display the Line style drop-down box by clicking on the down arrow and then clicking on a line choice.

147

5 To colorize a line, select the sample line next to one of the check boxes, and select a color from the Line color drop-down box.

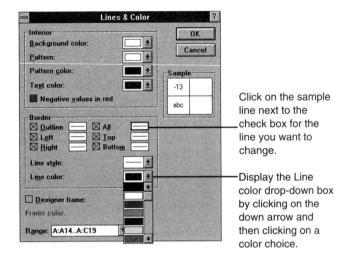

Click on the sample line next to the check box for the line you want to change.

Display the Line color drop-down box by clicking on the down arrow and then clicking on a color choice.

 Choose OK.

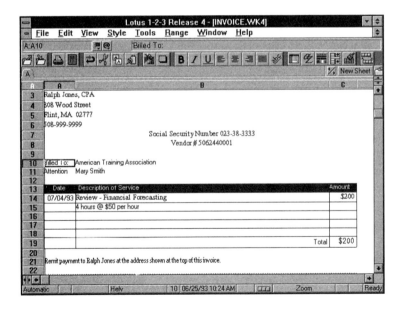

Range A13..C19 with lines-a-poppin'.

FRAME IT YOURSELF

If you don't think that lines and borders are hype enough to do the job, then use designer frames to pump up your cells. **DESIGNER FRAMES** are like custom picture frames you hang around on your worksheet. You can choose from a variety of designer frame styles, and then go one better and make them any size or color you want. To put things in a proper framework:

There is a SmartIcon in the Formatting set that you can select to display the Lines & Color dialog box so that you can select one of the **DESIGNER FRAMES** or add color and borders to your worksheet. You can also use the quick menu to add color, borders, or frames by selecting the range and then pressing the right mouse button to display the quick menu. Then select Lines & Color.

 Select the cell or range of cells you want to frame.

Select the whole range you want to frame.

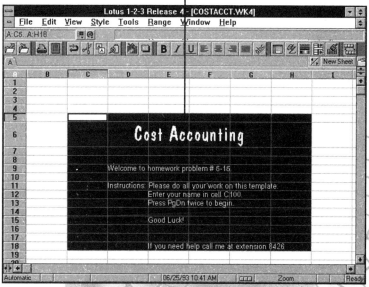

 Choose Style Lines & Color.

 Select the Designer frame check box by clicking on it.

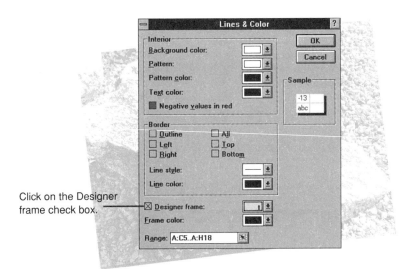

Click on the Designer
frame check box.

4 Select a frame from the Designer frame drop-down box by clicking on the
drop-down arrow and clicking on a frame style.

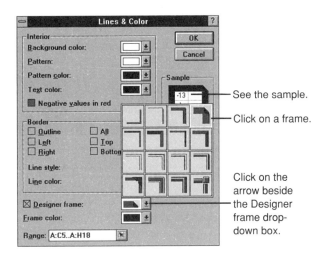

See the sample.

Click on a frame.

Click on the
arrow beside
the Designer
frame drop-
down box.

5 Select a color from the Frame color drop-down box by clicking on the drop-
down arrow and clicking on a color choice. (OK, Sherlock, the box drops up
instead of down.)

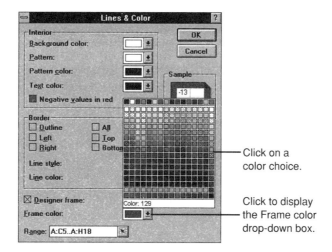

Click on a
color choice.

Click to display
the Frame color
drop-down box.

 Choose OK.

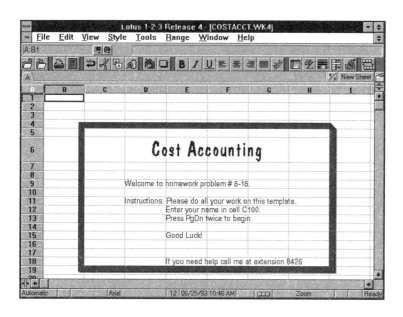

You paid big money for this feature . . . a designer frame encloses the information to call special attention to it.

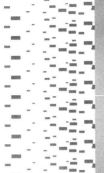

FORMATTING—See "12. You Look Mahhvelous!" p. 119, "13. Number Formats to Go," p. 131, and "15. We Be Stylin'," p. 153.

PRINTOUT—See "19. Putting Out the Output," p. 186.

TRIP EXPENSE REPORT—See "Project 4. Travelin' Man," p. 341.

TURN OFF ON-SCREEN GRIDLINES—See "23. It's Your Display, You Can Change It," p. 222.

HYPERLINKS

WE BE STYLIN'

Throw away all your old issues of GQ and Cosmo. You don't need one nanosmidgen of fashion sense to be successfully stylin' in 1-2-3. If you can muster any patience and organizational skills whatsoever, you can cut down the work it takes to format your worksheets —by using and creating styles.

As you *format worksheet cells*, you create a certain collection of attributes. For example, you might make a range bold, 14-point Arial font, with a red cell background. If you want to use this style on several ranges in your worksheet, you don't have to choose all the Style menu commands each time. When you apply several formats to a cell or range and achieve the look you like, you can save that collection of formats as a style and give it a name. Then, rather than apply formats to other ranges, you can select the range and select the named style from a list. Ba-da-bing, ba-da-bang; your range has just the formatting you want.

MONIKER-FREE STYLING

Before you actually create a style of your own, take a minute to learn the lazy way to blot a cell's **STYLING** all over the worksheet without actually saving it as a file:

 Apply the formats you want to a cell or range. Use the Style menu to apply the number format, font and attributes, colors, patterns, alignment, and everything else you want.

 Select one or more of the cells you formatted.

 Click on the SmartIcon that copies a range's styling to another range. This icon is part of the Formatting SmartIcon set, but you can *customize any SmartIcon set* to include it.

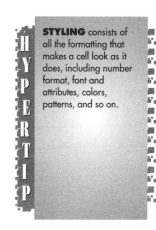

HYPERTIP

STYLING consists of all the formatting that makes a cell look as it does, including number format, font and attributes, colors, patterns, and so on.

Click on this Formatting set
SmartIcon, which lets you copy a
cell's formatting to another cell.

Select a
formatted cell.

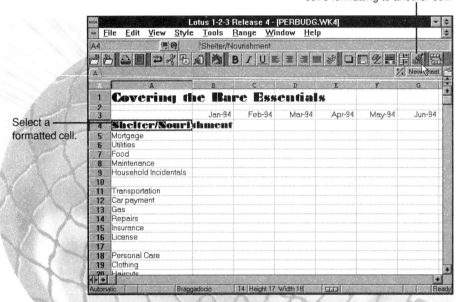

4 Point to the area where you want to copy the format. The mouse pointer looks like a paintbrush. Note that you can press Esc at this point to cancel the styling operation.

Click on one cell,
or press the left
mouse button,
and drag over
several cells.

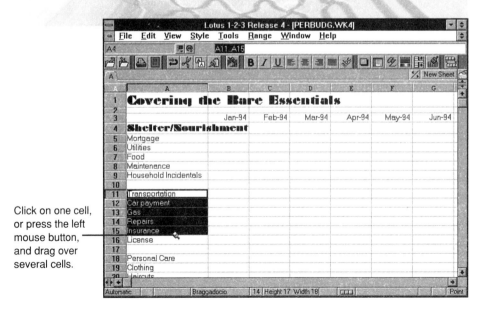

Click to format a single cell, or drag over all the cells you want to format.

BRAVE NEW STYLES

Saving the formatting of a cell or range is as easy as falling off your mountain bike. To name a style so you can use it again later:

 Apply the formats you want to a cell or range. Use the Style menu to apply the number format, font and attributes, colors, patterns, alignment, and everything else.

 Select one or more of the cells you formatted.

 Choose Style Named Style. The Named Style dialog box appears.

Formatted cell

 Enter a name for the named style in the Style name text box. You can enter up to 15 characters for a style name.

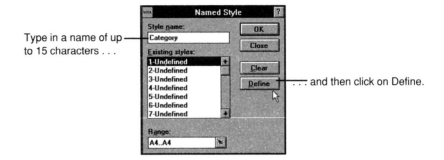

Type in a name of up to 15 characters . . .

. . . and then click on Define.

 Choose Define.

 Choose OK.

CELLS OF STYLE

If the **STATUS BAR** is not visible, use **View** Set View **Preferences** to display it.

Now that you've named several hundred styles for your worksheet, you're ready to apply those styles to the three or four blank cells that are left. There are a couple of ways you can do this. You can select the cell or range to format, choose Style Named Style, or click on the SmartIcon for naming and applying styles, and then double-click on the name of the style you want to apply in the Existing styles list of the Named Style dialog box. But like the preceding sentence, that procedure's too complicated, and the *status bar* offers a better way. You can use the **STATUS BAR** to take the easy way out:

 Select the range or collection to format.

 Click the style selector on the status bar at the bottom of the 1-2-3 window.

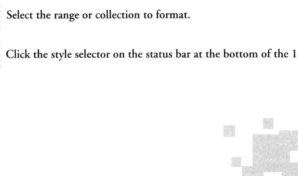

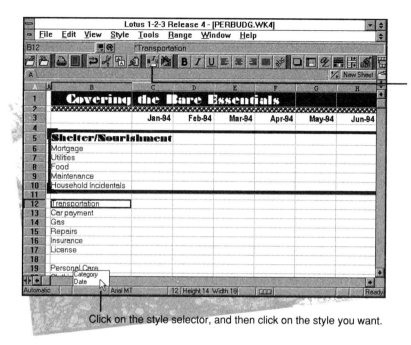

Add this SmartIcon to the current set, and then click on it to display the Named Style dialog box to save or apply a style.

Click on the style selector, and then click on the style you want.

 Click on the style you want to apply.

CELLS THAT FORMERLY HAD STYLE

Sometimes, the darn mouse just goes crazy in your hand, and you end up spreading the wrong style all over the worksheet. (The mouse is like sports equipment . . . it's always your golf club's or bowling ball's fault when things go ballistic.) Don't despair. To **STRIP STYLES** from cells, select the cell or range, and click on the SmartIcon for deleting styles from a range. This icon is in the Formatting SmartIcon set, but you can move it to other SmartIcon sets, too. To strip styles from cells, select the cell or range, and click on the SmartIcon for deleting styles from a range. This icon is in the Formatting SmartIcon set, but you can move it to other SmartIcon sets, too.

You can also **STRIP STYLES** from a range by using the Edit Clear command. First select the range that you want to strip styles from, and choose Edit Clear. Then select the Styles only option, and select **OK**.

Add this SmartIcon to the current set, and then click on it to remove a named style from the selected cell or range.

THAT STYLE'S HISTORY

You don't have to keep a named style forever. You can clear it from the list. Keep in mind that when you do, ranges previously formatted with the named style will no longer be displayed with the same characteristics. Clearing a named style also clears that style from those ranges formatted with the named style. To euthanize a named style:

 Choose Style Named Style. You can also click on the SmartIcon for creating and applying styles if it's displayed on the current set.

 Click on the style to delete in the Existing styles list box.

Click on the style name to delete . . .

. . . and then click on Clear.

 **Click on Clear.**

GOING THE TEMPLATE ROUTE

Getting a range to look exactly the way you want it to look can be a trial-and-error process. You try some formatting—maybe some patterns, lines, boldface, italics and so on. Maybe the range looks good . . . nah, it doesn't look quite right . . . maybe I'll just try this . . . oh, I've boned it up completely!

Let's be honest. Not all of us have developed a great sense of worksheet style. Therefore, for those of us who don't have the knack for creating stylish worksheets or who don't have the time or patience to play with it until it's right, there is the 1-2-3 **Style Gallery** command. With **Style Gallery**, you can format ranges with one of ten style templates. Some of the templates have the chiseled look, some have patterns that replicate the look of computer printouts from the "old days," and one template looks like a Post-it Note.

Click on this SmartIcon in the Formatting set to see the Gallery styles.

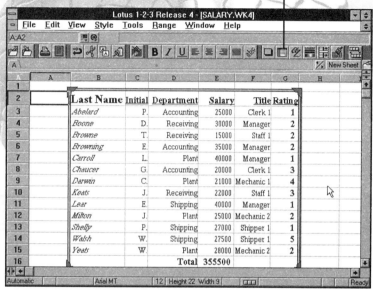

Impress your boss! Keep your job! Format your worksheets with one of the cool Gallery Styles offered in 1-2-3.

To apply one of the Style Gallery templates to a range:

 Select the range you want to format.

 Choose Style Gallery. (Or click on the SmartIcon to do so if it's on the current SmartIcon set.)

 Select a style template from the Template list box. A sample of the template appears in the dialog box so you can get an idea of how it will look.

You get a snappy sample.

Click on one of
these handy dandy
Gallery styles.

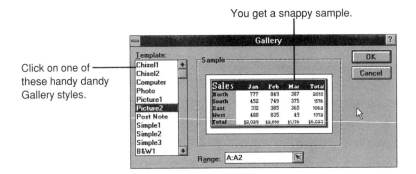

 Choose OK.

CUSTOMIZE ANY SMARTICON SET—See "31.
Even Smarter SmartIcons," p. 301.

FORMAT WORKSHEET CELLS—See "12. You Look
Mahhvelous!" p. 119, "13. Number Formats to
Go," p. 131, and "14. Color, Shading, Lines, and
Shadows," p. 141.

STATUS BAR—See "1. Tuning In to 1-2-3 for
Windows," p. 3.

HYPERLINKS

Copy Crazy

Getting Your Fill of a Good Thing

Drag Until You Drop

16

THE NAKED TRUTH ABOUT COPYING AND MOVING

How many times in school did you hear, "If you are caught copying, you will FAIL THIS EXAM"? You bought into the "do your own work" philosophy hook, line, and sinker . . . until you hit the working world. In one of those sick twists that life deals out with regularity, you discovered that the key to success in a job is copying as much as you can so you don't have to reinvent the wheel for every project . . . so much for the educational system preparing anyone for reality.

Copying and moving your 1-2-3 data and formulas saves time and minimizes errors. Get the formula right the first time, and every copy works just the way you want it to. When you copy (or move) data or objects, 1-2-3 places a copy (or the original) of the data and related styles on the Windows Clipboard. The **CLIPBOARD** is a temporary storage area that helps you transfer information between worksheets and other applications.

There are four ways of copying data in 1-2-3: by using Edit Copy (or *Edit Cut* for moving data), Edit Copy **R**ight, or Edit Copy **D**own, or by using a mouse action called drag-and-drop. This lesson covers all four methods of copying data.

You can view the contents of the Windows **CLIPBOARD** by double-clicking on the **Clipboard Viewer** icon found in the Main group window of the Windows Program Manager.

HOLD ON THERE, BABALOOEY!

Before you embark on a rampant copying frenzy, however, you need to pause and think about the effect that copying and moving has on formulas. (Remember that junk about *relative, absolute, and mixed references* in Lesson 8?) To keep it simple, here's what you need to remember:

◇ Moving doesn't affect a formula whatsoever, no matter what kind of references it contains.

◇ Copying adjusts relative references based on how many rows and columns from the original formula you place the copy. Say the formula in cell B4 is **@sum(B2..B3)** and you copy the formula across columns C, D, and E in the same row. The copy in cell C4 would read **@sum(C2..C3)**, cell D4 would contain **@sum(D2..D3)**, and cell E4 would read **@sum(E2..E3)**. Get it?

COPYING COPYING COPYING AND MOVING

1-2-3 offers the Edit Copy command for copying and the Edit Cut command for moving. When you copy, the source data remains intact on the worksheet—only a duplicate of the data is placed on the Clipboard. When you cut the data, it's removed from its original location, and the original is placed on the Clipboard. You can paste the **CLIPBOARD CONTENTS** into other ranges, worksheets, or applications using the Edit Paste command.

To copy or move data:

 Select the range or drawn object.

The **CLIPBOARD CONTENTS** are only temporary. They only remain on the Clipboard until you use Edit Copy or Edit Cut again. The moral of the story: Be careful when cutting data, because if you nuke what's on the Clipboard, you don't have an original to copy again. And remember the magic Edit Undo command.

HYPERTIP

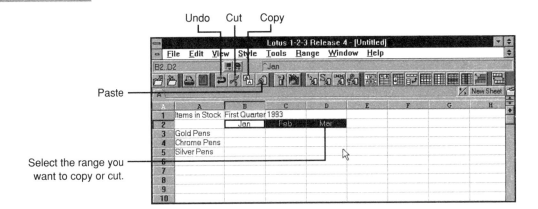

Paste ———

Select the range you want to copy or cut.

 Choose Edit Copy, or press Ctrl+C. Note that if you prefer to move data rather than copying it, choose Edit Cut or **Ctrl+X**. This command removes the data from the worksheet and places it on the Clipboard for pasting. Instead of this command, you can click on either the **Copy** or the **Cut** SmartIcon.

3 Click on the upper left cell that you want to copy the range to. Because you're copying a range of data, make sure the cells you're copying to are blank (unless you don't mind copying over the cell entries that are there).

. . . and then click on this SmartIcon to paste.

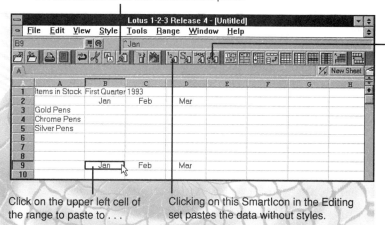

Clicking on this SmartIcon pastes formula results, not the formulas themselves.

Click on the upper left cell of the range to paste to . . .

Clicking on this SmartIcon in the Editing set pastes the data without styles.

4 Choose Edit Paste. Or click on one of the Paste SmartIcons. 1-2-3 pastes the data from the Clipboard to the new location.

FILL 'ER RIGHT

Entering reams of data bites. No one wants to do it. So if you have a column of data that you want to copy into columns to the right, the Edit Copy **Right** command can save your fingers. This command copies the contents of the leftmost column across the columns in the *selected range* to fill the entire range.

That is, if the selected range is **B3..D5**, the contents of cell B3 would be copied to C3 and D3; cell B4 would be copied to C4 and D4; and B5 would be copied to C5 and D5. The *Editing SmartIcon set* also offers a SmartIcon that mimics Edit Copy **Right**.

So Get Smart! Type in one column, then copy it over:

 Select the range. The range must include the cells you want to copy and the range of cells to the right you want to fill with the copied data.

Select a range that includes the cells you want to copy and the cells you want to copy to. ┌── Copy Right SmartIcon

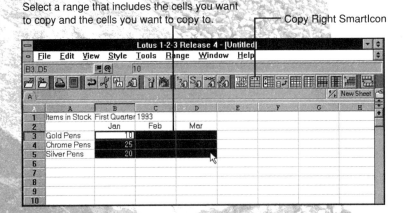

 Choose Edit Copy Right. You can also click on the **Copy Right** SmartIcon from the Editing SmartIcon set. 1-2-3 copies the contents of the cells in the leftmost column across the row.

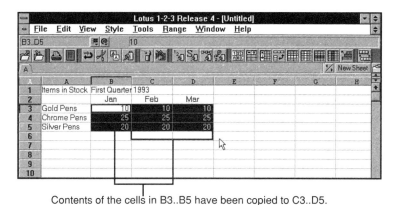

Contents of the cells in B3..B5 have been copied to C3..D5.

GETTING DOWN TO COPYING

It doesn't take an expert in quantum-chromodynamics to figure out that copying to fill down in the selected range works like filling to the right. The Edit Copy Down command (and its companion SmartIcon on the editing set) copies the contents of the top row in the selection to fill the entire selection. You can probably figure this out on your own, but we'll make it obvious for you:

 Select the range or collection. The range must include both the cells you want to copy and the range below those cells that you want to copy the data to.

Copy Down SmartIcon

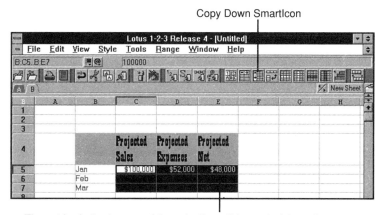

The entries in the top row of the selection will be copied down the range.

 Choose Edit Copy Down. The entries in the top row are copied down the column.

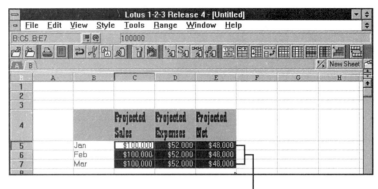

Entries are copied down the columns.

DRAGGING YOUR STUFF AROUND

To join the rest of the application world, 1-2-3 for Windows now offers **DRAG-AND-DROP**. Drag-and-drop lets you move or copy data simply by using the mouse pointer to grab the selection and drop it where you want it. With drag-and-drop, you don't access menu commands nor do you use the Clipboard. So, how does that grab you? If you are good with the mouse, drag-and-drop is the fastest and easiest way to move or copy data.

MAKING YOUR MOVE

To move data by using onl y your mouse:

 Select the cell or range of data that you want to move.

 Position the mouse pointer on the border of your selection. The mouse pointer changes from an arrowhead to an open hand.

3 **Press and hold down the left mouse button.** The mouse pointer that is a hand grabs the border of the selection. This means you can now begin the drag-and-drop.

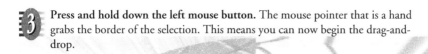

4 **Drag the selection to its destination.** While you drag, your selection is outlined by a dotted rectangle.

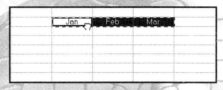

5 **Release the mouse button when you reach the destination to drop the data.**

EVEN BETTER THAN THE REAL THING: COPYING BY DRAGGING

You also can copy data with a little drag-and-drop action. As with Edit Copy, copying using drag-and-drop places a copy of the data in a new location and leaves the original data intact. Drag on:

1 Select the cell or range you want to copy.

2 Position the mouse pointer on the border of your selection.

3 When the pointer changes to an open hand, press and hold the Ctrl key, and then press and hold the left mouse button. The mouse pointer turns into a hand with a plus in it and grabs the border of the selection.

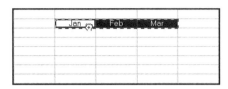

 Without releasing the mouse button, drag the selection to its destination. While you drag, your selection is outlined with a dotted rectangle.

 Release the mouse button when you reach the destination.

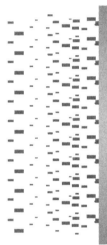

EDIT CUT—See "11. Techno-Subversive Activities: Removing and Hiding Data," p. 109.

EDITING SMARTICON SET—See "5. SmartIcons: Pictures on SmartDrugs," p. 49.

RELATIVE, ABSOLUTE, AND MIXED REFERENCES—See "8. Calculate This!" p. 77.

SELECTED RANGE—See "7. It's the Range (Not the Frequency)," p. 66.

TOOLS FOR THE INDECISIVE

The world's an imperfect place. People die. Dogs bark. And worksheets seldom turn out perfect with the first try. More often than not, you'll need to copy, cut, move, and paste data as you go along, and sometimes make more room for new data by inserting blank columns, rows, and ranges. This lesson can help you do it with a minimum of fuss.

SHOOTING BLANKS INTO A WORKSHEET

It never fails. Just when you've created the perfect spreadsheet, you realize you need an extra column between G and H, or two more rows following row 18. If you were doing the worksheet by hand with graph paper and a pencil, you'd probably wad up the paper and make a perfect rim shot into the trash. Fortunately, you're working with 1-2-3 instead.

HERE A ROW, THERE A ROW

Give your worksheet the gift of an extra row or column with the Edit Insert command. It puts a new row (or several) above the one(s) you've selected, or a new column (or several) to the left. Do this:

 Select a whole row or column, or several of them. Remember, new rows are inserted above the ones you select, and new columns are inserted to the left.

To select a row, click on its number in the worksheet frame.

To select a column, click on its letter in the worksheet frame.

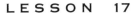

After selecting a row or column, instead of selecting **EDIT INSERT**, you can hold down the Ctrl key and type + on the numeric keypad. (The plus sign above the Enter key won't work.)

Choose **EDIT INSERT**. It's as easy as that; you'll immediately get a new row or column, whichever you selected.

The new column. Notice how the data in the old column F moved to column G to make room.

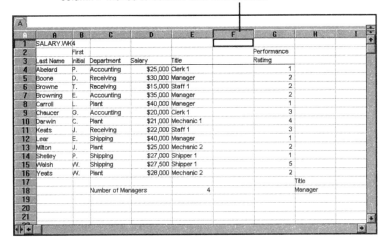

INSERTING RENEGADE CELLS

Some cells just won't cop to the system. They won't fit neatly into rows or columns, but insist on being stuck directly into the heart of an otherwise-perfect worksheet. This procedure tells you how to handle these rebels.

To insert a range of cells into a worksheet, first select an existing range that's the same size and shape as the blank range you want to insert. (The ones you select will move to the right or below to make room, depending on how you play it.) Then you issue the **Edit Insert** command. Here's the play-by-play:

 Select the range where you want to insert the new cells. Make sure it's the same size and shape as the range you want to insert, and make sure it's in the right place so that everything will align correctly when the selected cells move to the right.

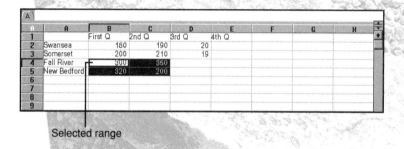

Selected range

Choose Edit Insert. You'll get the Insert dialog box, because 1-2-3 isn't sure what you want to insert.

Select the Insert selection check box.

Select Column or Row. If you select Column, the existing data will move to the right. If you select Row, the existing data will move down.

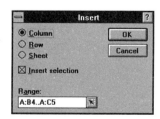

You can insert an entire **WORKSHEET** with Edit Insert. For all the gory details about *inserting worksheets*, see Lesson 21.

 Choose OK, and check your **WORKSHEET** to see the new cells in their new homes.

	A	B	C	D	E	F	G	H
1		First Q	2nd Q	3rd Q	4th Q			
2	Swansea	150	190	20				
3	Somerset	200	210	19				
4	Fall River			300	350			
5	New Bedford			320	200			
6								
7								
8								
9								

Four new cells have been inserted.

The opposite of inserting, of course, is *deleting*. Duh. It was covered in Lesson 11.

INSERTING WITH SMARTICONS

Now that you've seen the rest, take a look at the best way to insert rows, columns, and ranges—with SmartIcons. Just position your cursor, and click on the SmartIcon. There are separate ones for rows, columns, and ranges, so you don't even have to select a row or column first to tell 1-2-3 your intentions. If you need to select a different group of *SmartIcons* to see these icons, look back at Lesson 5.

These three SmartIcons for inserting rows, columns, and ranges can save you a ton of time and energy.

DATA TILT

Have you ever fantasized about turning your monitor on its side so the rows would be columns and vice versa? Don't rush off to your therapist; it's a perfectly normal dream. It's called *transposing*, and in this section, you'll learn how to make it a reality.

The range—before transposing.

Notice how the column headings . . .

. . . turned to row headings.

The range—after transposing.

Here's a caveat: Before transposing data, look to see if the CALC indicator appears in the status line. If it does, press **F9** (CALC) to update formulas. If there are linked formulas in the range, you also need to use **Edit Links** to make sure the values are up-to-date. This is important! The transposed range's data is *converted to values,* so you want the values up-to-date before you go off transposing. The formatting of a range that you are formatting goes with it. For example, if you have a column of text that's centered and you transpose it, the text will be centered in the rows when it's transposed.

 Select the range to transpose.

 Choose Range Transpose. You'll get the Transpose dialog box.

You don't need to specify the complete To: range—only the cell in the top left corner. ———

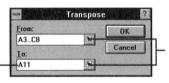

You can click on a range selector and use the mouse to select ranges, if you want.

 Put the destination range in the To: text box. You can use the whole range if you want, but it's easier to just specify the first cell and let 1-2-3 do the rest.

 Select OK. It's a done deal. It looks something like the "after" example if you did it right.

A CLIPBOARD FULL OF PASTE

The Clipboard is pretty marvelous, all in all. Anything that can be selected (and some things that can't) can be placed on the Clipboard and pasted anywhere else, not just in 1-2-3 but in any Windows-based app. It's a two-step process: First you use the *Cut* or *Copy* command from an app's Edit menu to get the stuff onto the Clipboard; then you use the **Paste** command (Edit menu) in the same app or a completely different one (your choice) to fetch the material.

1. **Select the item(s) you want to place on the Clipboard.** For instance, if you want to cut your Aunt Mathilda's phone number out of your Business Client Call List worksheet, highlight it.

2. **Choose Edit Copy or Edit Cut to put it on the Clipboard.** In Auntie's case, you'll probably prefer to Cut rather than Copy. (What was she doing on your worksheet in the first place?)

3. **Select the new location for the item(s).** For instance, dear old Mathilda might feel more at home in your Personal Phone Numbers worksheet. If you are pasting text, numbers, or formulas, you can select either a range or just the top left cell of the range. If you are pasting a chart or **DRAWN OBJECT**, though, you have to select the exact range.

4. **Choose Edit Paste or press Ctrl+V.** Thud. The Clipboard holdings are dumped into place.

You can use 1-2-3 to create **DRAWN OBJECTS** (see Lesson 25) that you can use to jazz up your worksheets. The command that gives you access to the 1-2-3 drawing capability is Tools Draw.

Don't forget the Cut, Copy, and Paste SmartIcons: they're at your service if you want to avoid the menu route.

	Cut to the Clipboard
	Copy to the Clipboard
	Paste Clipboard contents

Your old friends—the Cut, Copy, and Paste SmartIcons—are ever ready to assist you.

PASTING FROM ANOTHER APP

Pasting from another app is just as easy as pasting from 1-2-3, because the Clipboard works equally well everywhere you go. (Kind of like how the major credit cards want you to believe their card works. Yeah, right.) All you have to do is use the Paste Special command instead of the regular Paste.

1. **Cut or copy the data using the Edit menu of the other app.**

2. **Switch to 1-2-3 and select the location where you want the goodies to be pasted.**

3. **Choose Edit Paste Special from 1-2-3.**

 Choose a Clipboard format from the list. 1-2-3 makes its best guess about the format, but it's up to you to make the final decision. If you choose **Text**, **WK1**, or **WK3**, the data gets pasted into the selected range as if it were regular 1-2-3 type info. These types of links are called DDE (Dynamic Data Exchange), a format that allows you to share data between Windows applications. If you choose **Picture**, **Bitmap**, or **DIB**, the item comes in as a drawn object. And finally, if you pick **Object**, it gets pasted as an OLE embedded object. These are cool because you can double-click on the object from within 1-2-3 to revise it using its native program.

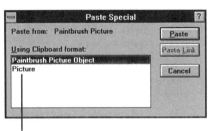

The choices here vary depending on what
1-2-3 guesses the format might be.

 Choose Paste or Paste Link to finalize the pasting. Paste plops it in place "plain," while Paste Link maintains a link to the pasted thing, so if it changes, the version in 1-2-3 will change, too. If you're not planning on changing anything, **Paste** is a lot less hassle.

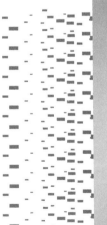

SMARTICONS—See "5. SmartIcons: Pictures on SmartDrugs," p. 49.

CUTTING (TO THE CLIPBOARD)—See "11. Techno-Subversive Activities: Removing and Hiding Data," p. 109.

DELETING ROWS AND COLUMNS—See "11. Techno-Subversive Activities: Removing and Hiding Data," p. 109.

COPYING (TO THE CLIPBOARD)—See "16. The Naked Truth About Copying and Moving," p. 161.

INSERTING WORKSHEETS—See "21. Managing Worksheet Proliferation," p. 206.

CONVERTING FORMULAS TO VALUES—See "13. Number Formats to Go," p. 131.

PREPRINTING ANXIETY AND HOW TO OVERCOME IT

Printing your worksheet is more than just choosing File Print. Have you considered headers and footers, margins and page breaks? What about gridlines? Do you want those to print? And after you have taken the time to set up the printed page, will you use those page settings again? If you think you will, you can name the settings, save them, and use them again.

DECORATIVE TRIM

You can trim a tree, and you can trim your nose (or at least your nose hair), but can you trim your friend's document? Sure you can. Just add a header and/or footer across the top or bottom of each page. A header is **TEXT** that appears at the top of each printed page, while a footer is the same thing except at the bottom.

1-2-3 makes it easy to use headers and footers. It provides some preset ones that you can pick, or you can type your own. Once you've got a header or footer, 1-2-3 automatically leaves two lines of blank space between your worksheet and your header or footer, so it won't look all scrunched up. Follow along with these steps to make one:

 Choose File Page Setup.

 Enter header and/or footer text in one or more of the text boxes provided.
The box you pick determines the alignment of your text when printed—left box for the left side of the header or footer, center box for the center of the header or footer, and so on.

HYPERTIP

Your choices of what **TEXT** to put in a header or footer are mind-bogglingly vast. Some people like to use the name of the worksheet as the header and the page number as the footer. Others like to use the headers and footers to time and date stamp their worksheets by putting the date in the header and the time in the footer. It's up to you.

Enter text to be left-aligned in these boxes.

Enter text to be center-aligned in these boxes.

Enter text to be right-aligned in these boxes.

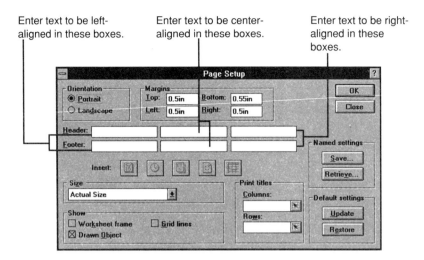

 Choose OK.

Instead of entering text in the **H**eader or **F**ooter text boxes in step 2, you can insert a preset header or footer. Just select a text box, and then click on one of the Insert buttons in the Page Setup dialog box to include the date, time, page number, file name, or contents of a particular cell. Take a look at the following table to see what each button does.

Button	Inserts
📅	Current system date, in day-month-year format
🕐	Current time, in hour:minutes:seconds format
📄	Page numbers
📄	File name
▦	Cell contents

These are all pretty obvious except for Cell contents. When you select the **Cell contents** button, 1-2-3 inserts a \ (backslash) in the **H**eader or **F**ooter text box, after which you specify a *cell address* or *range name* whose contents you want to insert. Then, whenever you print the worksheet, 1-2-3 takes the value from that cell or range and pastes it into the header or footer where you specified.

178

TALKIN 'BOUT MARGINS

You can set the amount of white space on the sides of your worksheet by setting the **MARGINS**. It's just like with a word processor (or typewriter, for that matter).

If you've got a 1" margin all around, that means you'll have 1" of **BLANK SPACE** on all sides of the worksheet when it's printed.

Here's how to change margins in 1-2-3:

 Choose File Page Setup.

 Under Margins, specify margins in inches in the Top, Bottom, Left, and Right text boxes. If you want to use millimeters or centimeters, type **mm** or **cm** after the number. Otherwise, 1-2-3 assumes you want inches.

Click on a text box, and type the margin setting you want.

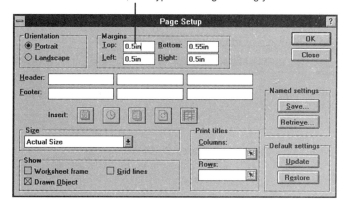

 Choose OK.

You're done. To see what the worksheet looks like with the new margins, select File Print Preview.

TEAR, FOLD, SPINDLE, MUTILATE

It's inevitable. If your worksheet grows bigger than can be printed on one page, it's going to have to be broken. And

unless you decide where to break it, 1-2-3 will decide on your behalf, and you may not be happy with its decision. Either

---

HYPERTIP

You can set the **MARGINS** and make other page settings by choosing the SmartIcon for setting the page layout. When you click on that icon, 1-2-3 displays the Page Setup dialog box.

HYPERTIP

As you probably remember from high school English class, margins (**BLANK SPACE** around the edge of the page) can be exploited to your advantage. For instance, a two-page essay need only be four sentences if you set large enough margins. Keep margins in mind when you're trying to figure out how to make a worksheet come out to a specific number of pages when printed.

You can also set the **PAGE BREAKS** by clicking on one or both of the SmartIcons that will insert a page break into your worksheet. One of the icons inserts a horizontal break while the other inserts a vertical one.

you can go with the flow and hope the **PAGE BREAKS** turn out okay, or you can follow these steps to take control of the situation:

 Select a cell below the row or to the right of the column where you want the page to break.

	A	B	C	D	E	F	G	H	I
16	Accum. Depr.--Building				2,000		0	0	2,0
17	Land			50,000				50,000	
18	Accounts Payable				2,000			0	2,0
19	Mortgage Payable				30,900			0	30,9
20	Proprietor, Capital				50,000			0	50,0
21	Sales				100,000			0	100,0
22	Sales Returns & Allowances			15,000	0			15,000	
23	Purchases			50,000				50,000	
24	Purchase Returns & Allow.				2,000			0	2,0
25	Purchase Discounts				3,000			0	3,0
26	Advertising Expense			1,000				1,000	
27	Salary Expense			4,000			0	4,000	
28	Miscellaneous Expenses			5,000				5,000	
29	Utilities Expense			2,000				2,000	
30	Interest Revenue				1,000			0	1,0
31									
32				$344,000	$344,000				
33									
34	Bad Debts Expense						0	0	
35	Insurance Expense						0	0	
36	Depr. Exp.--Furn. & Fixt						0	0	

In this example, the page break will happen after row 32.

 Choose Style Page Break.

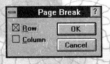 Select the check box for Row, Column, or **BOTH**. Selecting Row inserts a horizontal page break; selecting Column inserts a vertical one.

Here's a shortcut: to set **BOTH** vertical and horizontal page breaks at once, select the cell that you want to be in the bottom right corner of the printout, then mark both check boxes in step 3.

Choose OK.

SOME REASSEMBLY REQUIRED

Things change. People change. Page breaks outlive their usefulness. To remove a page break:

 1 Select the cell directly below the row or to the right of the column where the errant page break lies.

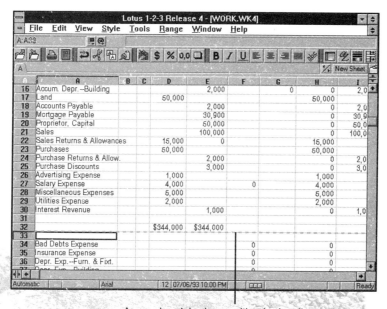

A page break is shown with a broken line.

 2 **Choose Style Page Break.** You'll get the Page Break dialog box.

 3 **Deselect the check boxes to remove the page breaks.**

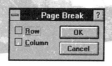

 4 Choose OK.

GRID LINE GLORY

Grid lines are exactly what they sound like: lines on the grid (the worksheet) that help your eye follow the rows and columns of data. On the screen, **GRID LINES** are the dotted lines that outline each cell. Grid lines help your eye follow data down long columns and across wide rows on the screen. They would help on paper too, but unfortunately they don't print by default. If you want 1-2-3 to print the grid lines, you must say so.

The same is true for the worksheet frame, which is the border around the work area that contains column letters and row numbers. It's handy on-screen (how else would you know where cell E182 was?), and it could be handy on a printout too, if only you could get it to *print*.

To have either or both of these things print, follow these steps:

 Choose File **PAGE SETUP**.

 Under **Show, select the check boxes for Worksheet frame or Grid lines.** Either or both; it matters to no one but you, at this point.

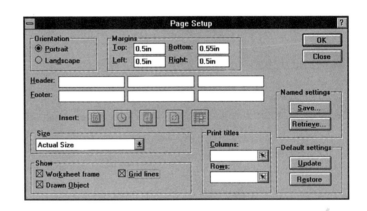

Choose OK.

To see what life would be like without **GRID LINES**, try this: Choose Set View Preferences from the **View** menu, and deselect the Grid lines check box. Select **OK** to return to your worksheet. Pretty bleak-looking, huh? Repeat the procedure to get them back.

You might have noticed in the **PAGE SETUP** dialog box that you can also tell 1-2-3 whether or not to print drawn objects. (You can draw objects on your 1-2-3 worksheets by choosing **Tools Draw**.) By default, 1-2-3 will print them.

182

ROW AND COLUMN REPEATERS

If you're printing rows and columns that are so long that they don't fit on one page, wouldn't it be nice to have your row and column titles from page 1 automatically repeat? Well, it's possible. Just follow these steps:

 Choose File Page Setup.

 Under Print titles, specify cells in the Columns and Rows text boxes. Enter only one cell from the column you want to use in the vertical heading, and one cell from the row you want to use in the horizontal heading.

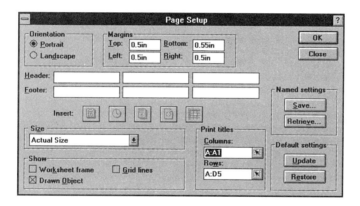

 **Choose OK.**

PAGE SETTINGS BY ANY OTHER NAME

The Page Setup dialog box you've been working with is chock full of page settings you can mess with—the orientation of the printed page (landscape or portrait), the size of the margins, headers and footers—it's all there. Getting all the settings exactly right can take an entire afternoon if you get carried away.

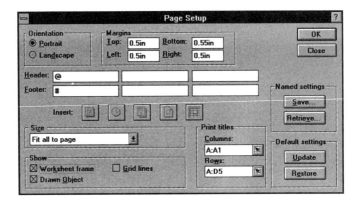

A plethora of page setting choices beckon you.

Once you've got it right, you can assign a name to the setup and retrieve the page settings the next time you need them.

That means fewer wasted afternoons and more time to play Solitaire. To save page settings, follow these steps:

 Choose File Page Setup. You'll see the old, familiar Page Setup dialog box.

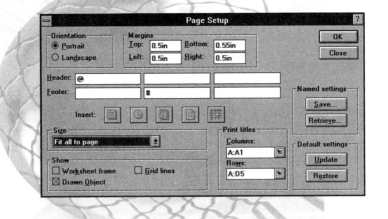

Under Named settings, click on the Save button. The Save Named Settings dialog box appears.

Type the name of the file to save the settings to in the File name text box. 1-2-3 automatically adds the extension .AL3 to it.

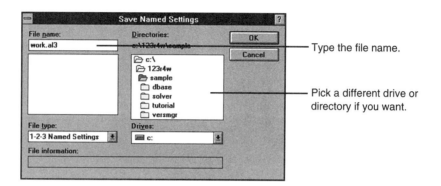

Type the file name.

Pick a different drive or directory if you want.

Choose OK twice to close everything.

That's all there is to it. To retrieve the page settings that you have named, click on the Retrieve button instead of the Save one in step 2, and pick the file that you saved.

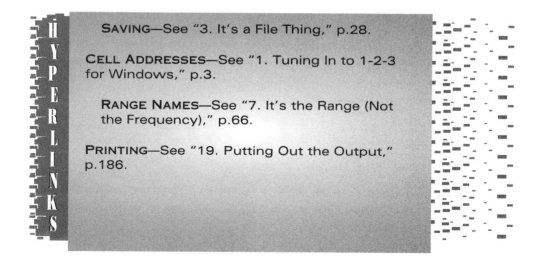

SAVING—See "3. It's a File Thing," p.28.

CELL ADDRESSES—See "1. Tuning In to 1-2-3 for Windows," p.3.

RANGE NAMES—See "7. It's the Range (Not the Frequency)," p.66.

PRINTING—See "19. Putting Out the Output," p.186.

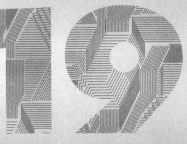

PUTTING OUT THE OUTPUT

So, you've waded through the quagmire of page setup in the last lesson and are ready for the big time. Congratulations!

In this chapter, you'll iron out a few last details and issue that Print command.

COMING SOON TO A PRINTER NEAR YOU

After you have your *page settings* the way you like them, you're ready to print. But wait! What if something's wrong? Do you really want to kill another tree by printing out a copy that you might have to reprint later? Of course, you don't. You're an ethical citizen of the world, after all.

With 1-2-3, you can *select a range* or an entire worksheet and then use **PRINT PREVIEW** to step back and see how your pages will look when printed. That means you can check on the placement of things, such as headers and footers, which don't normally show up on-screen, and see how your charts and drawn objects look.

Ready to preview? Go for it.

 Select what you want to preview. It can be a range of cells, a whole worksheet, or all of the worksheets in the file. (Yes, there can be *multiple worksheets in a file.* You'll learn about it in Lesson 21.)

 Choose File Print Preview, or click on the Print Preview SmartIcon.

HYPERTIP

In the **PRINT PREVIEW** dialog box, there's a Page **Setup** button you can select to bring up the Page Setup dialog box if you need to change the margins, headings, or other page settings. Once you get into Print Preview mode, there's an icon at the top of the screen (the one that looks like a page with a ruler on it) that'll do the same.

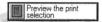

3 Under Preview, select Current worksheet, All worksheets, or Selected range. If you want the current worksheet or all worksheets in the file, it's pretty obvious what your choice should be here. If you want anything else (for instance, a chart or drawn object by itself), choose Selected range.

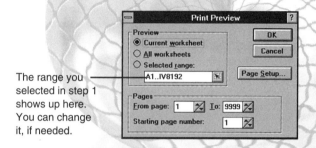

The range you selected in step 1 shows up here. You can change it, if needed.

4 Under Pages, specify the pages to preview by entering page numbers in the From page and To boxes. You can also click on the up or down arrows of each box to increase or decrease the value. Don't get confused; pages here means sheets of paper, not worksheets. If you have a huge worksheet that requires four pieces of paper to print, it's four pages, but only one worksheet.

5 Choose OK, and the **PRINT PREVIEW SCREEN** opens, in all its glory.

You can also get to the **PRINT PREVIEW SCREEN** from the Print dialog box (File Print) by clicking on the Preview button.

Margin settings appear as dotted lines.

187

Once you're in the Print Preview screen, you'll notice some icons at the top. Here's what to do with them.

Icon	Purpose
	Displays the next page.
	Displays the previous page.
	Magnifies the preview contents.
	Reduces the preview contents, if magnified.
	Opens the Page Layout dialog box.
	Prints the preview contents.
	Closes Print Preview without printing.

AN EMBARRASSMENT OF RICHES: CHOOSING AMONG YOUR PRINTERS

If you're one of those poor suckers who only has one printer, skip this part. It's for the wealthy or lucky user who has more than one printer and needs to choose among them for a print job.

If you've got a dot-matrix printer and a laser printer, you have probably discovered by now that a new toner cartridge for your laser costs anywhere from $50 to $200, where a new ribbon for the dot-matrix costs about $5. So, when thinking about which printer to do your rough drafts on, the choice seems pretty clear—go with the one that's cheaper to maintain. Then use the good-quality printer for the final output.

When you installed Windows, you picked the printers you wanted to use, and **PRINTER DRIVERS** were installed for them. So now that you're ready to print, it's a simple matter of picking from among the installed drivers and making sure that the correct printer is hooked up to your computer.

Assuming you've got printer drivers for your printers installed, here are the steps for choosing among them. (If you need to install a driver, see your Windows manual.)

PRINTER DRIVERS are translator programs that help a computer program and your printer communicate. Some printers can speak more than one language—usually their own, plus the language of a more popular printer (like Epson or IBM). That way, if Windows doesn't come with a driver made exactly for that printer's own language, it can scrape by with its second language.

HYPERTIP

Choose File Printer Setup.

 Select the printer you want to use from the Printers list box.

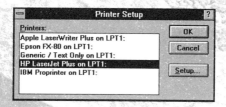

Choose OK.

Well now, that was certainly easy, wasn't it? But of course, there's more to it than that, if you choose to make a big production out of selecting the printer. Each printer model has its own list of options, fonts, and settings you can tinker with, if

you so desire. After you perform step 2 (selecting the printer from the list), you can click on the Setup button to open a dialog box for the printer you're using. Here's one for mine; yours will probably have some different options.

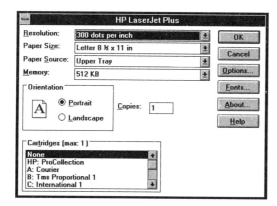

Resolution: The higher the resolution, the better the quality of any graphics that you print. (Resolution doesn't affect text.) Lower resolutions print faster.

Paper Size: This one's pretty obvious. Common choices are standard letter (8 1/2" x 11") and legal (8 1/2" x 14").

Paper Source: Most printers only have one paper tray, so you don't have to worry about this. If yours has more than one, you get to choose from this list.

Memory: Windows needs to know how much memory your printer has built-in, so it'll know how fast to send information to the printer.

Orientation: Your choices are portrait (tall) or landscape (wide). The picture in the Orientation box helps you remember which is which.

Copies: Normally, the printer is always set for **1** copy, and then you specify multiple copies in a particular app. Leave this at **1** unless you always want to print multiple copies of everything you do.

Cartridges: Most laser printers have one or more slots where you can plug in **FONT CARTRIDGES**. If you've got a cartridge, match its label to an item on the list of cartridges here.

Options: If you see this button in your dialog box, it means there are even more options you can set for your printer. Click on it to see them. For instance, there might be settings for dithering (shading for graphics) and intensity (the darkness of the printout).

Fonts: If you have other fonts on your system that are compatible with your printer, you can manage them by clicking on the Fonts button. Try it; you ought to know what's there, even if you don't have any.

When you're done tinkering, choose **OK** as many times as it takes to get back to your worksheet.

JUST PRINT IT

Well, it's about time. Send your perfectly crafted worksheet to the printer with these steps:

 If you haven't already done so, select the range of data you want to print. If you want to print the entire worksheet or all the worksheets in the file, you can skip this step.

 Choose File Print, press Ctrl+P, or click on the Print SmartIcon. Any way you do it, the Print dialog box appears. It looks a lot like the Print Preview dialog box, if you went through that process earlier in the lesson, except there are two more options: Preview and Number of copies.

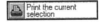

Print the current selection

Click on the button under Print for the area you want to print: Current worksheet, All worksheets, or Selected range.

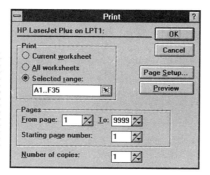

 Type the number of copies you want (up to 999) in the Number of copies text box.

 Choose OK.

After you have given the command to print your work, 1-2-3 displays a box that tells you that your data is being sent to the printer. That box contains a Cancel button. If you suddenly change your mind, click on the **Cancel** button to stop the printing.

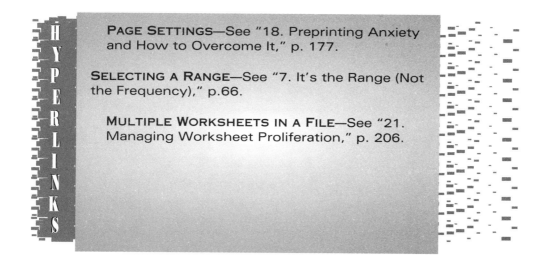

PAGE SETTINGS—See "18. Preprinting Anxiety and How to Overcome It," p. 177.

SELECTING A RANGE—See "7. It's the Range (Not the Frequency)," p.66.

MULTIPLE WORKSHEETS IN A FILE—See "21. Managing Worksheet Proliferation," p. 206.

Part IV

LOCAL AND GLOBAL QUESTIONS

Whenever you use a program, there's a certain amount of time you spend actually producing something, and a certain amount of time you spend noodling around under the guise of "setting things up so you can be more productive." This part has the lessons that teach you how to noodle around: arranging windows on-screen, creating or nuking worksheets and files, and changing your display settings and global options that affect all files. Enjoy!

BORDER DISPUTES: ARRANGING WINDOWS

As you're working along in 1-2-3, the open windows tend to multiply like rabbits. (Surely, your office is paperless and everything's on-line so your only alternative is to open other files . . . Not!) Every time you *open a file*, 1-2-3 places it in a new window without closing any other windows (files) that are already open. You can open as many files as you need, assuming your PC has the memory to handle it.

Having **OPEN FILES** hanging around is a good thing because you can jet back and forth from one active file to another . . . revising, reviewing, printing results, and sharing data. Hey, it's as big a thrill as bungee jumping! But, when you have multiple windows open, you'll have to do a little housekeeping, learn how to navigate, and so on. So, strap on a helmet, and get started with this lesson.

Opening and working with multiple files is different from working with multiple worksheets. Files contain worksheets (up to 256 worksheets). So don't confuse worksheets with files—they are not same. To make an analogy, worksheets are like the papers in your Pendaflex files. Files contain worksheets! The procedures described in this lesson don't affect worksheets. That's the next lesson.

You'll be accomplishing most of your window operations with various commands and mouse shortcuts. But every window also offers a Control menu for performing various operations, such as resizing and moving windows.

> **HYPERTIP**
>
> Remember that you can **OPEN FILES** with the Open SmartIcon, which appears in nearly every set. It looks like a file folder that's opening as an arrow emerges.

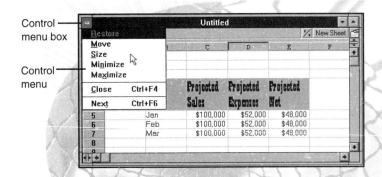

Control —
menu box

Control —
menu

Mr. Obvious reminds you that the Control menu lets you perform these commands on windows.

As you may know, to choose any of the Control menu commands, you must display the Control menu box by either clicking on it or by pressing the key combinations in Table 20.1. A window's Control menu drops down from its Control menu box, which is always in the top left-hand corner of a window.

TABLE 20.1 *Keyboard Control*

Control Menu for	Materializes When You Press
1-2-3 window	Alt+ Spacebar
A File window	Alt+ - (hyphen)
Transcript window	Alt+ - (hyphen)
Help window	Alt+ Spacebar
Dialog box	Alt+ Spacebar

Though the Control menu's available, it's easier to use the mouse and/or other commands to perform many window operations, so this is the method the rest of the lesson focuses on. But just for your own peace of mind, Table 20.2 gives a brief rundown on using Control menu commands. Note that available Control menu commands change based on the window types (see Table 20.1).

TABLE 20.2 *Those Darn Controls . . .*

Command	Using and Abusing It
Restore	Go to a minimized or maximized window, then choose this command to return the window to its previous size and position.
Move	Changes the pointer to a four-headed arrow. Use the arrow keys to move the window or dialog box, and then press **Enter**.

Command	Using and Abusing It
Size	Changes the pointer to a four-headed arrow. Use the arrow keys to size the window, and then press **Enter**.
Minimize	Makes the window an icon but doesn't make it inactive.
Maximize	Blows the window up to its max size.
Close	Closes the file or cancels a dialog box.
Next	Goes to the next open window.
Switch To	Displays the Windows Task List so you can go to another Windows application.

WHADDAYA WANT, ANOTHER WINDOW?

If you have any short-term memory at all, you usually can recall what files are open. When the open file names have slipped your mind (your existence is chemically altered, eh?), you can check the **W**indow menu, which lists up to nine open windows. A check mark appears beside the active window, which is the one you're working in. Only one window can be active at a time, and you can easily identify the **ACTIVE** window because the color in its title bar is different from the title bar color of nonactive windows.

If you lack restraint and open more than nine windows, the **W**indow menu will still show the names of nine open windows but will also show the **M**ore Windows command. Click on this command to list the other windows.

The **W**indow menu also lets you choose to go to another window when you want to work on the file it contains. Here's how to get there:

If your open windows are arranged so you can see part of each window, you can make any one of them **ACTIVE** by clicking on it or by pressing **Ctrl+F6** until the one you want becomes active.

 **Choose Window.**

Click on the name of the window you want to go to.

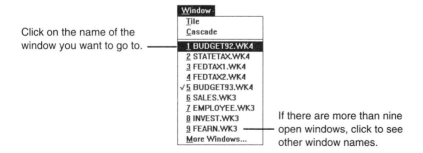

If there are more than nine open windows, click to see other window names.

 Click on the name of the window (file) you want to go to. That window moves to the front, and its title bar changes color.

FANNING 'EM OUT

Have you ever been sucked into a "friendly" card game, where the first dealer starts to flip the cards around faster than an Asian chef with a Ginsu knife and then finishes by fanning the cards in a perfectly overlapping pattern in front of you for the cut? Well, when you are working with multiple windows, you can have the same control . . . without the risk of losing every bit of currency in your wallet and your favorite watch.

You can cascade all open windows, which arranges them one on top of the other in a slightly fanned-out pattern. When you choose **W**indow **C**ascade, 1-2-3 resizes open windows and then neatly arranges them one on top of the other. Other than the active window (the one containing the cell pointer which is placed on top of the pile), just the title bars of the neatly overlapping open windows appear. Cascading open windows can help you see all your open windows at once, making it possible for you to move between windows by clicking on the title bar of the window you want to move to.

To arrange your open windows in a cascade (one on top of another):

 Choose Window Cascade. Or click on the Cascade SmartIcon if you've added it to the current set. The active window is placed in front, with the other windows arranged neatly underneath.

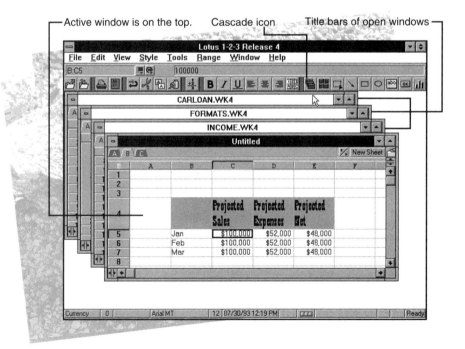

INFORMATION OVERWHELM

If you're really comfortable with the Information Age and don't go into overwhelm when you have to compare sets of data side-by-side on-screen, then the tiled look is for you. The **W**indow **T**ile command arranges open windows side-by-side so you can see some part of the content of every open file as opposed to seeing only the title bars of the nonactive windows. The active window moves to the upper left corner of the work space. If you think you can handle it, here's how to tile:

 Choose Window Tile. Or click on the **Tile** SmartIcon if you've added it to the current set. 1-2-3 places the active window in the upper left corner of the work space.

Active window is in the upper left corner.   Tile icon

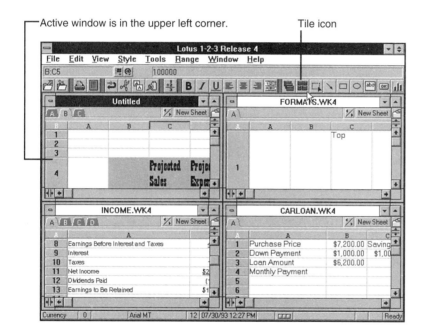

WARPING DIMENSIONS

You're an individual! You don't have to live with the tiled, cascaded, or maximized windows. Express your unique outlook on the world by adjusting the dimensions of a window.

You can make a window smaller to **MOVE** it around, or **RESIZE** it to see more of a window's contents. To change the size of a window:

You can't **MOVE** or **RESIZE** a window that has been enlarged to its maximum size. So if the window is enlarged to its maximum size, before changing its size, you need to restore it to a smaller size by choosing **Restore** from the **Control** menu or by clicking on the **Restore** button.

 Make the window you want to size the active window.

 Point to a border or corner of the window until the mouse pointer changes to a two-headed arrow. Point to a side or bottom border if you just want to move the side or bottom. Point to a corner to resize a side and bottom together.

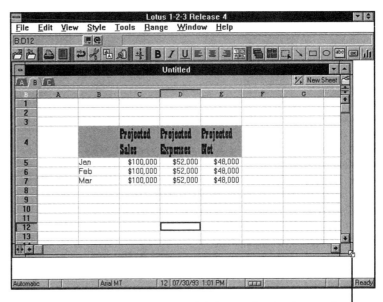

Pointing to a border changes the mouse pointer to a two-headed arrow.

 Press the left mouse button, drag the border, and then release. As you're dragging, a border shows the changing window size.

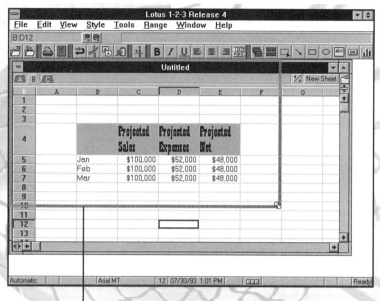

A border shows how the window size changes.

A MOVING EXPERIENCE

When working with 1-2-3, there are times when you need to move a window. For example, you may want to *move the Help window* to see a certain part of your worksheet. You can move all these kinds of windows (if the ones that can be maximized aren't):

◇ 1-2-3 application window

◇ Any file window

◇ *Macro Transcript window*

◇ Help window

◇ Dialog boxes (yes, you can move them even though you can't size them).

Repositioning a window or dialog box is a drag (literally):

 Point to the title bar of the window or dialog box that you want to move.

 Press and hold the left mouse button, drag, and release the mouse button when the window hits the position you want.

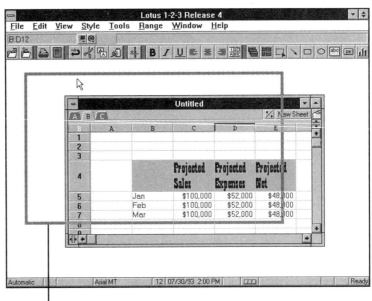

A border shows where the window's going when you drag.

SPLIT PERSONALITY

The **V**iew **S**plit command divides a Worksheet window horizontally or vertically into two panes. 1-2-3 panes are like the panes in the glass windows of your home or office. They divide the window into sections. Here's the advantage of dividing your worksheet window into sections. Let's say that you are working on some data in column A that is related to some data out in column N. You can't see all those columns in one screen. So rather than jump back and forth between column A and N, you can split your screen into two panes and keep column N data displayed while you work within column A.

There are two ways to divide your worksheet window into panes. One is by using the **V**iew **S**plit command while the other method allows you to split the window by using your mouse to drag the horizontal splitter (found at the top of the right scroll bar) or the vertical splitter (found at the far left of the bottom scroll bar). Remember, whatever method you use to split your worksheet, 1-2-3 saves a file's window settings when you save the file. So if you want the split to be temporary, **CLEAR THE SPLIT** before saving the file.

To move the cell pointer between panes using the keyboard, press **F6** (PANE) in Ready or Point mode. To move the cell pointer between panes using the mouse, click on a cell in the pane you want to move to. You can enlarge the current pane (the one your cell pointer is in) to the current size of the active window by pressing **Alt+F6** (ZOOM PANE). You can also press **Alt+F6** again to shrink the pane to its original size.

SPLITTING YOUR VIEW

 Position the cell pointer in the row or column where you want to split the window. The cell pointer cannot be in column A or row 1.

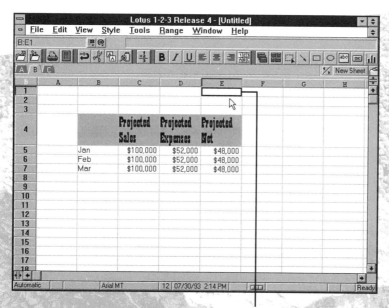

By selecting a cell in column E, you can vertically divide the worksheet between column D and E.

 Choose View Split.

 Under Type, select either Horizontal or Vertical. Horizontal makes the split follow the row of the selected cell. Vertical splits along the column.

 (Optional) Select the Synchronize scrolling check box to cause views to scroll together. If the check box is already selected, that means you will have synchronized scrolling unless you uncheck the box.

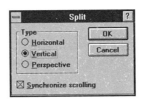

 **Choose OK.**

Screen is spilt vertically just before column E.

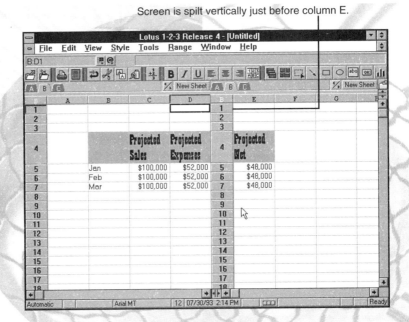

MOUSE OF PANE

To create a window pane horizontally with the mouse:

 Point to the horizontal splitter at the top of the right scroll bar. The pointer changes to a black two-headed vertical arrow.

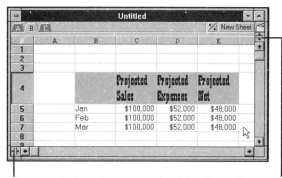

Vertical splitter—drag over to the column where you want to divide the window.

Horizontal splitter—drag down to the row where you want to divide the window.

 Drag the mouse pointer to the row at which you want to divide the window and release the mouse button.

To divide a window vertically:

 Point to the vertical splitter at the far left of the bottom scroll bar. The pointer changes to a black two-headed arrow.

 Drag the mouse pointer to the column at which you want to divide the window.

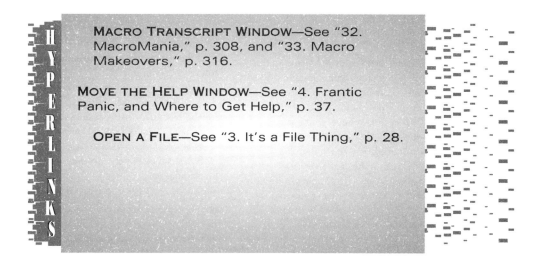

MACRO TRANSCRIPT WINDOW—See "32. MacroMania," p. 308, and "33. Macro Makeovers," p. 316.

MOVE THE HELP WINDOW—See "4. Frantic Panic, and Where to Get Help," p. 37.

OPEN A FILE—See "3. It's a File Thing," p. 28.

MANAGING WORKSHEET PROLIFERATION

There should be a TV show called "Lifestyles of the Zoned Out and Infamous" that profiles people who can't control their need to save stuff, like some senior citizens who get lost in their own houses because they have so many stacks of newspapers. One dip in Indianapolis saved 2,500 tires in his yard. And Howard Hughes saved all his fingernail and toenail clippings in jars (don't even ask about the toe jam).

Anyone could easily fall victim to this phenomenon when it comes to the worksheets in 1-2-3 files. You can organize data in up to 256 worksheets per *file* (depending upon your system's memory). Although you may never need 256 worksheets, you will probably find breaking up the data on separate worksheets is as irresistible as a fly strip is to flies. This lesson clues you into the best tactics for working with multiple worksheets in a file: moving around, changing the display, and throwing them out when you don't need them.

The ability to create multiple worksheets in each file gives you flexibility in organizing and formatting data. In a one-dimensional (one worksheet per file) system, you must think in blocks; constantly having to consider how inserting or deleting rows in one block might endanger other worksheet areas. Because you can create 3-D (three-dimensional) worksheets with 1-2-3 for Windows, the threat of endangering worksheet areas when you delete or insert rows can be minimized; each important module can occupy its own worksheet. Also, with the multiple worksheet capability, you are better able to share information between related worksheets. *Copying and linking cells* in related worksheets is extremely easy with 1-2-3 for Windows.

When you start 1-2-3, a file with only one worksheet is displayed. To create three-dimensional files, you insert or add worksheets to the file—stacking them one on top of the other. When you insert a worksheet, 1-2-3 assigns a letter from **A** (for the first worksheet) to **IV** to each worksheet in the file. For example, if you want to prepare a consolidated sales forecast for two regions, you need to add two worksheets, and 1-2-3 will name the new worksheets letters **B** and **C** (the

original one becomes worksheet **A**). One sheet can show the consolidated sales totals, one sheet can hold the sales forecasts for one region, and the last sheet can hold the sales forecasts for the other region.

MORE IS MORE

You can add one worksheet at a time by clicking on the **New Sheet** button.

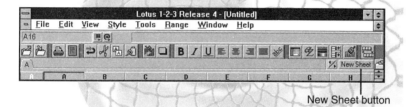

New Sheet button

Add a single worksheet.

If you want to be really radical, you can insert several worksheets at once with the **Edit Insert** command:

 **Choose Edit Insert.**

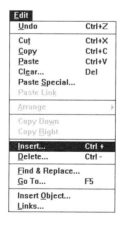

 Select Sheet.

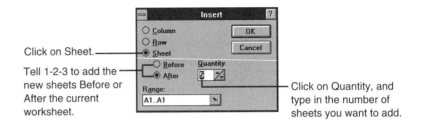

Click on Sheet.

Tell 1-2-3 to add the new sheets Before or After the current worksheet.

Click on Quantity, and type in the number of sheets you want to add.

Select Before or After. This tells 1-2-3 to insert new worksheets before or after the current worksheet.

Enter in the Quantity text box the number of worksheets to insert.

Choose OK.

New sheets

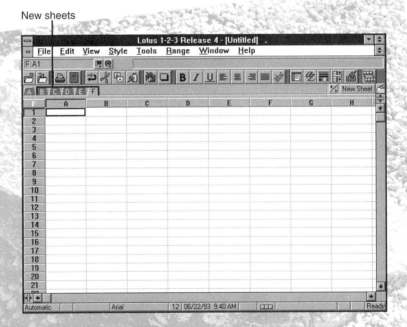

Call Robin Leach, we've got another one.

DISPLAYING THREE WORKSHEETS IN A FILE AT ONCE

You can **VIEW** three worksheets at once by using the **VIEW SPLIT COMMAND** to choose the **P**erspective view.

The perspective view is a layered display of three contiguous worksheets from a file. To change your perspective:

 Choose View Split.

```
View
  Zoom In
  Zoom Out
  Custom - 87%

  Freeze Titles...
  Split...

  Set View Preferences...
```

 Under Type, select Perspective.

Select the Perspective option to display three worksheets on the screen at once. ——————

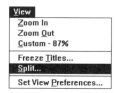

Choose OK. To get back to normal view, choose **View S**plit, and select Clear Split.

There's another way to change the worksheet **VIEW**: zooming in and out. Each time you choose View Zoom In, 1-2-3 magnifies the display by 10%. Shrink the display size of a worksheet by 10% with View Zoom **O**ut.

Rather than use the **VIEW SPLIT COMMAND** to display three contiguous worksheets, click on the Perspective View SmartIcon, which you can add to the current set.

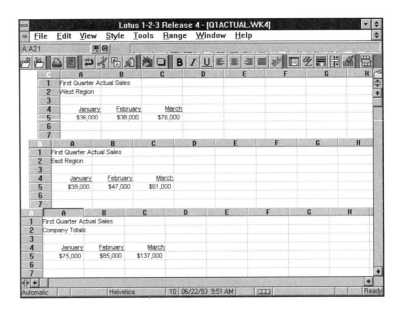

Getting some perspective on your worksheets.

YOU'VE GOT 'EM, HOW DO YOU GET TO 'EM?

Each worksheet has a tab which identifies the worksheet (except in perspective view). A **WORKSHEET TAB** looks like a tab on a file folder. It appears just above the worksheet you are working on to let you name the worksheet and to make it easy to move to a worksheet. To tab to a worksheet, just click.

You can relabel a **WORKSHEET TAB** with a meaningful name. Just double-click on the worksheet tab, and then type the name and press **Enter**. The name can be up to 15 characters long. To delete a worksheet name, double-click on the worksheet tab, press **Del**, and then press **Enter**.

H
Y
P
E
R
T
I
P

Click on a tab to jump to another worksheet.

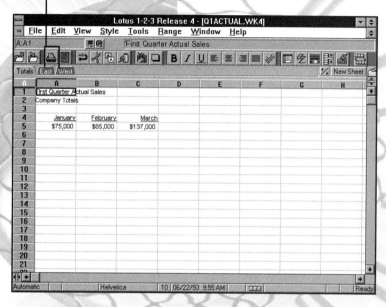

You have to use other ways **TO MOVE BETWEEN WORKSHEETS** while in the perspective view:

◇   Press **F6** (PANE).

◇   To move the previous or next worksheet into view, press **Ctrl+Pg Dn** or **Ctrl+Pg Up**.

   You can use **Ctrl+PgUp**, **Ctrl+PgDn**, **Ctrl+Home** and **End+Ctrl+Home** in normal view or in perspective view. The key

combinations cycle through all worksheets in all open files—not just the worksheet in the file you're currently working in.

◇   To move the first worksheet into view, press **Ctrl+Home**.

◇   To move the last worksheet into view, press **End+Ctrl+Home**.

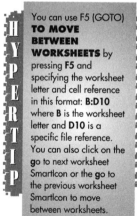

You can use F5 (GOTO) **TO MOVE BETWEEN WORKSHEETS** by pressing **F5** and specifying the worksheet letter and cell reference in this format: **B:D10** where **B** is the worksheet letter and **D10** is a specific file reference. You can also click on the **go** to next worksheet SmartIcon or the **go** to the previous worksheet SmartIcon to move between worksheets.

ZOT! THEY'RE GONE

As ye shall add, so ye shall take away . . . otherwise, extra worksheets make it harder to find the sheet your data's on,

and the size of your file becomes so large that it slows your system down. Here's how to rub out a worksheet:

 Click on the tab of the worksheet you want to delete.

2 Select the whole worksheet. You do this by clicking on the sheet letter at the intersection of the row and column headers.

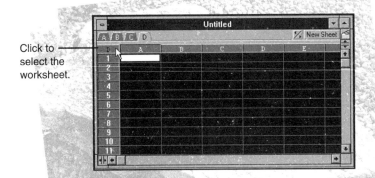

Click to select the worksheet.

3 Choose Edit Delete or press the right mouse button to display the quick menu, and then click on Delete. You can also press **Ctrl+ -** (minus on the numeric keypad) to delete.

Edit	
<u>U</u>ndo	Ctrl+Z
Cu<u>t</u>	Ctrl+X
<u>C</u>opy	Ctrl+C
<u>P</u>aste	Ctrl+V
Cl<u>e</u>ar...	Del
Paste <u>S</u>pecial...	
Paste Link	
Arrange	▸
Copy Do<u>w</u>n	
Copy <u>R</u>ight	
<u>I</u>nsert...	Ctrl +
<u>D</u>elete...	Ctrl -
<u>F</u>ind & Replace...	
<u>G</u>o To...	F5
Insert <u>O</u>bject...	
Links...	

A HAVEN FOR CONFORMIST WORKSHEETS: GROUPS

By default, each worksheet in a file can have its own style. One worksheet can have fonts, column widths, colors and so on that are different from any others in the file. The flexibility to customize the style of each worksheet in a file is usually a good thing. However, if you want consistency of style among worksheets in a file, you can have it by grouping worksheets. Then you can **UNGROUP** them later, at your whim.

To **UNGROUP** worksheets, follow the same steps as grouping except deselect (uncheck) the Group mode check box in the Worksheet Defaults dialog box.

HYPERTIP

212

Grouping worksheets together means you can assign the same styles and settings to all the worksheets in the group. For example, if you have 12 monthly budget sheets in a file, you'll probably want all those sheets to look the same—to have the same number formats, fonts, and colors. After the worksheets are grouped, if you change the styles or settings of any worksheet in the group, all the worksheets change. For example, if you change the font in B10 of one of the worksheets in a group to Times New Roman 12, then all the worksheets in the group will use Times New Roman 12 as the font in B10. If you change the column width of C to 15, then all the worksheets in the group will have a column C that is 15 characters wide.

When you group worksheets, you better be sure that you really want to change the styles of all the worksheets because it's permanent. When you ungroup the worksheets, the styles don't change back. Here's how to get a group together:

 Choose Style Worksheet Defaults.

 Under Other, select the Group mode check box.

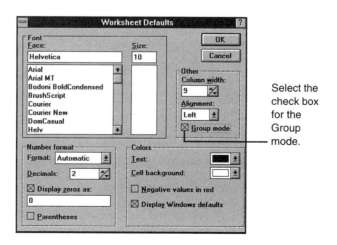

Select the check box for the Group mode.

 Choose OK.

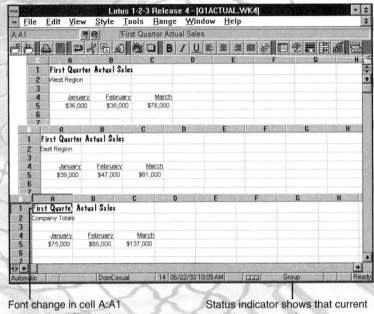

Font change in cell A:A1
appears in all files in the group.

Status indicator shows that current
worksheet is part of a group.

SHEETSMART ICONS

1-2-3 has some SmartIcons you can use
to work with multiple worksheets. To
access most of them, you need to add

them to an existing or *custom SmartIcon
set.*

SheetSmart icons.

H Y P E R L I N K S

COPYING AND LINKING CELLS—See "8. Calculate This!" p. 77, and "16. The Naked Truth About Copying and Moving," p. 161.

CUSTOM SMARTICON SET—See "31. Even Smarter SmartIcons," p. 301.

FILE—See "3. It's a File Thing," p.28, and "22. File Today, Gone Tomorrow," p.216.

FILE TODAY, GONE TOMORROW

Before you buy into the miracles that computer and software companies are trying to sell you, stop and use your own circuitry. Electronic data technology is here, and we all have to live with it, but it's not 100 percent reliable. It's inevitable that you'll lose data. That's why it's a good idea for you to know a little more about your file options in 1-2-3: how to save parts of files and save in other formats, how to delete unneeded files, and how to use the prophylactic of file management—backups.

"3. It's a File Thing" told you how to *save your 1-2-3 files* using the **File Save** and **File Save As** commands, but it didn't tell the whole story. This lesson gives you a lowdown on the other techniques you need to protect your electronic data and to share it with others.

IN PART, AND IN ANOTHER LANGUAGE

Rather than saving the **WHOLE FILE**, you can save just a range of data from a file, and you can do it in three different ways: including formulas and their values, with **VALUES ONLY**, or as a **TEXT FILE (.TXT)**. You may want to save a part of a file that you can use to build another worksheet or to import into another program. Saving to make a molehill out of a mountain:

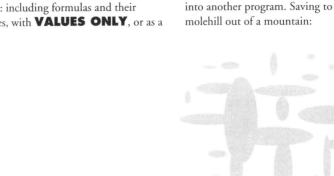

Select the range you want to save.

 Choose File Save As.

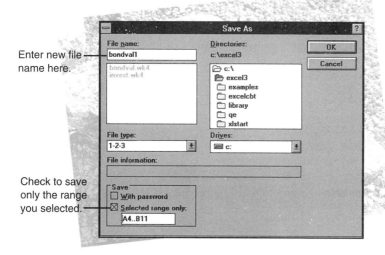 Enter the file name (to which you want to save the range) in the File name text box. To specify a text file, enter the file extension (**.TXT**) when you enter the file name in the File name text box.

To specify a text file, choose Text (txt) from the File type drop-down list box, and the TXT extension will be automatically added to our file name.

Select the Selected range only check box.

Enter new file name here.

Check to save only the range you selected.

 Choose OK. If you specified a worksheet file (**.WK***) in step 3, the Save Range As dialog box appears.

 Select Formulas and values or Values only.

Saves the file with the formulas intact.

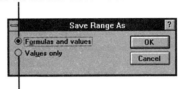

Saves the file with formulas converted to values.

 Choose OK.

BACKUP PLAN

People with any common sense whatsoever usually create a backup plan for significant events, so they don't freak out when something goes wrong (which it does 90% of the time). You can demonstrate your common sense when it comes to file accidents if you ask 1-2-3 to create a backup version every time you save a file. The **F**ile Save **A**s command gives you the option of not only saving the new version of the file, but also saving the old version (sans the changes you just made) to a backup file with the .BAK extension. For example, if you're working on a file that you had previously saved as **CLASSAVE.WK4**, and you save the file with a backup copy, 1-2-3 saves your changes to **CLASSAVE.WK4**, and the original file as **CLASSAVE.BAK**. Here's how to set this up:

 Choose File Save As. 1-2-3 displays the Save As dialog box. Remember that for normal saving, you would've just chosen **F**ile **S**ave. Do not change the File name in the Save As dialog box.

 Click on OK.

 Select the Backup button.

Assigns the extension .BAK to the file on disk and saves new file (with changes).

SHORT-CIRCUITING OLD FILES

When you delete a 1-2-3 file, you remove the electrical charges that make it up from the disk. You can't delete 1-2-3 files from within the 1-2-3 program. Instead, you must use the Windows File Manager or use the DEL command at the DOS prompt to delete your 1-2-3 file. Here's the best method, à la Program Manager:

 Close the file you want to delete and switch to the Windows Program Manager. *Changing to another application* is covered in Lesson 3.

 Double-click on the Main group icon to open the Main window.

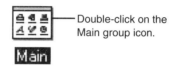

Double-click on the Main group icon.

 Open the File Manager by double-clicking on its icon. The Directory Tree window becomes active.

Double-click on the File Manager icon to open it.

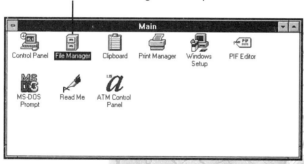

 Select the drive name of the disk that contains the 1-2-3 file you want to delete.

Click on the drive icon for the disk
containing the file you want to delete.

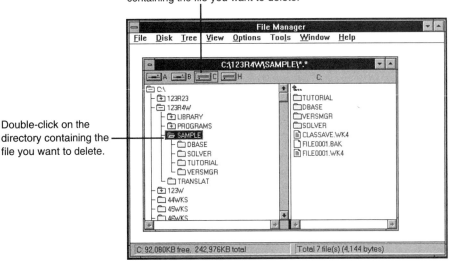

Double-click on the
directory containing the
file you want to delete.

 Select the directory that contains the file you want to delete. A window
displaying the subdirectories and files in the directory becomes active. If the file
is in a subdirectory, select the subdirectory.

 Select the 1-2-3 file you want to delete. Just click on the file's icon.

Choose File Delete
after you have
selected the file.

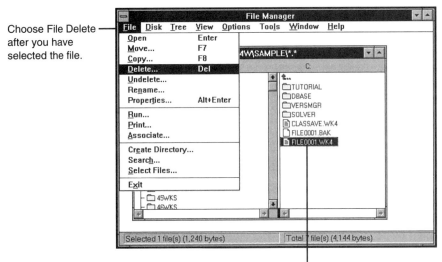

Select the file you want to delete.

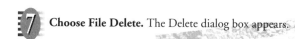

Choose File Delete. The Delete dialog box appears.

Click on OK. The File Manager dialog box appears and asks you to confirm that you want to delete the file.

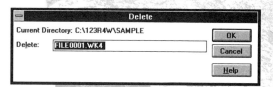

Click on Yes.

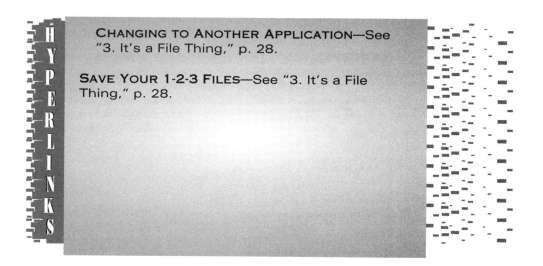

CHANGING TO ANOTHER APPLICATION—See "3. It's a File Thing," p. 28.

SAVE YOUR 1-2-3 FILES—See "3. It's a File Thing," p. 28.

IT'S YOUR DISPLAY, YOU CAN CHANGE IT

Fess up! You've got file folders you haven't looked in since last July laying on your desk, paper clips are buried like land mines, and you've got quite a science experiment growing in the bottom of a coffee cup you never bothered to empty out all the way. Sooner or later, this is going to have some impact on your efficiency.

At least, you can make an effort to keep your 1-2-3 work area streamlined, and this lesson tells you how to do it. You'll get ideas on how to see what you need to more clearly, be it rearranging or putting away parts of the 1-2-3 screen. All of this involves *changing worksheet defaults*.

STATIONARY TITLES

One of the problems you have scrolling around large worksheets is losing sight of column and row titles. The View Freeze Titles command eliminates that problem by freezing the contents of the top rows and/or the left-hand columns of the worksheet in place so you can scroll through the worksheet without losing sight of what your data represents. The rows and columns remain frozen (and the entries they contain visible) until you **UNFREEZE** them. To put the freeze on:

 Select a cell one cell below the rows you want to freeze, one cell to the right of the columns you want to freeze, or (to freeze both rows and columns) just below the rows and to the right of the columns you want to freeze.

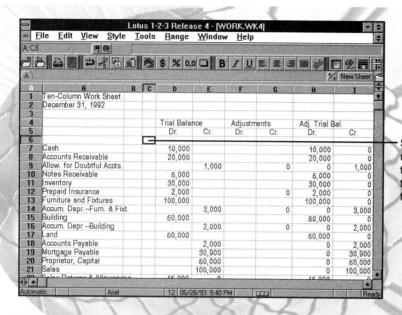

Selected cell is both below the rows to be frozen (rows 1 through 5) and to the right of the column (column B) to be frozen.

2 Choose View Freeze Titles.

3 **Select Rows, Columns, or Both.** Selecting **Rows** freezes the rows at the top of the sheet containing column titles. Selecting **Columns** freezes the columns at the left that contain titles that label rows. Selecting **Both** freezes both the rows and columns that contain labels.

4 **Choose OK.** After this is done, if you scroll anywhere on the worksheet, the frozen titles are always displayed.

LINES ON THE WORKSHEET

Grid lines outline the rows and columns in your worksheet. Isn't that special? They make it easier for you to read across rows and down columns. For example, if you are working with a 10-column worksheet, it is sometimes difficult to read across the rows. In such a worksheet, grid lines can help guide your eye across and down the page. If you don't want to see the grid lines, you can turn off this option and others. (And it logically follows that you can turn all **OPTIONS** back on.) To send your grid lines into oblivion (or bring them back again):

 Choose View Set View Preferences.

 Under Show in current file, click the check box for Grid lines.

Click, and then click on a color to change the grid line color.

Check so grid lines appear in your current file and others you open.

Other display items you can toggle on or off

Set View Preferences

Show in current file
- ☒ **W**orksheet frame   Standard ⬍
- ☒ Worksheet **t**abs
- ☒ **G**rid lines
- ☒ **S**croll bars
- ☒ **P**age breaks
- ☒ **C**harts, drawings, and pictures
- Custom **z**oom %:   87

Show in 1-2-3
- ☒ Smart**I**cons
- ☒ **E**dit line
- ☒ Status **b**ar

OK
Cancel

3 To change the color of grid lines, click on the arrow by the drop-down box, and then click on a color on the palette. There are 255 colors in the palette. The exact number of colors may be less than 255, dependent upon the monitor and the configuration of your system.

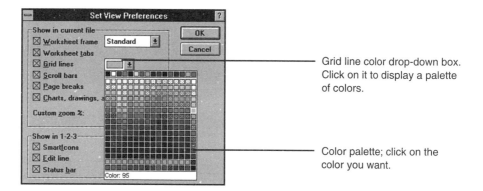

Grid line color drop-down box. Click on it to display a palette of colors.

Color palette; click on the color you want.

 Choose OK.

I'M TOO SEXY FOR MY FRAME

The worksheet frame is the horizontal bar that initially contains a worksheet's tabs (A: through IV:), the column letters (A through IV), and the row numbers (1 through 8132). You can choose to display or hide the worksheet frame or change the type of frame by using the View Set View Preferences command. The frame format of letters for columns and numbers for rows is the Standard frame type—the default. You can choose one of the following other types of frames:

> Character   Shows how many characters will fit in a column or row.

> Inches   Shows measurements on the frame in inches. For example, it shows the width of columns and the height of rows in inches.

> Metric   Shows distances on the frame in centimeters.

> Points/Pica   Shows measurements in points (1/72nd of an inch) and Pica (approximately 1/6th of an inch). For example, it shows the height of characters in points and the width in Pica.

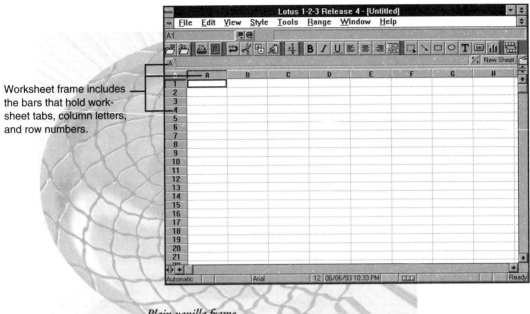

Worksheet frame includes the bars that hold worksheet tabs, column letters, and row numbers.

Plain vanilla frame.

To try on a new frame:

 Choose View Set View Preferences.

 Under Show in current file, select the check box for Worksheet frame. This box is checked by default. Make sure it is checked if you want the frame displayed and unchecked if you don't want a frame.

Select a frame type from the drop-down list.

Check to display the frame.

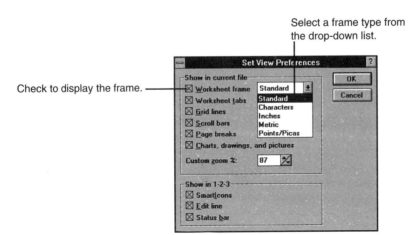

(Optional) If you want the frame to show, and you want to change the frame type, select a frame type from the drop-down box. Standard is the most popular and traditional setting—columns as letters and rows as numbers.

 Click on OK. You get what you paid for.

This is the Character frame type.

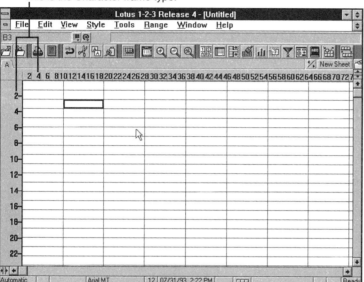

WHO'S ZOOMING WHO

Hacked late into the night and are having problems seeing your worksheet today? (Let me guess whose fault it was. Could it be . . . Satan?) You can increase the display size of cells by as much as 400%. Or you can decrease the screen size of cells to as small as 25% of the normal size. The effects of the View Zoom In and View Zoom Out commands should now be obvious to you (with the exception of the fact that they zoom you in or out by increments of 10% when selected). To zoom in or **ZOOM OUT**, just choose the appropriate command from the View menu (hopefully, you can at least see the menus and commands).

HYPERTIP

To get an aerial view of a large worksheet, **ZOOM OUT** until you can see what you want to look at. If you zoom out to 25% of the normal cell display size, you'll see almost 2,000 cells on one screen. Before you delete columns or rows in a large worksheet, you may want to "step back" a bit by zooming out. That way you can see what parts of the worksheet, if any, will be jumbled if you delete.

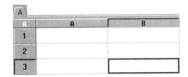

Big cells and little ones.

DE DEFAULT

You can set the screen display size of cells (and return it to normal if you've been screwing around with it) by using View Set View Preferences and entering a percentage in the Custom Zoom % text box. For example, if you want the cells to be 87% of their normal size, choose View Set View Preferences, and enter **87** in the Custom Zoom % text box. Then, any other time you need to reset the cells to the default (custom) percentage, choose View Custom. (By the way, 87% of normal is the default).

A FEW GOODIES FOR YOUR DISPLAY

The Goodies SmartIcon set offers some icons to let you mess with the display even faster. Just *change the SmartIcon set* to display Goodies, and click away.

Display changers.

CHANGE THE SMARTICON SET—See "5. SmartIcons: Pictures on SmartDrugs," p. 49.

CHANGING WORKSHEET DEFAULTS—See "24. Enhancing the Global Environment," p. 229.

HYPERLINKS

ENHANCING THE GLOBAL ENVIRONMENT

The world would be scary if hair professionals all used those suck-cut vacuum haircutters so that everyone came out with an identical shag cut. But no, you tell your cutter what to do so you (with any luck) get the look you want. Software companies are finally getting the message that we're not all happy, shiny people who want shag haircuts.

There are certain 1-2-3 options, such as the default settings, which affect entire worksheets and files. A specific example of a default setting is the **GRID LINES** option. You choose whether or not *grid lines* appear in every worksheet and file.

In older programs, you had less control over the defaults. Now, you have control, but you have to hunt around on different menus to pick up the settings you want. This lesson helps you find and clean up your worksheet defaults.

A CLEARER VISTA

The View Set View **P**references command gives you quite a bit of control over the *view of your current file* or all worksheets. Turning off some options lets 1-2-3 display more cells on-screen and to speed up your work. Globally, you can choose to see (or not) SmartIcons, the **EDIT LINE**, and the status bar.

 Choose View Set View Preferences.

To make information in your worksheets easier to read, you can display **GRID LINES** between columns and rows by choosing **View** Set **View** Preference **G**rid lines.

If you're done entering all the formulas in your worksheet and you're just formatting it, put away the **EDIT LINE** by using **View** Set **View** Preferences.

 Under Show in 1-2-3, check to turn options on and off. For example, if you don't want SmartIcons to be displayed on all your currently opened files or in new files, click on the SmartIcons check box to uncheck it. Or click on a check box to turn an option back on.

These settings affect all files you open.

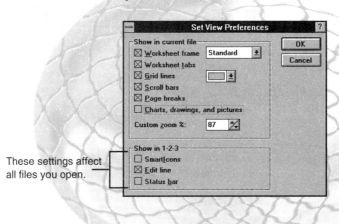

 Choose OK.

TOOL TIME

You also can choose Tools **USER SETUP** to customize 1-2-3. Changes in the User Setup dialog box turn special working features on and off. For example, the Save files every __ minutes feature saves all open files frequently so they don't disappear if the power goes out while you're working happily along. But having 1-2-3 pause to save every three minutes can annoy the hell out of you. To stop 1-2-3 from being such a tool:

 **Choose Tools User Setup.**

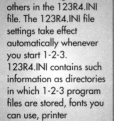

1-2-3 stores the **USER SETUP** settings and others in the 123R4.INI file. The 123R4.INI file settings take effect automatically whenever you start 1-2-3. 123R4.INI contains such information as directories in which 1-2-3 program files are stored, fonts you can use, printer information, and page size.

Click options to turn them on and off. Options that are turned on have checked boxes while options that are off have unchecked boxes. Here are the flavors to choose from:

Drag-and-drop cells   Turns the *drag-and-drop* feature on and off.

Use **A**utomatic format   Sets the 1-2-3 default number format to Automatic, which means 1-2-3 determines how to format an entry by examining the way you enter the data. For example, if you enter **$50**, 1-2-3 formats the cell as Currency. Unchecking this option changes the default *number format* to General.

Save files every   Check this and enter a number of minutes to have 1-2-3 save open files automatically at the specified interval.

Undo   Turns **E**dit **U**ndo on or off.

Run autoexecute **m**acros   Tells 1-2-3 whether or not to run autoexecute macros when you open files that contain the *macros.*

Beep on error   Lets 1-2-3 beep when you blow it or when the {Beep} macro command is encountered in a macro.

Number of recent **f**iles to show   Enter a number from **0** to **5** in the text box. The number tells 1-2-3 how many of the most **RECENTLY OPENED FILES** to list at the bottom of the **F**ile menu.

Worksheet directory   Lets you enter the default directory where you want 1-2-3 to save files.

You can open one of the **RECENTLY OPENED FILES** that appear on the File menu by clicking on its name.

 (Optional) Click International, change the settings, and click on OK. In the International dialog box, you can change:

◇ International date and time formats.

◇ How 1-2-3 will read and save characters in 1-2-3 for DOS Release 2 (.WK1) files.

◇ The appearance of decimal points, thousands separators, argument separators, and negative numbers.

◇ The currency symbol and its position.

(Optional) Choose Recalculation, change options, and click on OK. You can make these changes to how 1-2-3 recalculates formulas:

Natural   This will recalculate all the formulas that you used to make the current formula first. Then, it will calculate the current formula.

By column   This option recalculates formulas by the order they appear in the worksheet. It starts in the first cell or the first column

(A:A1) and goes from left to right. When it's done with one worksheet, it moves to the next one in the file.

By row   This option recalculates formulas in order, too, but it starts in cell A:A1 and moves from top to bottom. When the first worksheet has been recalculated, it moves on to the next one in the file.

Choose OK.

IT'S NOT HOW YOU FEEL, IT'S HOW YOU LOOK

Gravity controls much of human existence. Not only do our butts and other parts sag as we age, but we also settle into our habits, like always, always cutting the grass in precisely the same pattern and always reading the paper in the same order. (Let's hope this doesn't apply to your sex life.) When it comes to the look of your worksheets, gravity compels you to settle into giving your worksheets a look you're comfortable with. You probably choose the same fonts, the same number formats, and even the same text colors time after time.

Most of the commands for *changing cell styling* in individual files fall on the **S**tyle menu. You also can use a **S**tyle menu command to change these settings for all new files: **S**tyle **W**orksheet Defaults. If you use this command to set up 1-2-3, all the worksheets you create from that point forward will sport your favorite fonts, colors, and more.

 Choose Style Worksheet Defaults.

 Select the options you want to always apply. Here are the settings you can have 1-2-3 apply to all new files you open:

Font   Select a default letter style from the **F**ace list, and then enter or choose a **S**ize.

Number format   Choose a **F**ormat from the drop-down list, type in or click on the arrows to set the **D**ecimals (decimal places), and enter a character in the Display **z**eros as text box to display that character instead of zeros. Or turn off this check box to hide zeros, or indicate whether to show all new numbers in **P**arentheses.

Colors   To choose colors for **T**ext and the **C**ell background, click on the appropriate down arrow to display a palette, and then click on the color you want; turn check boxes to display

The initial default colors for data and background in 1-2-3 are the **WINDOWS DEFAULTS** (the colors currently set on your Windows Control Panel Color palette). Turning on the Display Windows defaults check box in the Worksheet Defaults dialog box reverts the colors of your 1-2-3 worksheets to what's currently selected for Windows.

Negative values in red or Display **WINDOWS DEFAULTS** on or off.

Other Use the arrows or type to change the default Column **w**idth from the original default

of 9, specify the **A**lignment you want in cells, and tell 1-2-3 whether or not you want to use **G**roup mode in the current file so that style and alignment changes will apply to every worksheet in a file.

 Choose OK.

CHANGING CELL STYLING—See "12. You Look Mahhvelous!" p. 119.

DRAG-AND-DROP—See "16. The Naked Truth About Copying and Moving," p. 161.

GRID LINES—See "23. It's Your Display, You Can Change It," p. 222.

MACROS—See "32. MacroMania," p. 308, and "33. Macro Makeovers," p. 316.

NUMBER FORMAT—See "13. Number Formats to Go," p. 131.

VIEW OF YOUR CURRENT FILE—See "23. It's Your Display, You Can Change It," p. 222.

Part V

GETTING GRAPHIC

Hey, no one said your spreadsheets had to be boring. The next few lessons explain how you can give your data oomph! by adding drawings and charts. Just don't add too much of your artistic talent to any given worksheet . . . people still need to read the data, after all.

THE AMAZING LINE AND SHAPE MAKER

Bend it, shape it—any way you look at it, computer drawing is a blast. Most spreadsheet programs let you import pictures that you've drawn with other programs, but 1-2-3 is one of the few that actually give you a drawing program built in. Granted, it's not an overly sophisticated drawing program, but what do you expect for free? It all happens through the **D**raw command off the **T**ools menu—you don't even have to leave 1-2-3.

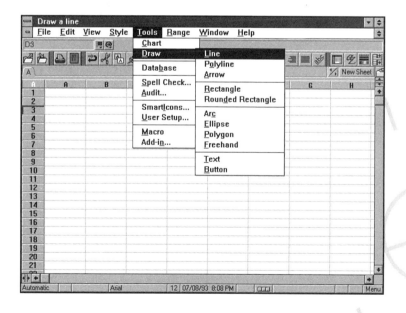

There's a plethora of choices on the **D**raw menu for your drawing pleasure. (Plethora, what a great word!) And for each object that you can draw from the Tools Draw submenu, there is a *SmartIcon*. Here's a quick rundown:

	Line	Draws a single straight line. (That's right, only straight ones. If you want more freedom, try **F**reehand.)
	P**o**lyline	Draws a series of connected, straight lines that don't form a closed polygon. (If you want a completed shape with no open ends, try **P**olygon instead.)
	Arrow	Draws a single straight line with an arrowhead on one end or both.
	Rectangle	Draws a rectangle or a square. (Duh.)
	Roun**d**ed Rectangle	Draws a rounded rectangle or rounded square. These are kind of like rectangles with the points of their corners filed off.
	Ar**c**	Draws an arc. (Notice I said an arc, A-R-C, meaning a curved line, not an ark, meaning a large boat filled with smelly animals.)
	Ellipse	Draws an ellipse or a circle. (An ellipse is an oval or lopsided circle.)
	Polygon	Draws a series of connected lines that end up being a closed polygon (shape). If you leave the last connecting line undrawn, 1-2-3 connects the two ends for you.
	Freehand	Draws a freehand object. This is where you can go crazy and draw ugly, wobbly lines.
	Text	Draws a text block (a block you can type text into).
	Button	Creates a macro button (a button that you can click on in the worksheet to run a macro).

THE STRAIGHT AND NARROW: LINES AND ARROWS

If straight lines are your thing, follow these steps:

 Select Draw and then Line from the Tools menu, or click on the Line SmartIcon. Either way, your mouse pointer turns into a dotted sort of cross hair.

 Move the mouse pointer to where you want to begin drawing the line. Hold the left mouse button down to anchor the line.

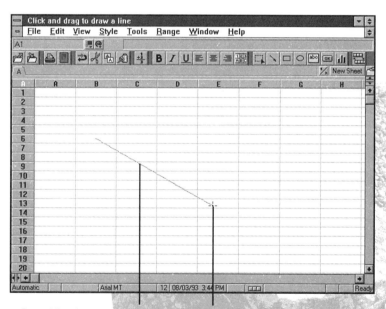 **Drag across the worksheet until the line is the right length and in the right position.** The line you're creating shows up dotted. If you need the line to be exactly horizontal, vertical, or at a 45-degree angle, hold down the **Shift** key as you drag.

Dotted line (under construction)   Mouse pointer

 Release the mouse button. The line turns solid, and your cursor changes from the cross hair to a four-headed arrow that you can use to reposition the line (as you'll see later).

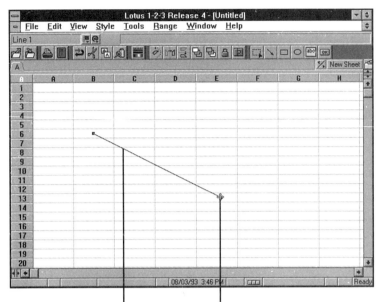

Solid line (that means it's finished)   Mouse pointer

Drawing a line with an arrow at the end is as easy as drawing a line without one. You just select Arrow instead of Line from the Draw menu, or click on one of the Arrow SmartIcons. There are two Arrow SmartIcons: double (an arrow at both ends of the line) and single (an arrow at just the ending point of the line).

POLY WANT A LINE?

No, a polyline isn't a line designed by a parrot, or even a clothesline on which to hang man-made fabric. It's a bunch of line segments connected together. Sort of like a polygon, except it forms an open shape since the starting and ending points aren't connected. Here's how to make one:

 Choose Select Draw and then Polyline from the Tools menu, or click on the Polyline SmartIcon. Your mouse pointer turns into the same dotted cross hair as with a single line.

 Move the mouse pointer to where you want to begin drawing the first line segment. Click on the mouse button once to anchor the line.

3 **Drag across the worksheet to draw a line segment.** For a plain, straight line, just drag. To make the line exactly horizontal, vertical, or 45-degrees, hold down **Shift** while you drag. To free yourself from linear thinking and draw a nonstraight line, hold down **Ctrl** while you drag.

4 **Click on the mouse button at the point where you want the line segment to end.**

5 Repeat steps 3 and 4 until you've drawn all the lines you care to.

6 Double-click to complete the polyline.

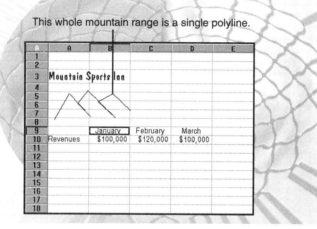

This whole mountain range is a single polyline.

SHAPELY ALTERNATIVES

You can fiddle with a polyline all day long trying to create a perfect square or rectangle, but it's much easier to use the right tool for the job. (Sounds like one of those do-it-yourself shows where Handyman Bob shows you how easy it is to create a $10 stool with $5,000 worth of power tools.) To draw a rectangle or a square, follow these steps:

1 **Choose Tools Draw Rectangle, or click on the Rectangle SmartIcon.** Your mouse pointer, once again, turns into that funky, little, dotted cross hair.

2 **Move the mouse pointer to where you want to begin drawing the rectangle or square.** Hold the left mouse button down to anchor a corner.

 Drag across the worksheet to make your rectangle. If you want an exact square, hold down **Shift** while you drag.

 Release the mouse button when the rectangle or square is the size you want.

As you might have guessed, a rounded rectangle works the exact same way, except you choose Rounded Rectangle from the menu or click on the **Rounded Rectangle** SmartIcon. (Another duh.)

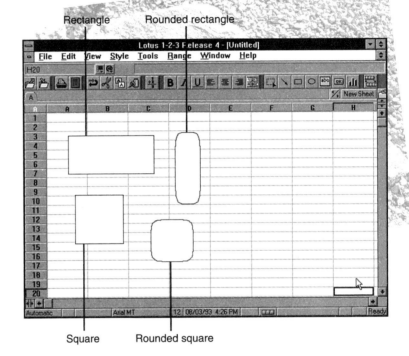

Rectangle   Rounded rectangle

Square   Rounded square

TRIUMPHANT ARCS, ELLIPSES, AND CIRCLES

Ellipses and circles work the same way as squares and rectangles; do it plain for an ellipse, or hold down **Shift** for a perfect circle every time. Arcs are a little different. To make one, you drag the mouse as if you were drawing a box (sort of), and then pivot the sucker around until it's the right angle. Not terribly efficient, but it gets the job done.

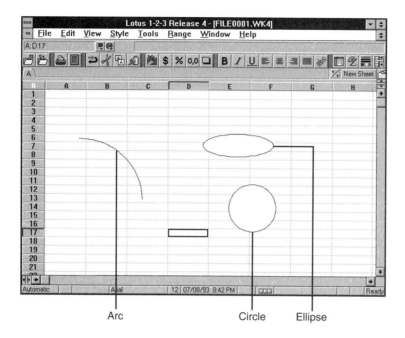

Arc   Circle   Ellipse

POLY'S GONE

Yes, Poly's pretty far gone. A polygon is a collection of line segments that form a closed shape. It can have any number of sides and can include straight or crooked (freehand) segments, whatever works best for you. You draw them kind of like a polyline:

 Choose Tools Draw Polygon, or click on the Polygon SmartIcon.

 Move the mouse pointer to where you want to begin drawing the first line segment. Click on the mouse button to anchor the first line.

 Draw whatever line segment you feel compelled to, just as you have done with regular lines and polylines. (Remember, hold down **Shift** for horizontal, vertical, or 45-degree lines, and hold down **Ctrl** for a freehand line.)

 Click on the mouse button where you want the line segment to end.

Repeat steps 3 and 4 until the whole polygon is done.

Double-click to complete the polygon. If you haven't connected the starting and ending points, 1-2-3 makes the connection for you.

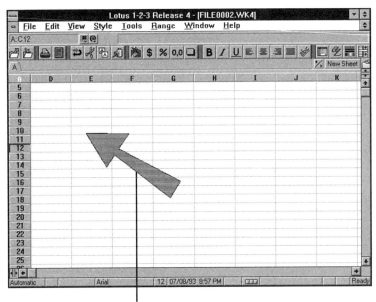

Here's one of the many cool things you can do with polygons.

FREEHAND: THE ULTIMATE CREATIVE TOOL

With the Freehand tool, there are no rules. There are no guidelines. You just start moving the mouse and make things happen. The results may not be especially pretty, but they're guaranteed to be your very own.

Choose Tools Draw Freehand.

Move the mouse pointer to where you want to begin the freehand drawing. Hold the left mouse button down to anchor the line.

Drag across the worksheet. You're free! Move it any which way you choose.

 Release the mouse button where you want the drawing to end.

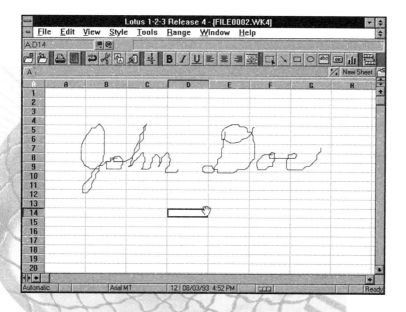

BE THE FIRST ONE ON YOUR (TEXT) BLOCK

Text blocks are like cyber Post-it Notes. Stick them onto worksheets to make either snide or earnest comments, or to point out the important parts of a huge worksheet filled with tiny numbers. Once you've got your **TEXT BLOCK**, you can put text in it, change the font, and change the color.

To change the appearance of a **TEXT BLOCK** (once you've created it), click on it, and then choose **Style Font & Attributes**.

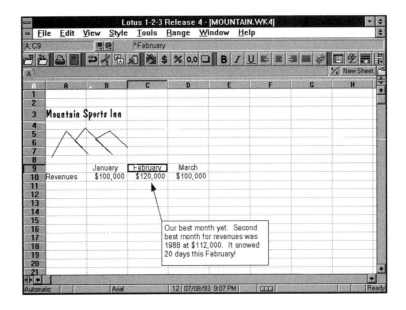

Here are a text block and an arrow used to show off an impressive number.

Here's how to add a text block:

 Choose Tools Draw Text.

 Move the mouse pointer to where you want to begin the text block.

 Do one of the following:

⬦ Click on the worksheet to create the text block in the default size.

⬦ Drag across the worksheet, and release the mouse button when the text block is the size you want.

Either way, the text block appears with a blinking insertion point in the top left corner so that you can begin typing text or pasting it.

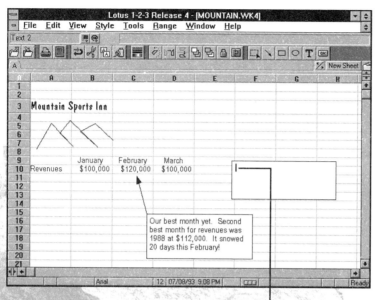

A blinking insertion point points the way.

4 Type text into the block, or paste it in using Edit Paste.

5 Click on the worksheet outside of the text block when you finish entering **TEXT**.

HYPERTIP

Did you screw something up? You can edit the **TEXT** in your text block by double-clicking on the block.

COLOR MY STUFF

You can *change the color* of a text box, or any other drawn object, by selecting the object, choosing Style Lines & Color, and selecting the color drop-down boxes. If you missed the complete story in Lesson 14, turn back there now.

THE INCREDIBLE SHRINKING OBJECT

Don't kid yourself—you're probably not going to get the drawing sized perfectly the first time. After you draw an object, you'll probably have to resize it at least once before it's the perfect size for the worksheet. Here's how:

 Select the object by clicking on it. When an object is selected, it sprouts small black handles.

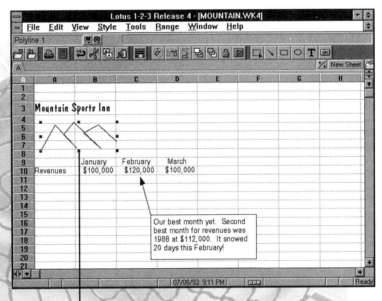

They may look like squares, but to 1-2-3 they're handles.

 Drag a handle in the direction you want to size the object. If you drag one of the handles in the middle of a side, the object stretches in the direction you drag, with no regard to the proper proportion. If you drag a corner handle, the object stretches both sides at once, again with no proportion. If you want to keep the original proportion, hold down **Shift** while you drag one of the corner handles.

 Release the mouse button when the object is the size you want.

DUPING OBJECTS

No, your objects are not necessarily gullible creatures, but you can clone them fairly easily without them even noticing. It works just like copying data—you use the *Windows Clipboard* **COPY** and Paste features.

 Select a drawn object.

 Choose Edit Copy, or click on the Copy SmartIcon.

 Select a cell where you want to paste the object.

 Choose Edit Paste, or click on the Paste SmartIcon.

Here's an easier way to make a **COPY**; just select the drawn object, and press the **Insert** (Ins) key. The duplicate object appears on the screen next to the original, and you can move it or drag it wherever you like. You can delete drawn objects in sort of the same way—by pressing the **Delete** (Del) key.

IT'S A MOVEMENT

You can move a drawn object anywhere you want—to a different place in the same worksheet, to another worksheet in a file, or even (using Windows' Clipboard) to a different file or a different application. Stay tuned for the gory details.

DRAGGING ALONG

Moving a drawn object around in a worksheet can be a real drag:

 Select a drawn object.

 Drag it to its new location. Position your mouse cursor inside the object rather than on a handle, so 1-2-3 won't think you're wanting to resize the thing.

 Release the mouse button when the object is where you want it.

LONG-DISTANCE MOVING

With the Clipboard, you can move an object anywhere at all (within Windows, of course. Every program has its limits after all).

 Select a drawn object.

 Choose Edit Cut, or click on the Cut SmartIcon.

 Open up the worksheet or other app where you want to put the object.

 Choose Edit Paste, or click on the Paste SmartIcon.

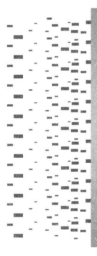

CHANGING THE COLOR OF A TEXT BOX—"See 14. Color, Shading, Lines, and Shadows," p.141.

WINDOWS CLIPBOARD FOR COPYING, CUTTING, AND PASTING—See "11. Techno-Subversive Activities: Removing and Hiding Data," p. 109, and "16. The Naked Truth About Copying and Moving," p. 161.

SMARTICONS—See "5. SmartIcons: Pictures on SmartDrugs," p. 49.

THE CHART OF THE MATTER

When people see huge spreadsheets full of tiny, little numbers, their eyes sort of glaze over, and their minds start thinking about what to have for lunch or whether to take the dog to the vet for his flatulence problem. The same data in a chart, however, makes that same reader sit up and take notice. A chart tells the reader, at a glance, what he needs to know—no fine print, no deep thoughts.

Best of all, with 1-2-3 for Windows, charts are easy to create and update. Just follow a simple procedure for creating the chart out of existing data on your worksheet. If that data changes, you can arrange to have the chart updated automatically. You can also switch among the various chart types easily, without re-creating or relabeling anything. You can also use the charting SmartIcons to modify your charts, such as set colors, patterns, borders, and frames, and change chart types. The charting SmartIcons appear in the SmartIcon bar when you create or select a chart.

GO AHEAD, MAKE MY CHART

Before you get started, you should know the full story about X and Y. Basically, X means horizontal and Y means vertical. Memorize that, because it'll come in handy. Most charts (except pie charts) plot worksheet data on a two-dimensional plane that shows the data against a horizontal X-axis and a vertical Y-axis. A few of the more complicated chart types plot data in the third and remaining dimension, Z.

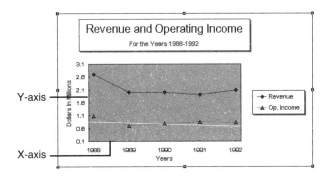

This is a two-dimensional chart; the data is plotted against the X-axis and Y-axis.

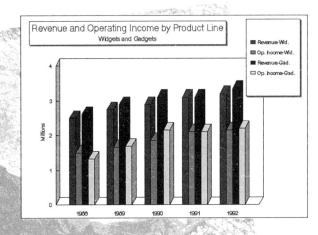

3-D charts are even more active and attractive.

To create a chart, you first *select the range(s)* that you want to plot. 1-2-3 follows a set of rather complicated rules when creating a chart from the data that you select. They're a pain to learn, but they simplify things in the end: these rules make it possible for your range selection to include the titles, legend labels, and data to be plotted. For instance, if the selected range contains more rows than columns, 1-2-3 plots the data by columns. This means it will use the first column as the X-axis labels and the remaining columns as the data to be plotted. For more on the rules that 1-2-3 uses to plot your data, see your *1-2-3 Release 4 for Windows User Guide.* This lesson carefully sidesteps the entire issue by selecting only the data to be plotted, and adding the titles, labels, and legends separately.

Let's get down to business. To plot some data in a chart, follow these steps:

 Select the range or collection that contains the data you want to chart.

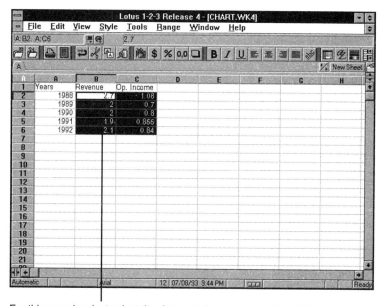

For this exercise, just select the data, not the row and column labels.

 Choose Tools Chart.

 Hold down the mouse button, and drag across the worksheet where you want the chart to appear. 1-2-3 creates a default chart type. If you're not happy with the default chart type, keep moving through this lesson, and you'll learn how to change it.

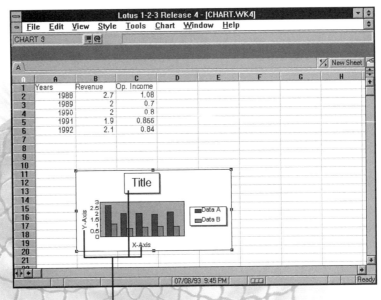

Notice the dummy text used as placeholders.

BUT WHAT DOES IT MEAN?

For a chart to be effective, the reader needs to understand what your point is. A bunch of unlabeled bars or pie slices doesn't accomplish anything at all. When you add titles, footnotes, labels, and legends, however, the point you're trying to make comes shining through:

◇ The title and subtitle of the chart are known also as headings—they are essential to communicating the purpose of the chart.

◇ Labels tell you what each axis represents, which is important to know because most data is plotted against the X- and Y-axes.

◇ Legends are explanations of the symbols, patterns, or colors used to depict data in the chart.

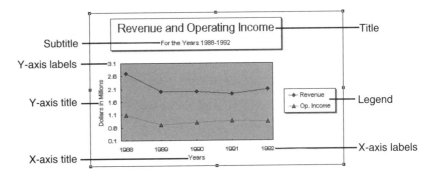

A Catchy Title

The title and subtitle tell the reader what it is that's being shown. Without a title, a chart plotting IBM's market share in the PC industry over the last 10 years could easily be mistaken for a chart of Brazilian rain forest acreage over the same time period. (A mere coincidence? You be the judge.) To add a title and subtitle to a chart, follow these steps:

 Select the chart by clicking on it.

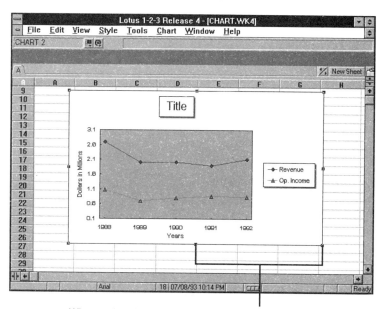

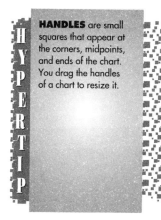

HANDLES are small squares that appear at the corners, midpoints, and ends of the chart. You drag the handles of a chart to resize it.

When a chart is selected, **HANDLES** appear around it.

 Choose Chart Headings. The Headings dialog box appears.

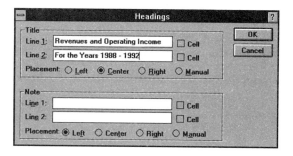

3 Under Title, type the chart title in the Line 1 text box, and enter the subtitle in the Line 2 text box. If you prefer, you can reference a worksheet cell for the title instead, so that if the title on the worksheet changes, the title on the chart will automatically change, too. Just type a valid cell or range address on Line 1 or Line 2. If you use a cell address or range, select the Cell check box.

4 Select a placement option under Title to change the location of the title and subtitle. Centered is the most common way to go.

5 Choose OK to close the **HEADINGS DIALOG BOX**.

LEGENDARY CHARTS

Legends are handy for charts that are plotting more than one series of data (that is, multiple rows and multiple columns). The legend shows the colors, symbols, or patterns that appear on the chart and tells what each one means. For instance, a legend might tell you that the green bars show the number of times you have gotten airsick on domestic flights, where the brown bars show the same for international flights. To add legends to a chart, follow these steps:

1 Select the chart by clicking on it.

2 Choose Chart Legend. The Legend dialog box appears.

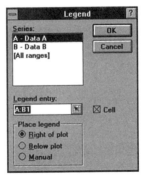

3 Select a data range from the Series list box. To change all legend labels, select All ranges.

Type the text for the legend label in the Legend entry text box (if you selected All ranges from the Series list box, you cannot enter text), or specify the range name or address of a cell (or range, if you selected All ranges) that contains a label you want to use for the legend entry. If you use a cell address or range, select the Cell check box.

 Select an option under Place Legend to change the location of the legend.

 Choose OK.

ADDING AXIS TITLES

The Y-axis and X-axis of a chart need to be labeled so that you describe what it is that is being plotted. For instance, in the chart below, is the Y-axis showing millions of dollars? Number of insect parts found in canned vegetables? We have no way of knowing. Ditto with the X-axis.

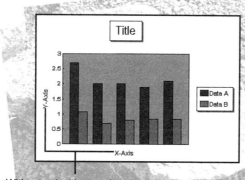

Without axis titles, we have no clue what's being plotted.

A chart without titles is nearly impossible to decipher.

 Select the chart by clicking on it.

 Choose Axis from the Chart menu, and then X-Axis, Y-Axis, or 2nd Y-Axis, depending on which axis you want to title.

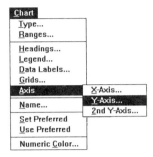

3 Type a title in the Axis title text box, or specify the range name or address of a cell that contains a label you want to use for the **AXIS TITLE**. If you use a cell or range address, select the Cell check box.

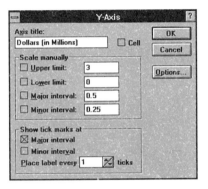

 Choose OK.

ADDING X-AXIS LABELS

When you create a chart, 1-2-3 automatically adds Y-axis labels, but you have to add the X-axis labels yourself. Fortunately, it's not difficult.

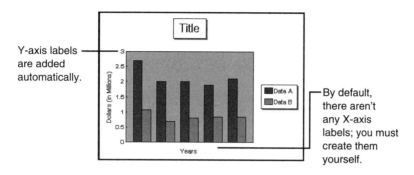

Y-axis labels are added automatically.

By default, there aren't any X-axis labels; you must create them yourself.

1-2-3 does only half the work for you assigning axis labels.

In most cases, the labels for your X-axis are already typed into a row or column on your worksheet. All you need to do is tell 1-2-3 that you want to use them as X-axis labels on the chart. Follow these steps:

 Select the chart by clicking on it.

 Choose Chart Ranges. The Ranges dialog box appears.

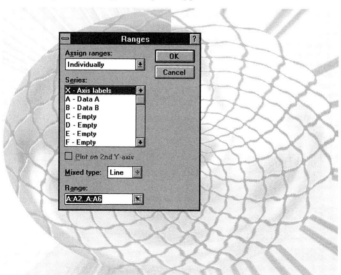

 Select the X-Axis data labels from the Series list box.

 Specify a range for the X-Axis data labels in the Range text box.

 Choose OK.

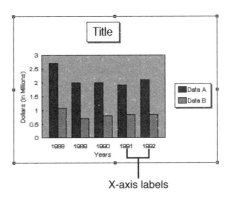

X-axis labels

NOT YOUR TYPE

Selecting the right **CHART TYPE** is important, because each type is very good at showing some kinds of data and very poor at showing other kinds. For example, if you are plotting things that change over time, like your weight, your income, or the amount of time you spend exercising, line and bar charts are the best types. A pie chart would be no help at all. If you want to plot percentages, however, such as the percentage of the time that you're late for work, a pie chart is best.

There are 12 different 1-2-3 **CHART TYPES** and each type has a few alternative styles. For example, a 3-D Bar chart is one type, and it is available in three styles.

Chart Type	What It's Good for Showing
Bar	Frequencies of occurrences, trends, values at points in time.
Pie	Parts of the whole, percentages.
Line and Area Charts	Trends, changes over time.
Mixed	Items that change over time but are different by definition. For example, total revenues and net profits.
XY	Correlation between two sets of data.
HLCO	Track data that fluctuates over time, such as stock prices.
Radar	The symmetry or uniformity of data.

To make life simpler, 1-2-3 uses a default chart type when it first creates your chart. It's easy enough to change the chart type, however, so you can experiment with the various types until you clearly make your point. Here are the steps:

 Select the chart by clicking on it.

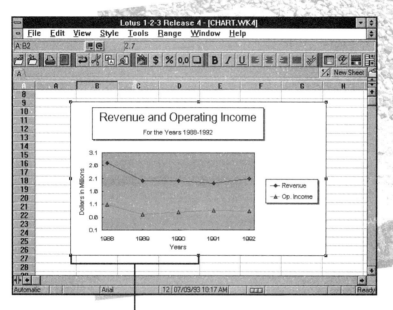

Handles around the chart show that it's selected.

 Choose Chart Type. The Type dialog box appears.

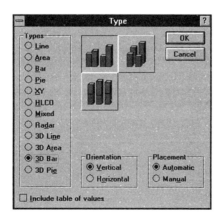

Under Type, choose a chart type by clicking on one. As you select a chart type, styles for each chart type appear as panels.

Select one of the option panels for the chart type. The selected panel will look like it has been pressed down.

Under Orientation, select an option—either Vertical or Horizontal. If you select Vertical, 1-2-3 will display the X-axis across the bottom of the chart, the Y-axis along the left edge of the chart, and the 2nd Y-axis (if there is one) along the right edge of the chart. If you select Horizontal orientation, 1-2-3 will display the X-axis along the left edge of the chart, the Y-axis across the top of the chart, and the 2nd Y-axis along the bottom of the chart. Got that? Good.

Select the Include table of values check box to display data values under the chart. (This option isn't available for pie charts, HLCO charts, radar charts, and XY charts).

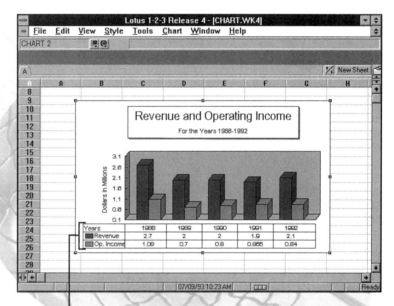

This is a table of data values. It looks like a piece of worksheet combined with a legend.

 Select OK.

NAMING A CHART

When you create a chart, 1-2-3 gives it a name. It's not necessarily a great name—the first one is Chart1, the second chart is Chart2, and so on. From those names, you can't tell what the **CHART** is about.

But if you were to rename your chart on airsickness, for example, to SkyBarf, you would have no trouble remembering its contents.

To assign a more descriptive name to a chart, follow these steps:

 Select the chart by clicking on it.

 Choose Chart Name. The Name dialog box appears.

 Enter a new name in the Chart name text box. A chart name can be up to 15 characters long and can include spaces.

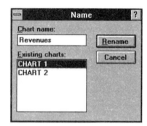

 Choose Rename.

You can go to a **CHART** just like you can go to a named range or a cell address by using the Edit Go To command.

GET THAT CHART OUT OF HERE

After you create a chart, you can move it to a new location by using the old drag-and-drop technique:

 Select the chart by clicking on it.

 Drag the chart by any part except the handles.

 Release the mouse button when the chart is where you want it.

You can also move a chart by using Edit Cut to place it on the Windows Clipboard and Edit Paste to place it in a new location, or use the **Cut** and **Paste** SmartIcons.

SIZING A CHART

Sizing a chart is the same as *sizing a drawn object* (which you learned in Lesson 25). After you create a chart, you can change its size by following follow these steps:

 Select the chart by clicking on it.

 Drag a handle in the direction you want to size the chart. Handles are small squares that appear at the corners, midpoints, and ends of the chart. For **MULTIPLE CHARTS**, dragging one handle in a given direction sizes all selected objects in that direction.

To change chart width, drag a side handle.

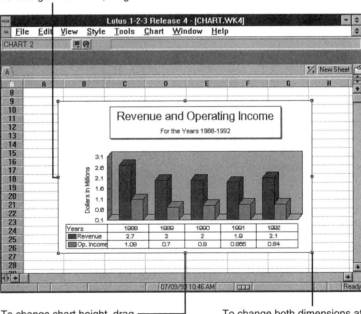

To change chart height, drag a top or bottom handle.

To change both dimensions at once, drag a corner handle.

 Release the mouse button when you have finished sizing the chart.

To select **MULTIPLE CHARTS**, click on the first one, and hold down **Shift** or **Ctrl** while clicking on the others.

HYPERTIP

CH-CH-CH-CH-CHANGES (TO CHARTS)

Creating a chart was fun. Heh-heh. Pretty much automatic. Heh-heh. Heh-heh. Got great results. That's cool . . . heh-heh.

Before you settle for the kind of chart any Beavis or Butt-head can make, take the time to look for ways to make it better, such as the ways described in this lesson.

ONE MATRIX, COMING UP

Adding grid lines to a chart can make that chart easier to read. Points on a line or bar chart are easier to trace back to an axis when you add grid lines. You can

have grid lines originate from each **INTERVAL** on each axis. To add grid lines that extend out from the interval tick marks on the chart:

 Select the chart by clicking on it.

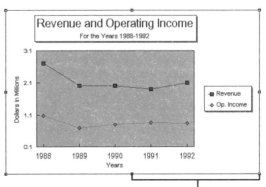

Handles mean the chart's selected.

2 Choose Chart Grids.

3 **Change the X-axis and Y-axis settings to something other than None.** The X-axis box controls vertical grid lines (originating from the X-axis). The Y-axis box controls horizontal grid lines (originating from the Y-axis).

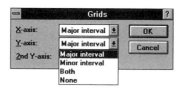

4 Choose OK.

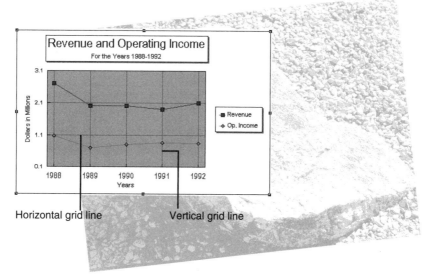

Horizontal grid line   Vertical grid line

A MODEL OF CONSISTENCY

When you *create a chart*, 1-2-3 uses a **DEFAULT CHART** type. For example, if the default chart is a bar chart, and you select a range of data, and then choose Tools Chart, 1-2-3 creates a bar chart. Then you have to use Chart Type to change the chart type. You can change the default chart type with the Chart Set Preferred command. For example, if you are going to be creating a lot of pie charts, then create a pie chart you like, and choose Chart Set Preferred.

If you create a chart that's not the default type and later decide that you want the preferred chart settings to apply to that chart, select the chart, and then choose Chart Use Preferred.

EXPLODING PIE SLICES

For spicier pie charts, you may want to add the exploding-piece special effect. For example, one piece of the pie may represent a very large portion of the data. To make that portion stand out from the rest of the pie, explode it.

The easiest way to explode a piece of pie is by using the mouse to drag the slice out of the pie like this:

 Select the piece of pie by clicking on it.

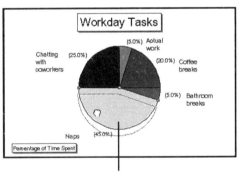

Dragging out a slice of pie to emphasize how well your time is spent.

 Drag the piece away from the pie. When you have it where you want it, release the mouse button.

EXPLODING THE WHOLE THING

If you're really radical, you can explode all pieces of the pie:

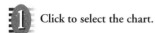 Click to select the chart.

Choose Chart Data Labels. You'll see the Data Labels dialog box.

Under Explode slices, click All by, and enter a percentage. The percentage specifies by how much you want to explode all the pieces.

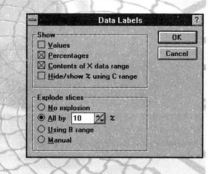

Choose OK.

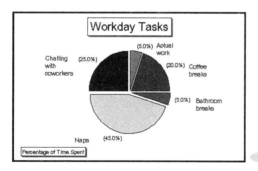

The miraculous exploding pie.

SETTING CHART COLORS AND PATTERNS

You can select **CHART ELEMENTS** and set the colors and patterns for them in much the same way as you can colorize and add patterns to *drawn objects*.

To color or add patterns to your charts:

 Select the element of the chart you want to color or add a pattern to by clicking on it.

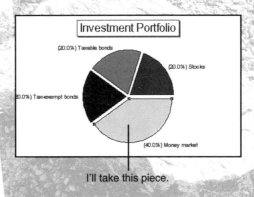

 Choose Style Lines & Color.

Select the options you want. Note that if you've selected a chart legend, title, or footnote for modification, you'll also have the option to change text color.

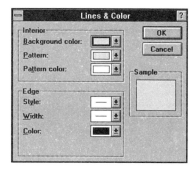

 Choose OK.

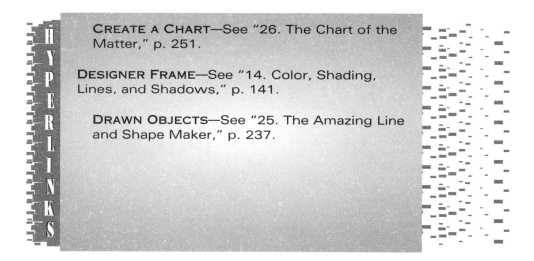

CREATE A CHART—See "26. The Chart of the Matter," p. 251.

DESIGNER FRAME—See "14. Color, Shading, Lines, and Shadows," p. 141.

DRAWN OBJECTS—See "25. The Amazing Line and Shape Maker," p. 237.

Part VI

DIGITAL DATA DOMINATION

The next three lessons can help you better manage and analyze your data. 1-2-3 is more than a spreadsheet—with its database capabilities and its Version Manager, advanced information management is only a few keystrokes or mouse movements away. You can design database tables, add records, search for data and extract reports, and you can perform high-power what-if analysis to discover the possibilities. It was Samuel Johnson who said: "Knowledge is of two kinds. We know a subject ourselves, or we know where we can find information upon it." In this age, when mastery of information is where it's at—learn to manage data by working through the three lessons of this part.

DATABASICS

You know that worn-out, nasty-lookin', out-of-date, semi-useless, little address book you have? It's a database. A database is a collection of related data organized in rows and columns. In 1-2-3, the databases are called *tables* because they consist of records (rows of data) whose parts are identified by labeled fields (columns). Each field contains one kind of information. For example, if you created a database table to catalog your multimedia CDs, you would build fields for title, distributor, date purchased, cost, and so on. You create database tables so you can find certain records quickly and sort data.

DATABASE TABLE FOUNDATION

Before you create a database table in a worksheet, you may want to give some thought to how you want to name the fields and scrawl out the **LAYOUT** on paper first. Then you are ready to create the table:

 In a blank area of a worksheet, enter the field names in the first row of the database table. Each field name must be unique within a database table.

	Stock Number	Description	Unit Cost	Retail Price	On Hand
2					
3					
4	Stock Number	Description	Unit Cost	Retail Price	On Hand
5					
6					
7					
8					
9					
10					
11					

Field names

 Enter data for each record in the rows below the field names. Use consistent *formats* and capitalization when you enter data in each field.

It's always a good idea to make the first field in your table **LAYOUT** a record number field. That way, you can always sort the records so they appear in the order you entered them.

Each row holds a record.

	Stock Number	Description	Unit Cost	Retail Price	On Hand
2					
3					
4	Stock Number	Description	Unit Cost	Retail Price	On Hand
5	1001	Computer	$500.00	$1,000.00	14
6	1003	Printer	$200.00	$400.00	22
7	1005	Monitor	$225.00	$420.00	35
8					
9					
10					
11					

 Use Range Name Add to name the 1-2-3 database table, but do not use a range name that matches a field name in the table. The row that contains the field names must be part of the *named range*. Naming a table makes referring to it easier when you use certain **T**ools Data**b**ase commands.

A FEW MORE RECORDS

After you create a database table, you can **ADD NEW RECORDS** to the bottom of a database table by entering the records in the row immediately below the last record in the table. Because you named your table using **R**ange **N**ame, you must use the **R**ange **N**ame command to redefine the range name so that it includes the new records. Here are all the steps:

 Enter data for each field in the row immediately below the last row in the table.

	Stock Number	Description	Unit Cost	Retail Price	On Hand
2					
3					
4	Stock Number	Description	Unit Cost	Retail Price	On Hand
5	1001	Computer	$500.00	$1,000.00	14
6	1003	Printer	$200.00	$400.00	22
7	1005	Monitor	$225.00	$420.00	35
8	1007	Diskettes	$5.00	$10.00	65
9					
10					
11					

Enter new records at the bottom; select the table, including new records.

Choose Range Name, or press the right mouse button to display the quick menu and click on Name.

Under Existing named ranges, click on the range name of the database table. If you have never named the database, type it in the **N**ame text box, and then select the **A**dd button.

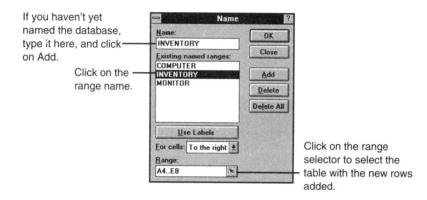

If you haven't yet named the database, type it here, and click on Add.

Click on the range name.

Click on the range selector to select the table with the new rows added.

 Specify the new range by entering it in the Range text box, or even better, click on the range selector to select the table with the new rows included.

 Choose OK.

MORE ENTRIES IN RECORD TIME

Let's say, you've got a huge database project, and there's a snowball's chance in hell that you'll finish all the entries before your boss's deadline. If you can con a coworker into making some of the entries in a separate file (this is gonna cost you,

isn't it?), you can add the coworker's records to the end of your database with the handy **TOOLS DATABASE APPEND RECORDS** command. Here's how you can use this technique to stitch together groups of records:

 Select the range that contains the records you want to add to the table. The first row of the range should contain field names that are the same as those in the table to which you are appending records.

When you use **TOOLS DATABASE APPEND RECORDS** to add a group of records to a database table, 1-2-3 appends (adds) the records to the bottom of the database table. The new records are included in the named database range.

The selected range must have field names that
match the database table you're adding to.

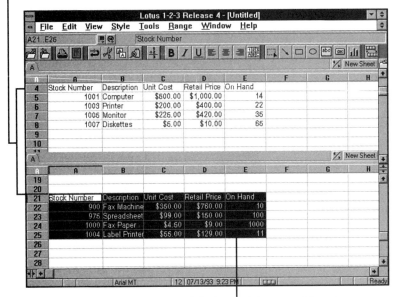

Select records to append them to
another database table.

2 Choose Tools Database Append Records.

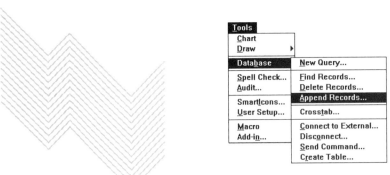

3 Specify the table to which you are appending the records in the To
database table text box.

278

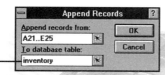

Enter the database
table range name here
or its range address.

 Click on OK. The original records remain in place, and copies are appended to the table.

3					
4	Stock Number	Description	Unit Cost	Retail Price	On Hand
5	1001	Computer	$500.00	$1,000.00	14
6	1003	Printer	$200.00	$400.00	22
7	1005	Monitor	$225.00	$420.00	35
8	1007	Diskettes	$5.00	$10.00	65
9	900	Fax Machine	$350.00	$760.00	10
10	975	Spreadsheet	$99.00	$150.00	100
11	1000	Fax Paper	$4.50	$9.00	1000
12	1004	Label Printer	$55.00	$129.00	11

GETTING RID OF RECORDS

Rather than scrolling around through a database for the records you want to delete, you can delete records from a 1-2-3 database table that meet particular **CRITERIA**. For example, you could delete all the records of customers who live in Hell, Michigan (that's a real city . . . Michigan's a tough state). That's the beauty of a database—1-2-3 can search through lots of data quickly and manipulate it much more quickly and reliably than you can. To delete a group of records, just:

 Select the range that contains the database table.

 Choose Tools Database Delete Records.

 Specify a criterion for the records you want to delete. For example, if you want to delete the records of everyone who lives in the state of Massachusetts, the criterion is **STATE=MA**, where **STATE** is the field, = is the operator, and **MA** is the value.

CRITERIA are conditions that you want records to meet when working with a database table. For example, to delete all customers that live in the state of Massachusetts, the criterion could be **STATE=MA**, where **STATE** is the field name and **MA** is the state of Massachusetts.

Select the field. Select the operator. Specify the value.

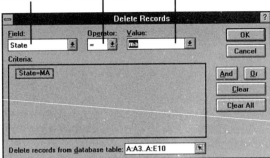

4 (Optional)**To further limit the records to delete, choose the And button and repeat step 3.** For example, if you also wanted to delete the records of everyone who lives in Rhode Island, you could choose the **And** button and repeat step 3 to specify the criterion **STATE=RI**.

5 (Optional)**To expand the number of records to delete, choose Or and repeat step 3.**

6 Choose OK.

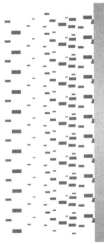

FORMATS—See "13. Number Formats to Go," p. 131.

NAMED RANGE—See "7. It's the Range (Not the Frequency)," p. 66.

DATA DRUDGERY: SORTING AND QUERYING

Imagine meeting the most intriguing woman (or man) you've ever seen, coolly walking over, casually getting this person to fork over their phone number, and mentioning that you'll call "some time." You wait precisely 24 hours (can't appear too eager, after all) to make the call, but you can't find the number. You're hosed, because a napkin isn't a very good database.

The whole point of a database is to make your data accessible and manageable. This lesson tells you how to get to it after you've entered it.

DATABASE INTERROGATION: BUILDING QUERY TABLES

You can extract information from a *database table* by creating a **QUERY TABLE**, or a workspace where you can create reports from the data from a database table. The query table looks like a smaller version of the database table, because it contains only the records that you want to extract from the database table. In a query table, you choose to display only those records that meet **CONDITIONS** (criteria) that you specify.

Here's how to find the answers you want:

 Choose Tools Database New Query.

There's a SmartIcon in the Goodies set that you can click on to create a **QUERY TABLE**.

Once you have set up a query table, you can change the **CONDITIONS** that a record must meet to be included in the query table. You change the criteria of a query table by selecting the query table and choosing **Q**uery Set Criteria.

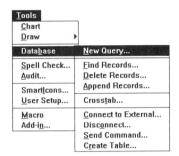

 Enter the range name of the table (if you already named it using Range Name) in the text box under 1. Select database table to query. Rather than type the table name, you can use a shortcut; press the **F3** key, and select the name of the table you want to query. To query an unnamed table, specify the range that contains the table by entering the range address in the text box under 1. Select database table to query, or use the range selector to select the database table.

Enter the database table range name or range address.

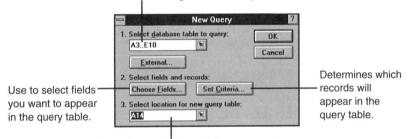

Use to select fields you want to appear in the query table.

Determines which records will appear in the query table.

Enter the cell in the top left corner of the range where you want to place the query table.

 If you don't want the query table to include all the fields of the database table, then select Choose Fields to determine which fields you want to appear in the query table, and in what order.

 Specify where you want 1-2-3 to place the query table. You can specify just the top left corner of the range where you want to locate the query table; just be sure that there is enough room for the table because it will overwrite any existing data in a range. If you *specify a range*, 1-2-3 displays only the records and fields that fit in that range. For example, if you specify a range of five columns by ten rows, 1-2-3 displays the first five fields and the first ten records in the order in which they appear in the database table.

You can then resize the query table to be larger so that 1-2-3 displays the additional fields and records.

Select **Set Criteria** to determine which records will appear in the query table.

Sample criterion tells 1-2-3 the query table is to contain the records of customers who live in the state of Massachusetts (MA).

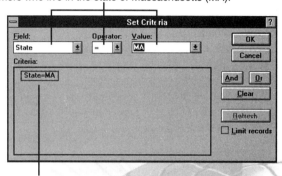

Specified criteria appear here.

 Choose **OK** in the Set Criteria dialog box.

 Choose **OK** in the New Query dialog box.

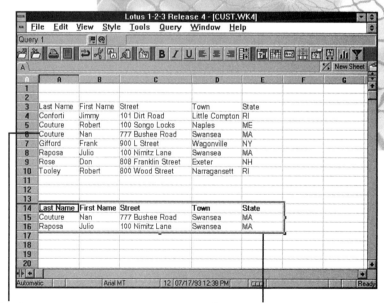

Database table

Query table with records extracted using the criterion State=MA.

SORT IT OUT

Sorting puts records in a specific order. You can sort data in **ASCENDING ORDER**, which is a sort from A to Z and from the smallest value to the largest, or in **DESCENDING ORDER**, which is from Z to A and from the largest value to the smallest. There are two ways to sort data. The method that you choose depends upon whether you are working with the records of a database table or a query table. If you are working with a named database range, use the **R**ange Sort command. If you are working with a query table, use the **Q**uery **S**ort command. Both methods are detailed in the sections that follow.

Whether you choose to **SORT YOUR RECORDS** in ascending or descending order, you should be aware of the way that 1-2-3 sorts through letters, numbers, blank cells, and symbols. Numbers are sorted first followed by:

◇ Blank cells.

◇ Labels that start with a space.

◇ Labels beginning with numbers (in numerical order).

◇ Labels beginning with letters (in alphabetical order with lowercase letters preceding uppercase letters).

◇ Labels beginning with other characters.

◇ Values in numerical order.

SORTING (THE RANGE METHOD)

You can sort any range of data on a worksheet, including the data in a database table:

 Select the range that you want to sort. If you are sorting records in a database table, do not include the field names.

2					
3	Last Name	First Name	Street	Town	State
4	Couture	Nan	777 Bushee Road	Swansea	MA
5	Gifford	Frank	900 L Street	Wagonville	NY
6	Tooley	Robert	800 Wood Street	Narragansett	RI
7	Rose	Don	808 Franklin Street	Exeter	NH
8	Couture	Robert	100 Songo Locks	Naples	ME
9	Conforti	Jimmy	101 Dirt Road	Little Compton	RI
10					

Select the range to sort sans field names.

 Choose Range Sort.

 Under Sort by, specify one cell in the column by which you want to sort data.

Enter one cell in the column by which you want to
sort the data; for example, choose a cell in the
Last Name column (field) to sort by last name.

Sorts A–Z
or smallest
to largest
values.

Sorts Z–A
or largest to
smallest
values.

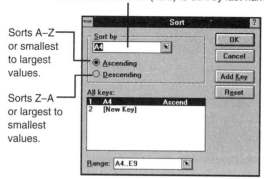

Select a sort option. Ascending order means that text will be sorted from A to
Z and values from smallest to largest. **D**escending order means that text will be
sorted from Z to A and values from largest to smallest.

**(Optional) If two or more records have the same entry for the sort key you
selected, specify another sort key.** For example, if more than one customer
lives in the same state and you want the customers sorted by state, choose Add
Key and repeat steps 3 and 4.

Choose OK.

A NEW ORDER IN A QUERY TABLE

To arrange the data in a query table:

Select the query table.

Before you can sort the data of a
query table, select the query table.

 Choose Query Sort. Note that the **Q**uery menu appears on the menu bar after you create a query table.

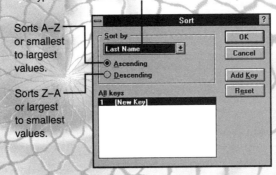

Type or select the name of the field to sort by.

Sorts A–Z or smallest to largest values.

Sorts Z–A or largest to smallest values.

Under Sort by, in the text box, select the name of the field you want to sort by.

 Select a sort option. Ascending order means that text will be sorted from A to Z and values from smallest to largest. **D**escending order means that text will be sorted from Z to A and values from largest to smallest.

 (Optional) To specify additional sort keys, choose Add Key and repeat steps 3 and 4. For example, if the State field is the first sort key, select the Last Name field as the second sort key.

 Choose OK.

ZEROING IN ON A FEW RECORDS

One of the advantages of organizing data in a database table is that you can locate information fast. You can specify certain criteria that you want records to satisfy and then let 1-2-3 rip through the database or query table with lightning fast speed to find the data.

To locate **RECORDS** in a 1-2-3 database table or query table that meet criteria you specify:

 Select the range that contains the database, including field names or query table.

 Choose Tools Database Find Records.

Specify a criterion for the records you want to find.

Use the Field, Operator, and Value drop-down boxes to specify
criteria; these criteria find the record with a Last Name of Rose.

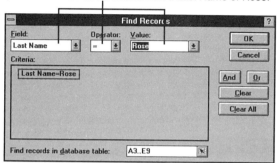

 To further limit the records to find, choose And, and repeat step 3.

 To expand the number of records to find, choose Or, and repeat step 3.

 Choose OK. 1-2-3 highlights the records that meet the criteria you specify.

1-2-3 highlights the records that
meet the criteria you specify.

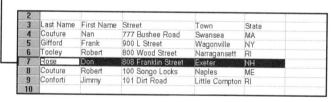

	Last Name	First Name	Street	Town	State	
2						
3	Last Name	First Name	Street	Town	State	
4	Couture	Nan	777 Bushee Road	Swansea	MA	
5	Gifford	Frank	900 L Street	Wagonville	NY	
6	Tooley	Robert	800 Wood Street	Narragansett	RI	
7	Rose	Don	808 Franklin Street	Exeter	NH	
8	Couture	Robert	100 Songo Locks	Naples	ME	
9	Conforti	Jimmy	101 Dirt Road	Little Compton	RI	
10						

287

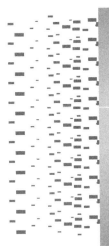

DATABASE TABLE—See "28. Databasics," p.275.

SPECIFY A RANGE—See "7. It's the Range (Not the Frequency)," p. 66.

HYPERLINKS

Same Range,
Different Way

Modified and Updated

What If?

The Cutting
Room Floor

It's My Version, and I'm Sticking to It

Have you ever read about those studies where researchers try to find out how reliable witnesses are? You'd bet big cash that the "witnesses" in these tests weren't in the same place at the same time. If the perp was a 5'10" male driving away in a black Porsche getaway car, witnesses report anything from a 5' older American driving a blue Chevy to a 7'2" Sasquatch taking off on foot. There are as many different versions of the same event as there are witnesses.

The Version Manager is a 1-2-3 feature that allows you to create versions, which are sets of different data, to plug into the same range in a worksheet to get a different take on your calculations. Version Manager makes it easy for you to do "what-if" analysis. By changing one or more of the assumptions (contents of cells) used in your worksheet, you create different versions which you can save using the Version Manager. Then you can step back and review the results of

each version because the Version Manager creates an index of all the versions you create for a particular range. You can select a version from the index and display it in your worksheet.

For example, maybe you're looking at three different forecasts for sales and you want to see how each affects the bottom line (net Income). Your net income is calculated using formulas with the projected sales being an important input. The Version Manager helps you to quickly and easily bring in each version's inputs (the three different sales forecasts), plugs them into the formulas, and shows you the bottom line (results of each version of data). While this example shows that the Version Manager can work different sets of data into the same set of formulas, it can also work the other way; it can generate versions by bringing in different formulas to work on a static set of data.

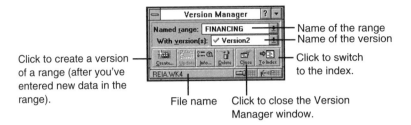

Click to create a version of a range (after you've entered new data in the range).

Name of the range
Name of the version

Click to switch to the index.

File name
Click to close the Version Manager window.

Versions: A different viewpoint of your calculations.

The name of the range (A3..B7) for which versions have been created: FINANCING

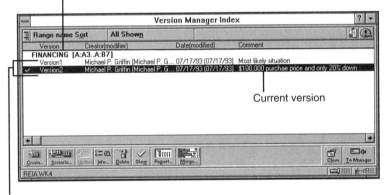

Versions created for a named range

Current version

Index of all the versions.

GO ON, GIRL!

There is a SmartIcon in the Goodies bar that you can click **TO START THE VERSION MANAGER**. See Lesson 5 to learn how to *display another* SmartIcon set.

When you're ready to create some versions, you have **TO START THE VERSION MANAGER**. But before you can work with the Version Manager, you must do two things:

◇   You must *open a file* that contains a worksheet that you want to use to create different versions, or you must create such a worksheet.

◇   With your worksheet model in place, you must use the **R**ange **N**ame command to *name the range* that you want to create versions of.

Now, you are ready to begin creating different versions of a range, like this:

 Enter the data that you want to include in the version.

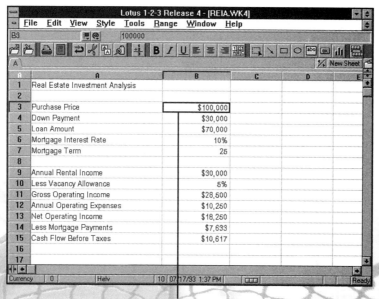

If you want this version to show a purchase price of $100,000,
enter that assumption before you create the version.

2 Select the range for which you want to create a version.

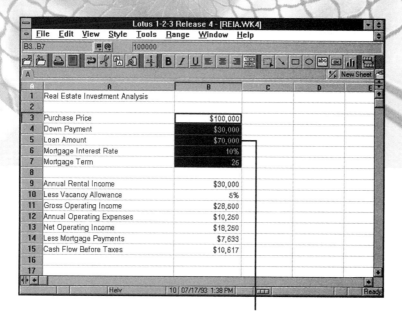

Select the range for which you want to create a version.

Choose Range Version.

Range
Version...

Fill...
Fill by Example
Sort...
Parse...
Transpose...

Name...

Analyze   ▶

Choose Create.

Click to create a new version.

(Optional) To rename the range, enter a new name in the Range name text box.

The range name; typing a new name here renames the range.

1-2-3 names the version.

Comments, please.

Select if you want the formatting (fonts, underlining, and so on) used in the version saved.

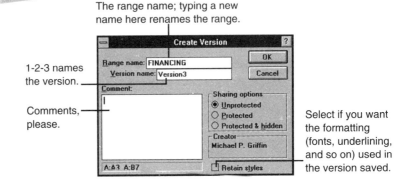

Enter a version name in the **Version name text box, or accept the name proposed by 1-2-3.** It is better to enter a version name that you can relate to rather than accept the 1-2-3 name of version1 or version2 and so on.

 (Optional) **In the Comment text box, enter a comment about the version.**

 (Optional) **To save formatting information with the version, select the Retain styles check box.**

 Think about whether you want others to have access to your versions, and then select a sharing option: Unprotected, Protected, or Protected & hidden.

 Choose OK.

To close Version Manager, double-click on its control box, or click on its **Close** button.

CHECKING OUT A VERSION

The advantage of creating versions is that you can play "what-if" analysis by quickly and easily displaying different versions of data in the same worksheet range. For example, if you are looking at different financing arrangements, you can see the effects of each proposal by creating versions. Then you can use **VERSION MANAGER** to display each version without ever leaving your worksheet. To get a different version of the range's story:

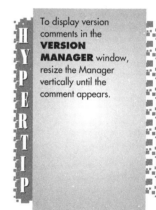

To display version comments in the **VERSION MANAGER** window, resize the Manager vertically until the comment appears.

 Choose Range Version. The Version Manager appears.

 Select the range for which you want to show a version from the Named range drop-down box.

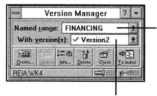

Select the range name.

Select the version to show in the worksheet.

 In the With version(s) drop-down box, select the version to show in the worksheet.

 Select Close.

THE VERSION MANAGER INDEX

The Version Manager Index helps you to keep track of the versions you have created, their names, and characteristics. You can go to the Index to look up what you have put there or you can use it to display a particular version. To display a specific version from the Index window, just double-click on its name. If you have had enough of the Index and want to go back to the Manager Window, choose the **To** Index button or **Alt+T**.

To move from the Version Manager to the Index or from the Index to the Version Manager, choose the **To** Index button (if you are in the Version Manager window) or the **To** Manager button (if you are in the Index).

CHANGING YOUR STORY

The range name, version name, comments, and range styles are the **VERSION SETTINGS**.

HYPERTIP

Lucky for most of us, there's no criminal penalty for changing a version. You can go back and modify any previously created version by changing the data upon which the version was created and then saving that updated version; or you can modify the **VERSION SETTINGS**. To change your version:

 Choose Range Version.

 Select the name of the version from the With version(s) drop-down box. If the name of the range you are working with is not selected, select the range name from the Named range drop-down box. In the Index, select the version by clicking on it.

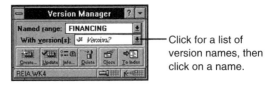

Click for a list of version names, then click on a name.

 In the worksheet range that you are using to create versions, enter the new data and styles to update the version. You can switch to the worksheet by clicking on it with the mouse pointer or by pressing **Alt+F6**.

Switch back to the Version Manager by clicking on it or by pressing ALT+F6.

 Choose Update.

 Choose OK.

The version settings are range name, version name, comments, and range styles. You can change any one of these settings. For example, you may want to edit a comment that you had previously entered for a version. To change the settings of a version, follow these steps:

 Choose Range Version.

 In the Version Manager, select the version that you want to modify from the With version(s) drop-down box. If the name of the range you are working with is not selected, select the range name from the Named range drop-down box. In the Index, select the version by clicking on it.

After choosing a version, choose Info to display the Version Info dialog box.

 Choose Info to display the Version Info dialog box.

 To rename the range, enter the new name in the Range name text box.

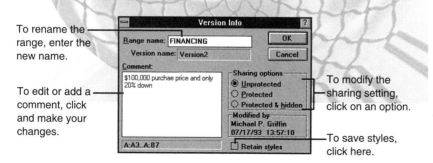

To rename the range, enter the new name.

To edit or add a comment, click and make your changes.

To modify the sharing setting, click on an option.

To save styles, click here.

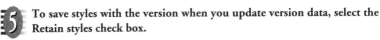

To save styles with the version when you update version data, select the
Retain styles check box.

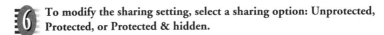

To modify the sharing setting, select a sharing option: Unprotected,
Protected, or Protected & hidden.

Choose OK. If you renamed the range, the Rename Range confirmation box
appears. Choose OK again.

THROWING OUT THE BOGUS VERSIONS

If a version isn't working for you, you can delete it:

Choose Range Version.

In the Version Manager, select the version that you want to delete from the
With version(s) drop-down box. If the name of the range you are working
with is not selected, select the range name from the Named range drop-down
box. In the Index, select the version by clicking on it. To select more than one
version in the Index window, hold down Ctrl while you click on additional
versions.

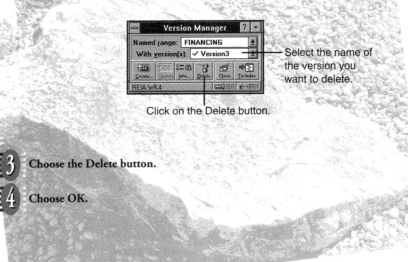

Select the name of
the version you
want to delete.

Click on the Delete button.

Choose the Delete button.

Choose OK.

HYPERLINKS

DISPLAY ANOTHER SMARTICON SET—See "5. SmartIcons: Pictures on SmartDrugs," p. 49.

OPEN A FILE—See "3. It's a File Thing," p. 28.

NAME THE RANGE—See "7. It's the Range (Not the Frequency)," p. 66.

Part VII
ELECTRIC ECLECTICA

With the first 30 lessons of this book, you can learn just about everything you need to know to really shake and bake with 1-2-3. To continue with the food theme, this last part contains four lessons that are the icing on the cake—other neat stuff that you might use, such as customizing SmartIcons, creating and running macros, adjusting macros, and protecting your work.

Even Smarter SmartIcons

Didn't you love the computer in the old Star Trek? Kirk just said something like, "Computer, compute the angle of the points of Spock's ears," and the computer would do the task, no matter how asinine or complex it was.

That example only relates to this lesson by the most tenuous of ties . . . authors' license, you see. While you can't bark out your commands to 1-2-3 quite yet, you can makes changes to the SmartIcons to get your job done with a click. This lesson explains everything you need to know to change the *SmartIcons* that display on the icon bar, to create your own SmartIcons from *macros*, and to save new SmartIcon sets you've created.

The Icon Shuffle: Discovering and Displaying Other Icons

You've already seen that 1-2-3 offers several sets of SmartIcons. It also offers numerous icons that don't appear on any one set. "But master," you ask, "what good are they if I can't get to them?" Relax, weedhopper, you can find and add available 1-2-3 SmartIcons to the icon bar (or take them **OFF**):

 Choose Tools SmartIcons.

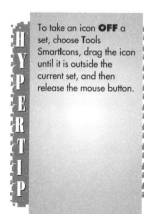

HYPERTIP

To take an icon **OFF** a set, choose **Tools SmartIcons**, drag the icon until it is outside the current set, and then release the mouse button.

2 Select the set of SmartIcons to customize from the drop-down box.

Select the SmartIcon set to which you want to add an icon.

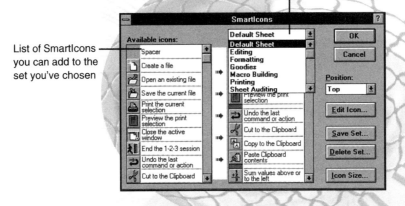

List of SmartIcons you can add to the set you've chosen

3 Drag an icon from the Available icons list box to a location in the set.

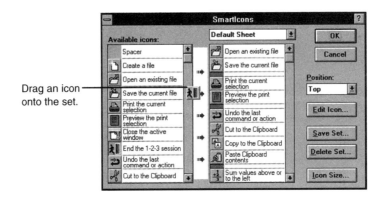

Drag an icon onto the set.

Choose OK. This saves the changes to the current set of SmartIcons and closes the SmartIcons dialog box.

SMARTICON MICRO-BREWING

To give you the ability to satisfy all your individualistic quirks, you can create a new SmartIcon by editing an existing icon or by creating one from scratch. Creating a working icon consists of two processes: creating the icon picture and assigning a macro to the picture.

The easiest and fastest way to tackle phase one of SmartIcon creation is to change the appearance of an existing icon (or another **BITMAP** you've created), as described next in the procedure for creating a SmartIcon:

You can use the Windows Paintbrush (or some other graphics program) to create **BITMAP** files for icons. The best approach is to open one of the available SmartIcons in Paintbrush and edit it. When you have created a custom icon using Paintbrush, save it in the \123r4w\program\sheetico subdirectory. Then it appears in the available icons list when you choose Tools SmartIcons, so you can assign a macro to it.

 Choose Tools SmartIcons.

 Click on the Edit Icon button.

Select an icon from the Available icons list box.

Click on the icon to edit.

Enlarged view of the icon.

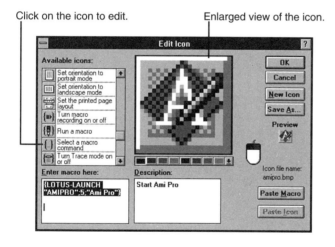

If the Create a New Icon dialog box appears, enter an icon File name, and click on OK.

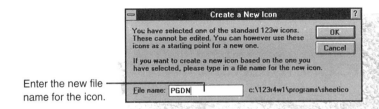

Enter the new file name for the icon.

If no dialog box appears, choose Save As, enter a name to Save the new icon as, and click on OK.

Modify the icon by painting it to change its appearance. You do this by assigning colors to the mouse buttons, then clicking on squares in the icon to change them to the new color. To change the color assigned to the left mouse button, click on a color with the left mouse button; to change the color assigned to the right mouse button, click on a color with the right mouse button. You can also change available colors by displaying the color palette drop-down box by clicking on the down arrow, and clicking on a color in the drop-down box to change the color assigned to the selected box in the top row.

Mouse shows colors currently assigned to the buttons.

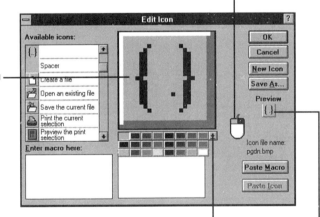

Click on the squares (pixels) you want to paint by clicking on the right or left mouse button.

Click to display a palette of colors; assign colors to the right and left mouse button by clicking on a color with either the right or left mouse button.

Shows what the icon looks like in normal size

6 **Click on the Enter macro here text box, and enter your macro.** If you previously copied an existing macro to the Windows Clipboard by selecting its range in the macro worksheet and using *Edit Copy*, you can click on Paste Macro to paste your macro into the Enter macro here text box.

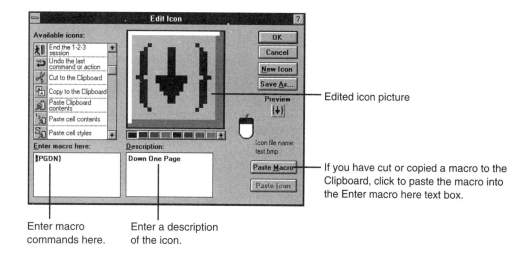

Edited icon picture

If you have cut or copied a macro to the Clipboard, click to paste the macro into the Enter macro here text box.

Enter macro
commands here.

Enter a description
of the icon.

 7 **Click on the Description text box and type a macro description.** I highly recommend doing this. Otherwise, you won't remember what your brand-spankin'-new icon does.

 8 **Choose OK.** 1-2-3 returns to the SmartIcons dialog box, and the new icon appears in the Available icons list box.

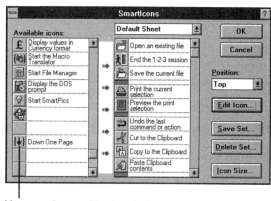

Your new icon and its description

SET SAVING

After you're done playing Three-icon-
monty (creating new icons and dragging
them on the current set in the
SmartIcons dialog box), you can save
your changes to the current set in a
special file that uses a **.SMI** extension.
This new set joins the original sets that
came with 1-2-3, and you can display it
or choose another set at will. A set of
icons reflect the work that you are
planning to do. For example, if you use
certain icons to prepare departmental

budgets, why not gather up those icons
and save them as a set you can display
when you need to?

As part of saving a set of icons, you
NAME the set. For example, your set of
icons that help you create a budget could
be called Budget Builder. After you save a
set under that name, the name appears in
the SmartIcons dialog box drop-down list
of sets and in the SmartIcons selector on
the status bar.

To save a set of icons in its own file:

 Choose Tools SmartIcons.

 Select a set of SmartIcons that you want to use as the basis for the new set.
Add, move, or remove icons to create the custom set you want.

 Choose Save Set. The Save Set of SmartIcons dialog box appears.

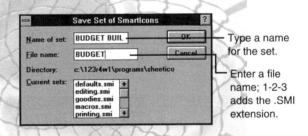

Type a name
for the set.

Enter a file
name; 1-2-3
adds the .SMI
extension.

 Enter a name for the set of SmartIcons in the Name of set text box. Because
this is not the file name but is a descriptive name that will appear in the
SmartIcons drop-down list and in the SmartIcons selector in the status bar at
the bottom of the worksheet window, it can include spaces.

 Enter a file name for the set of SmartIcons in the File name text box. 1-2-3
adds an .SMI extension to the file name.

Choose OK. 1-2-3 saves the set of SmartIcons and puts the .SMI file in the subdirectory according to what is currently selected. 1-2-3 returns you to the SmartIcons dialog box.

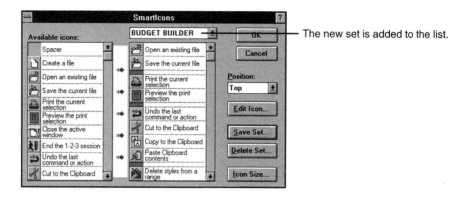

The new set is added to the list.

 Choose OK.

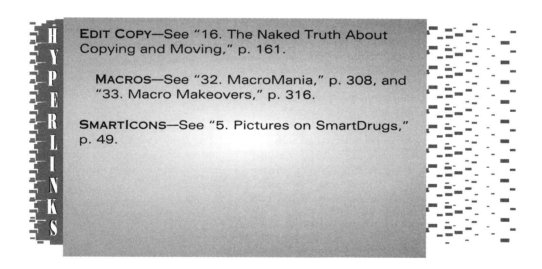

EDIT COPY—See "16. The Naked Truth About Copying and Moving," p. 161.

MACROS—See "32. MacroMania," p. 308, and "33. Macro Makeovers," p. 316.

SMARTICONS—See "5. Pictures on SmartDrugs," p. 49.

MacroMania

In the 50s, getting your booty in shape was excruciatingly boring. You had to do millions of situps, pushups, and jumping jacks. Up, down, repeat. Up, down, repeat. No wonder so many people were flab meisters until running, in-line skating, aerobics, and mountain biking came along.

Macros free you up from 1-2-3 calisthenics so you can deal with the exciting stuff. A macro is a set of instructions for automating a task. Macros are ideal for repetitive or complex chores, and the possibilities of macro applications are limited only by your knowledge of 1-2-3 and your imagination. Macros can automate tasks that you normally perform from the keyboard or mouse, such as choosing commands, selecting options, or entering data. They are especially helpful for guiding users who are unfamiliar with 1-2-3 through tasks and applications.

You can create macros in one of two ways: writing the macro by typing every macro command into a worksheet or by recording keystrokes and actions using the 1-2-3 **TRANSCRIPT WINDOW**. When you write a macro, you are actually performing a type of programming—you are creating instructions for 1-2-3 to follow. When you record a macro, you turn on a recorder and then perform the tasks you want to automate. 1-2-3 records **MACRO COMMANDS** as you execute the task so that the next time you want to perform that same task, you can simply play back the recording (the macro).

Before you create, you must plan. Give some thought to the tasks that you want the macro to automate. For complex tasks (or simple minds), the planning process may involve taking notes and writing down specifications. For simple tasks, the planning may be much more informal, with you mapping the macro out in your mind.

With a concrete idea of what you want the macro to accomplish, you can do one of two things:

◇ Perform the task manually and note each key that you press and each command that you choose so that you can go back and type the macro commands into a worksheet. Or you can . . .

◇ Use the 1-2-3 macro record feature, which records your keystrokes and command choices for you in the 1-2-3 Transcript window. Recording is an easier way to build a macro.

Once you have an idea of what you want the macro to do, you must decide where you want to put it. You enter macros down a column in a worksheet. However, you don't want to enter the macro in just any column. If you think the macro will

be used in only one file, you can enter the macro in a column of that file, in a somewhat remote area of the worksheet file away from the data that the macro will affect. Try a column below and to the right of the data. A position below and to the right of your data makes it unlikely your row/column insertions or deletions will disturb the macro.

A better location for a new macro is in a separate worksheet reserved just for macros. By locating a macro in its own worksheet, you can safeguard the macro from being destroyed by data movement.

If you anticipate that the macro will have broader applications and help you out with several files, you should create a **MACRO LIBRARY**—a worksheet file that contains only macros.

To create a **MACRO LIBRARY**, *open a new file*. Copy and paste your favorite macros to the file, and then save and name the file just like any other file. To use the macros of a macro library file, be sure the file is open before you try to run one of the macros.

NO WIMPS ALLOWED: ENTERING MACROS BY HAND

Although the fastest and most accurate way to create a macro is by recording your actions (a method which is detailed later in this lesson), if you're not a wimp or if you plan to create fairly complex macros, you'll need to learn how to type in macros and edit by hand. The easy part is typing it in. Just type in macro commands in consecutive cells in a column. You must start and end each macro command in the same cell;

however, more than one macro command can occupy the same cell. Macro commands begin with an open brace ({) and end with a close brace (}). The challenging part is finding out the commands you need and stringing them together in the right order. Some macro commands contain **ARGUMENTS**, which you enter using a prescribed syntax.

Macro command syntax can include **ARGUMENTS**. Arguments supply 1-2-3 with information needed to execute the macro command. There are four types of arguments: value, text, location, and condition.

You can cheat during macro entry by choosing the commands from a list and inserting them into a cell. To enter macro commands:

 Select a cell where you want to enter the first macro command.

 Type { (open brace).

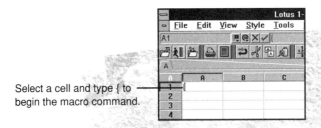

Select a cell and type { to
begin the macro command.

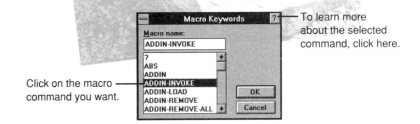 Press F3 (NAME) to display a list of macro commands and key names.

To learn more
about the selected
command, click here.

Click on the macro
command you want.

Click on a command in the macro name list.

To find out what arguments are needed for the macro command, click on the
question mark or press F1 (HELP). 1-2-3 displays the Macro Help window,
which contains explanations and structures (syntax) of macro commands.

Close the Help window by double-clicking on the control box.

Choose OK.

Enter any required arguments.

Type } (close brace).

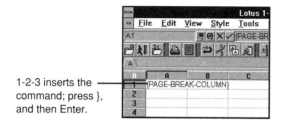

1-2-3 inserts the command; press }, and then Enter.

 Press Enter. 1-2-3 enters the macro command into the current cell.

 Press ↓ to move to the next cell. Macro commands must be entered in consecutive cells in the same column.

 Repeat steps 1–8 until you've entered the whole macro.

There are several SmartIcons that can help you with your macros. To use these macros, you have to choose the **Tools** SmartIcons to add them to an icon bar.

The macro icons include ones for selecting a macro command, running a macro, and turning a macro recording on or off.

PRESS RECORD

Even if you're too lazy to take the time to learn any commands, you can create a macro. You can **RECORD THE KEYSTROKES AND MOUSE ACTIONS** that you make to accom-plish a 1-2-3 task. They are recorded to the Transcript window, from which you can paste them to a worksheet to create a macro.

To record keystrokes and mouse actions, follow these steps:

 Choose Tools Macro Record.

There is a SmartIcon you can add to your icon bar that you can click to **RECORD THE KEYSTROKES AND MOUSE ACTIONS**.

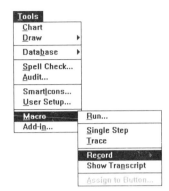

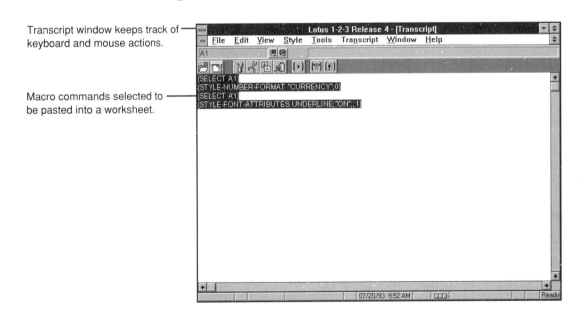

Enter the keystrokes or perform the mouse actions you want to record.

When you are finished with the task, choose Tools Macro Stop Recording.

Choose Tools Macro Show Transcript.

Select the macro commands that you want to copy by highlighting them.

Transcript window keeps track of keyboard and mouse actions.

Macro commands selected to be pasted into a worksheet.

Choose Edit Copy.

 Paste the macro into a worksheet using Edit Paste. You can also paste the macro into a *macro button* or use it to *create a SmartIcon*.

NAME IT, SAVE IT, ANY NAME YOU WANT IT

You can't just have a bunch of macros junking up a worksheet with no rhyme or reason. After you create a macro, you need to name it so you can tell 1-2-3 which set of instructions to run. To name a macro, you use the Range Name command to name the first cell of the macro.

 Click on the first cell of the macro.

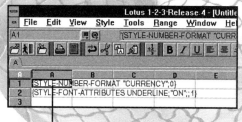

Before you can name the macro, select the first cell.

 Choose Range Name.

 In the Name text box, enter the name you want to assign to the range. Range names can be up to 15 characters long and cannot begin with an ! (exclamation point) or numbers and cannot include:

, (comma)	+ (plus sign)	< (less than)
; (semicolon)	– (minus sign)	> (greater than)
. (period)	* (asterisk)	@ (at sign)
? (question mark)	/ (slash)	# (pound sign)
(space)	& (ampersand)	{ (left brace)

Range names also cannot look like cell addresses or @function names, key names, or macro command keywords.

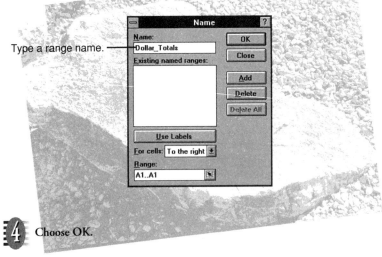

Type a range name.

 Choose OK.

 Use File Save or File Save as to save the file with the macro. When you save a file containing a macro, the macro is saved with the file, just like any other data contained in the file.

EXECUTE SEQUENCE

After you have created a macro and named it, you can **RUN** it. Running a macro means that you want 1-2-3 to perform the tasks that the macro automates. You can run macros in one of three ways: you can assign the macro to a SmartIcon and click on the icon to run the macro, you can assign the macro to a macro button and click on the button to run it, or you can use the Tools Macro Run command.

Setting up the macro to run it via one of the first two methods is covered in other lessons (31 and 33, respectively). Here's the fallback plan for now:

 Open the file that contains the macro you want to run.

Choose Tools Macro Run.

 Select a macro from the All named ranges list box, enter the macro name or address in the Macro name text box, or click on the first cell of the macro. If the macro is in another active file, select the name of that file from the In file drop-down box to see the range names from that file. Then select the macro name from the list.

Type the range name or select it from the All named ranges list.

If the macro you want to run is in another open file, click here, and then select it from the list.

 Choose OK. 1-2-3 executes your macro.

To stop a macro, press **Ctrl+Break**, and then press **Esc**. Or choose **OK** from the dialog box that appears to confirm that you want to stop the macro and return to the Ready mode.

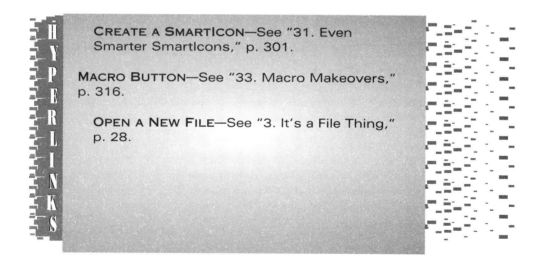

CREATE A SMARTICON—See "31. Even Smarter SmartIcons," p. 301.

MACRO BUTTON—See "33. Macro Makeovers," p. 316.

OPEN A NEW FILE—See "3. It's a File Thing," p. 28.

MACRO MAKEOVERS

You're not a perfect being. You don't always use your turn signals. You put dirty clothes under the bed to pretend like you've cleaned. You go without underwear rather than doing a load of laundry. Considering the evidence, there's a high likelihood that all your macros won't be perfect either.

You met the **TRANSCRIPT WINDOW** in the last lesson when you created macros. This is the place where it's easiest to edit your macros, which you'll learn to do in this lesson. You'll also learn how to attach your macros to a button in the worksheet so you can run them with a point and a click. Jam on!

BETTER THAN A STICK IN THE EYE: EDITING YOUR MACROS

The 1-2-3 Transcript window is where keystrokes and mouse actions are recorded. With a record of your keystrokes and actions in the Transcript window, you can copy, delete, or play back the commands and mouse actions to see how well the macro works. When you *create a macro* in the Transcript window, you may often find that you need to edit the macro to fit your specific needs.

For example, if you record a macro that applies certain styles to a cell or range of cells, the macro recording will include the command {**SELECT**} for whatever cell your cell pointer was in when you started recording the macro. So, if you were in cell A1 while recording, then your macro will include {**SELECT A1**} as the first macro command. However, you don't want cell A1 to be selected every time you want to run the macro; chances are that you want to select the cell or range yourself and then execute the macro. In this case, you'd have to edit the macro to fit your needs.

You can modify macros within the Transcript window using these steps:

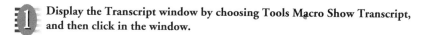

1   **Display the Transcript window by choosing Tools Macro Show Transcript, and then click in the window.**

2   **Edit the macro commands by using the Edit commands and typing your changes in the Transcript window.**

The macro you want to edit   Transcript window SmartIcon Bar

3   **Select the macro commands to copy them.**

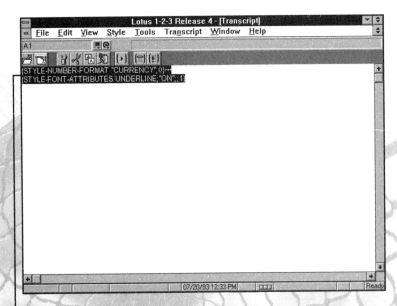

Select the macro commands to copy them back to a worksheet.

4 Choose Edit Copy.

5 Paste the macro into a worksheet using Edit Paste.

ON THE BUTTON

Even though you know perfectly well where you're putting your macros, if you share worksheets with coworkers (who you already know aren't as brilliant as you are), you can make running macros easier and more obvious for lamebrains. You can draw a rectangular button, with a label, in the worksheet and assign a macro to it. When you want to run that

macro, point your little mousy at it, and click the little button—just like clicking on a SmartIcon. To use a macro button in a worksheet, you must first draw the macro button with a *Draw menu* command, and then take the steps to assign the macro to the button.

To make a button out of a macro:

 Choose Tools Draw Button.

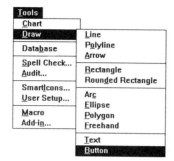

 Move the mouse pointer to where you want the macro button to appear.

 To create the macro button in the default size, click on the worksheet. To size the macro button, drag across the worksheet, and release the mouse button when the macro button is the size you want. The Assign to Button dialog box appears. You can choose **OK** and assign a macro to the button at a later time, or move onto to step 4 and assign the macro now.

To resize the button, drag the handles.

 Select Range in the Assign macro from drop-down box.

Click and select Range from the list.

Click on the macro name.

Enter the label for the button.

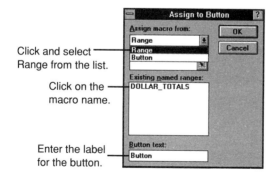

 Select the macro name from the Existing named ranges list box.

 In the Button text box, enter the text you want to appear on the Button.

 Choose OK.

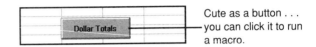

Cute as a button . . .
you can click it to run
a macro.

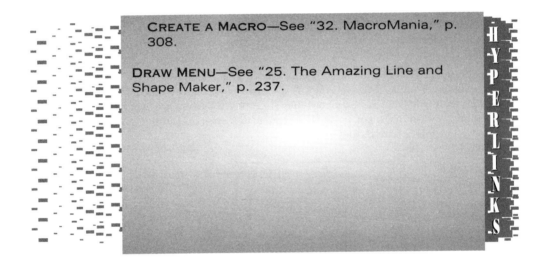

CREATE A MACRO—See "32. MacroMania," p. 308.

DRAW MENU—See "25. The Amazing Line and Shape Maker," p. 237.

HYPERLINKS

PROTECTING THE DATA YOU LOVE

If you're paranoid, you'll really enjoy this lesson. It tells you how to prevent others from seeing or changing data in your worksheets. When *saving a file*, you can assign a password so you're the only one who can open it. By sealing a file using the **File Protect** command, you can prohibit changes to cell contents, styles, and settings. Sealing a file also keeps others from seeing *hidden data*.

For example, if you are working with confidential employee salary data to prepare a budget, you may want to show the file to others, but you don't want them to see the salary numbers. You can hide those numbers by choosing **S**tyle **H**ide. If you don't seal the file, anyone can also unhide the numbers using the **S**tyle **U**nhide command, but if you seal

the file, only you can redisplay the hidden data. Here's the full impact of sealing a file:

◇ Cell contents, styles, and settings are protected.

◇ Hidden worksheets and columns can't be redisplayed.

◇ Rows, columns, or worksheets cannot be inserted or deleted.

◇ Protection settings, range names, formats, alignments, column width, row height, page breaks, frozen titles, or drawn objects cannot be changed.

FILE LOCKDOWN: PREVENTING OTHERS FROM CHANGING CELLS

If you don't want anyone to make any changes to a file that you may need to share with them, seal the file this way:

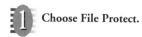 **Choose File Protect.**

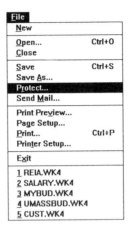

2 Under File Protection, select the Seal file check box.

Click this box to check it if you want to seal the file.

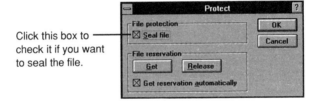

3 **Choose OK.** The Set Password dialog box appears asking you to supply a **PASSWORD** for the seal.

4 **In the Password text box, enter a password.** A password can be up to 15 characters long and is case-sensitive. Therefore, remember exactly how you entered the password—what was capitalized and what wasn't. Write down the exact password somewhere so you won't forget it.

Type the password.

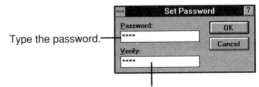

Type it here again, exactly as you did the first time.

In the Verify text box, enter the same password again—exactly the way you entered it the first time.

 Choose OK.

SELECTED TO STAY UNPROTECTED

There may be times when you create a file and want to protect the file from changes by other users, but you need to allow others to enter data in the worksheet. For example, you may have a form on a 1-2-3 worksheet and only want someone to be able to change or enter data into certain cells. No problem. You can protect a file by sealing it and allow others to enter data in the file by unprotecting some *ranges*. Before you seal the file (as just described), do this to leave some ranges unprotected:

 Select the range or collection of ranges that you want to leave unprotected.

		Lotus 1-2-3 Release 4 - [REIA.WK4]			
	File	**Edit**	**View**	**Style**	**Tools** **Range** **Window** **Help**

A:B9..A:B9   30000

A	A	B	C	D	E
1	Real Estate Investment Analysis				
2					
3	Purchase Price	$100,000			
4	Down Payment	$30,000			
5	Loan Amount	$70,000			
6	Mortgage Interest Rate	10%			
7	Mortgage Term	25			
8					
9	Annual Rental Income	$30,000			
10	Less Vacancy Allowance	5%			
11	Gross Operating Income	$28,500			
12	Annual Operating Expenses	$10,250			
13	Net Operating Income	$18,250			
14	Less Mortgage Payments	$7,633			
15	Cash Flow Before Taxes	$10,617			
16					
17					

Helv   10   07/21/93 10:20 AM   Ready

Select the ranges to leave unprotected.

 Choose Style Protection.

 Select the check box to allow changes to cell contents after the file is sealed.

Select so the range or ranges you selected remain unprotected.

 Choose OK.

 Seal the file using File Protect. Follow the prompts to enter and confirm your password, as described earlier in this lesson.

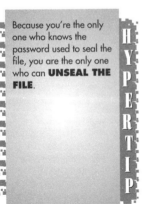

BREAKING THE SACRED SEAL

If you decide that you want to make changes to a sealed file, like if you realize you boned up some of the formulas and need to fix them (who, you?), you must first **UNSEAL THE FILE**. Here's the sacred ritual, known only to a few cloistered souls:

 Choose File Protect. The Protect dialog box appears.

 Deselect the Seal file check box (uncheck it).

 Choose OK. The Get Password dialog box appears.

In the Password text box, type the password you used to seal the file. Be sure to enter it exactly as you did when you sealed the file—using the exact combination of upper- and lowercase letters.

Type the password you used to seal the file.

 Choose OK.

BOOM, BABY! GIVING A FILE A PASSWORD

This is the ultimate! You can keep other users from opening your file at all by saving it with a secret password. Only those privileged people to whom you give **PASSWORD**:

the password will be able to open the file. (This is one way to get some control in your life.) To save a file with a

 Choose File Save As. The Save As dialog box appears.

 Under Save, select the With password check box.

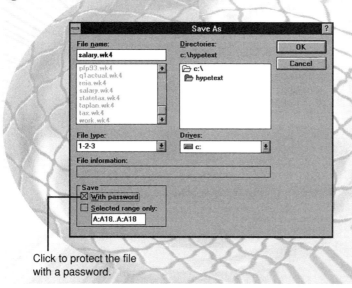

Click to protect the file with a password.

To delete a **PASS-WORD**, open the file and choose File Save As. Deselect the With password check box, and click on **OK**.

 Choose OK. 1-2-3 displays the Set Password dialog box.

 In the Password text box, enter a password. A password can be up to 15 characters long and is case-sensitive. Therefore, remember exactly how you entered the password—what was capitalized and what wasn't. Write down the exact password somewhere so you won't forget it.

In the Verify text box, enter the same password again—exactly the way you entered it the first time.

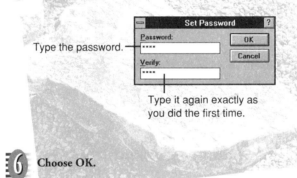

Type the password.

Set Password

Password:

Verify:

OK

Cancel

Type it again exactly as you did the first time.

Choose OK.

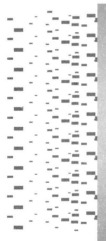

OPENING AN EXISTING FILE—See "3. It's a File Thing," p. 28.

HIDDEN DATA—See "11. Techno-Subversive Activities: Removing and Hiding Data," p. 109.

RANGES—See "7. It's the Range (Not the Frequency)," p. 66.

SAVING A FILE—See "3. It's a File Thing," p. 28.

HYPERLINKS

Part VIII
PROJECTS

So, you've learned all you need to learn and you're ready to do something practical. Or, more likely, you couldn't wait for the good stuff and skipped ahead to this part. Whatever the case, this is the part where you can really have fun. Using the pre-programmed worksheets and other stuff on the disk (see "Installing the Disk" at the back of the book), you can complete each of the projects that come next.

Hot Links

If you've worked your way through a good part of this book (or even if you haven't), you may have already realized that 1-2-3 for Windows can't do everything. In fact, one of the things it's worst at is handling long blocks of text. So what's a person to do if he or she wants to put a chunk of text in a 1-2-3 document? Type it in cell by cell? No way, José!

You can insert information created in another Windows application, such as a word processor, graphics application, and so on, into a 1-2-3 document using OLE technology (we're not talking bull here, either). OLE stands for Object Linking and **EMBEDDING**. It's a Windows feature that lets you link parts of documents together, or embed one document within another. OLE is superior to a plain old copy and paste because you can usually update the material you paste into another document from within 1-2-3.

This project explains how to create a link between 1-2-3 and another Windows application, using Windows Paintbrush as an example. (Bonus: You don't even need anything from the disk to follow along.) You can link 1-2-3 with any other Windows application that supports OLE. Here goes. . . .

> **EMBEDDING** lets you use the features of another application to create an object (graphic, piece of text, and so on) from within 1-2-3. This technique does not create a separate document file for the other application. Use the **Edit Insert Object** command, choose an application, create the object, choose **File Exit** or the equivalent, and click on **Yes** when you're asked whether to update the embedded object.

Start the application that you want to link material from. In this case, double-click on the **Accessories** icon in the Windows Program Manager, then double-click on **Paintbrush**.

Open the file that creates the material you want to link, or create a new file containing that material (be sure to save new files with File Save). You would either open an existing Paintbrush file, or create and save a drawing.

Select the material you want to link with 1-2-3. You can select all or part of the file you've created.

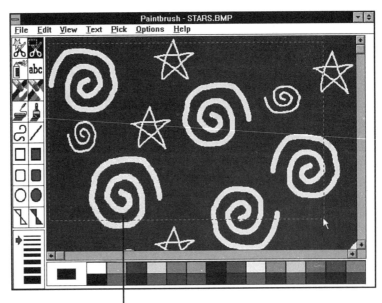

Selected portion of a drawing.

4 Choose Edit Copy.

5 Press Ctrl+Esc, and then double-click on Program Manager from the Switch to list.

6 Start 1-2-3, and then open or create the file you want to link to.

7 **Choose Edit Paste Link.** This pastes the information you copied from the other application into 1-2-3. However, the information is still linked to its original source, the Paintbrush file in this example. Therefore, remember to save both documents (the 1-2-3 document and the original) before exiting.

Note that this whole procedure can work the other way around, too. You can link information you create in 1-2-3 into other applications, such as a word processor like Ami Pro, a presentation program like Freelance Graphics, and more.

THE OBJECT UPDATE

You heard that the beauty of this whole deal is that you can **UPDATE LINKS**. That is, you can make and save changes in the original file—the Paintbrush file in our example—and those changes will appear in the 1-2-3 file. Here's how:

 Open the application where you created the object (such as Paintbrush) and the file that contains the object.

 Edit the object, and then choose File Save.

 Press Ctrl+Esc, and then double-click on Program Manager from the Switch to list.

 Start 1-2-3, and then open the file containing the link. The changes automatically appear in the linked object.

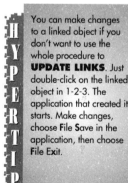

You can make changes to a linked object if you don't want to use the whole procedure to **UPDATE LINKS**. Just double-click on the linked object in 1-2-3. The application that created it starts. Make changes, choose File **S**ave in the application, then choose File Exit.

Changes made with the other application appear in the linked object.

 Save both files—the 1-2-3 file and the source file.

You can create a manual link so that 1-2-3 doesn't update your links automatically. This saves time and system resources and is useful if you're not changing your server file constantly. Here's how:

Choose **Edit Links**. In the list box, select the link you want to edit. Its description will show up in the Information box. Choose the **Edit** button, and set the Update mode to **Manual**. Select **OK**, and then close the Links dialog box.

Whenever you need to update the links, choose **Edit Links Update All**. If you only want to update one linked file, choose **Edit Links**. Then select the one you want from the list box, and choose **Update**. Close the Links dialog box when you're finished.

There are numerous ways to take advantage of Linking. Just think of the possibilities:

◇ Link a Windows Card file database with a 1-2-3 database so you can take advantage of Windows' number-dialing capabilities.

◇ Link your 1-2-3 data with graph slides in a presentation package like Freelance Graphics, for an easy way to update the presentation as data changes.

◇ Annotate your spreadsheet with full paragraphs, bullet lists, and column text . . . without worrying about wrapping text in cells and without disturbing existing data.

FONTS A PLENTY

Windows 3.1 has made it easier to use the fonts you want in documents. This version of Windows introduced TrueType fonts, which let you see on-screen exactly what will print out. The TrueType fonts that come with Windows can be used with any Windows application . . . that's why they can be a cost-effective way to jazz up your 1-2-3 worksheets. This project explains how you can install into Windows some TrueType fonts provided on the disk that came with this book (as part of a **SHAREWARE** program called

WinPak#1 by Rhode Island Soft Systems), so they'll be available for use in 1-2-3.

Bonus points! WinPak#1 also comes with four screen savers and a file that lets you choose more icons when creating program items in Windows' Program Manager. To learn about using these items (after you've installed WinPak#1, of course), double-click on the **Main Documentation** icon in the WinPak#1 Screen Savers group in Program Manager.

SHAREWARE programs are not free. They're typically distributed over on-line services and computer bulletin board systems. The idea is that you should test the program out, and if you plan to use it, you should send in the registration form— and a small fee. To register WinPak#1, double-click the Registration Form icon in the WinPak#1 Screen Savers group from Program Manager. Fill out the form, print it, and mail it in with your check.

INSTALLING WINPAK#1

To access the WinPak fonts, you'll need to install the program first. It's really a two-step process: You'll need to copy the winpak#1.exe file from the disk that came with this book to a directory on your hard drive (if you didn't do so

already according to the "Installing the Disk" page at the back of the book), and then set up the program. Installing copies the TrueType fonts (and a few other goodies, such as screen savers and a file of icons) to your hard drive.

COPYING WINPAK#1.EXE TO YOUR HARD DRIVE

 Take the disk from the back of the book, and place it in your floppy drive.

 Go to the Windows Program Manager, and double-click on the File Manager icon in the Main program group.

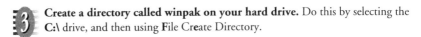

3 Create a directory called winpak on your hard drive. Do this by selecting the C:\ drive, and then using File Create Directory.

4 Double-click on the drive icon for the floppy drive that's holding the disk for this book. You should now have two windows on-screen. To make things easier, you may want to choose the Window Tile command, and then scroll down in the window for your hard drive until you see the winpak directory you just created.

5 Copy winpak#1.exe to the new winpak directory. You can drag the icon for the winpak#1.exe file from the floppy drive window over the winpak directory icon. Release, and click on OK at the dialog box that appears.

SETTING UP WINPAK#1

1 Still in the File Manager, double-click on the winpak#1.exe file in the winpak directory you created.

2 Choose Window Refresh or press F5.

3 Double-click on the setup.exe file in the winpak directory.

4 Click on OK, or enter another name for the Windows directory and then click on OK.

INSTALLING TRUETYPE FONTS

Now, you're certainly ready to install your WinPak fonts (or any that you've gotten from another source and have copied to the \windows\system directory on your hard drive), which are named FIBox and FIBoxBB. If you've purchased TrueType fonts from another source, they may come with their own installation program . . . so check the documentation before you proceed.

1 If you haven't copied the fonts to your hard disk, insert the diskette with the fonts into your floppy drive.

2 From the Windows Program Manager, double-click on the Main group icon, and then double-click on the Control Panel icon.

3 Double-click on the Fonts icon.

4 Click on the Add button. The Add Fonts dialog box appears.

(Optional) Use the Drives: list to select the floppy that contains the fonts to install. You don't need to do this at all if you've set up WinPak#1. This just applies if you're installing fonts from other sources.

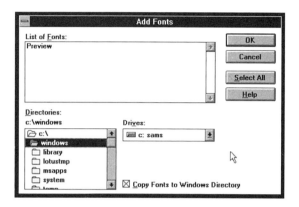

 Use the Directories list to change to the \windows\system directory. (Or change to another directory if you've copied font files somewhere else.) The available fonts in that directory appear in the List of Fonts.

 Scroll down the available fonts to find the ones you want to install, and then select them by clicking (use Ctrl+click after the first font). In this case, highlight **FIBox** and **FIBoxBB.**

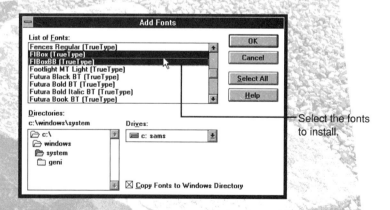

Select the fonts to install.

 Make sure the Copy Fonts to Windows Directory check box is checked. This way, if you're installing from a floppy disk or a directory besides \windows\system, the fonts are copied to windows\system so Windows doesn't look for the fonts on a floppy disk.

 Click on OK. This installs the fonts and makes them available for use in 1-2-3 for Windows and other Windows applications.

 OK all dialog boxes, and switch to an application to use the font(s).

New fonts to choose as headings.

BRIGHT IDEAS

Other ways to get TrueType fonts:

◇ Register your WinPak#1 product with Rhode Island Soft Systems. They'll send you a more complete version of their product (with more fonts). Rhode Island Soft Systems also offers two more sets of fun WinPak stuff, TrueType font packages, and more. . . . See the registration form that you get when you double-click the Registration Form icon in the WinPak#1 Screen Savers group.

◇ Download shareware fonts from on-line services and bulletin board systems (BBSs).

◇ Buy them in computer stores or from catalogs.

◇ Get other applications that come with TrueType fonts, such as CorelDRAW! In fact, if you have a CD-ROM drive, you can use the two CDs' worth of fonts and clip art that come with Corel.

SOUNDS GOOD TO ME

3

PROJECT

Windows 3.1 also lets you add sounds to your documents; if, that is, you've installed a driver file (a mini-program) that tells Windows how to output the sounds to your PC's speaker. Although you won't hear great, great sound quality from your speaker as it stands, this can give you a taste of what sound can add, particularly if you're considering adding a sound board to your system. So, without further ado. . . .

INSTALLING A SPEAKER DRIVER

PC Speaker is a sound driver distributed by Microsoft that lets Windows play back .WAV sound files. (You get a few of these with Windows 3.1, and there are more on this book's disk.) This procedure tells you how to copy the file that contains the speaker driver (and some bonus .WAV files) from the disk that comes with this book to your hard drive. Then keep going to install the speaker driver so it works with Windows, like this:

 Take the disk from the back of the book, and place it in your floppy drive.

 Go to the Windows Program Manager, and double-click on the File Manager icon in the Main program group.

 Create a directory called speaker on your hard drive. Do this by selecting the **C:** drive, and then using **F**ile **Cr**eate Directory.

 Double-click on the drive icon for the floppy drive that's holding the disk for this book. You should now have two windows on-screen. To make things easier, you may want to choose the **W**indow **T**ile command, and then scroll down in the window for your hard drive until you see the speaker directory you just created.

 Copy noise.exe to the new noise directory. You can drag the icon for the noise.exe file from the floppy drive window over the speaker directory icon. Release, and click on **OK** on the dialog box that appears.

6 Double-click on the noise.exe file in the noise directory you created.

7 **Choose Window Refresh.** You'll see there are several files there, including a file with a .DRV extension and several .WAV files.

8 Leave File Manager and go to Program Manager.

9 From the Windows Program Manager, double-click on the Main group icon. Double-click on the **Control Panel** icon, and then double-click on the **Drivers** icon. The Drivers dialog box appears.

10 **Click on the Add button.** The Add dialog box appears.

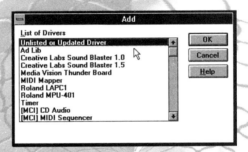

11 Click on Unlisted or Updated Driver, and then click on OK. This choice should appear at the top of the dialog box.

12 Type c:\noise in the text box of the dialog box that appears, and then click on OK. The Add Unlisted or Updated Driver dialog box appears.

13 Because the PC-Speaker driver is the only one listed, click on OK. You'll hear some screeching noises, and then see a box that lets you set up the driver.

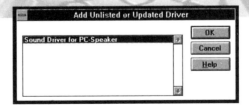

Change any settings you want, using the Test button as needed, and then click on OK. I recommend setting Seconds to limit playback to No Limit.

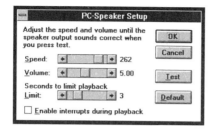

 Restart Windows when prompted for your changes to take effect.

GETTING A SOUND INTO 1-2-3

In addition to assigning sounds to Windows events (check out the Sound icon in the Control Panel group), you can embed them in your 1-2-3 for Windows files. When you click on the icon for the sound, you'll hear it. This gets more practical when you add a sound board to your system that lets you record your own sounds. Then, you can annotate your worksheets with personalized voice **MESSAGES**, recordings from other sources, and more!

Keep in mind that other users can hear the sound **MESSAGES** only if their systems have sound capability, and they may need to have your sounds on disk.

Here's a down-and-dirty way to embed a sound in your worksheet:

 Go to Program Manager, double-click on the Accessories group icon, and double-click on the Sound Recorder icon.

 Choose File Open, and select a .WAV file from any directory that has one. You can select one from the \noise directory, where you copied some earlier in this project, or from the \windows directory. After you click on **OK**, the WAV file appears in the title bar of the Sound Recorder dialog box.

Click here to play your sound.

 Choose Edit Copy.

 Go to your 1-2-3 worksheet.

 Choose Edit Paste Link. 1-2-3 pastes an icon into your document.

 Double-click on the icon to play the sound.

BRIGHT IDEAS

Other ways to sound off:

◇ Download shareware sounds from on-line services and bulletin board systems (BBSs).

◇ Play with the capabilities of the Sound Recorder Accessory to mix sound files together, edit them, and more!

TRAVELIN' MAN (OR FOR THE POLITICALLY CORRECT: TRAVELIN' PERSON)

Okay, so you're lucky enough to have an expense account, but that also means you travel so much that most of your plants are dead and your landlord thinks you've moved. Oh bother! And to top it off, you're forced to produce pages and pages of reports every month telling your boss just exactly how you spent her money.

Well, have we got a template for you! In case you didn't notice the reason why this book is so thick, there's a disk in the back that contains nifty templates to help you out of boring situations like creating expense reports. All the hard work's been done—and that leaves you free time to play, customize, whatever.

GETTING DOWN TO BRASS TACKS

Let's get started: first, follow the instructions at the back of this book to copy the files into the correct directories on your hard drive. For this project,

you're looking for TRIP.WK4. We'll start by opening it up and taking a look around.

 Open the TRIP.WK4 file from the \123R4W\HYPER directory.

 Choose File Save As, and save the file under a new file name, such as TRIP1.WK4. This is for your protection. Should you make some changes to customize the worksheet and then you hate them, you can go back to the beginning by using the original file.

Special icon bar   One worksheet for every   Monthly totals, too!
week, just like underwear.

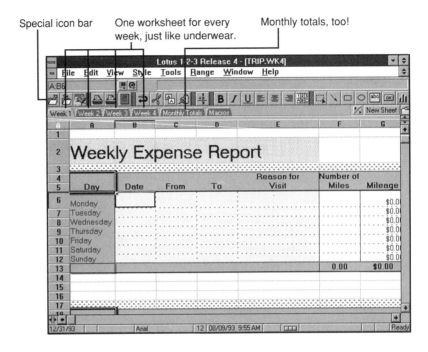

Taking a look around.

 Click on the SmartIcon selector in the status bar, and select the Trip Sheet.
It's a specialized icon bar just for this worksheet—it looks like the default icon
bar but there are two new icons. You can peek if you want, but an explanation
will have to wait just a sec until we've checked this baby out. Notice that there
are four weekly worksheets, and one **WORKSHEET** that holds monthly
totals (the last worksheet contains the custom-designed macros for this project
at no additional charge to you).

 Enter a date for Monday in the Week 1 worksheet, and press Ctrl+D. All
the other dates are entered for you automatically—bada bing, bada boom! I
wish my dishes could find their way to the dishwasher as easily, but they keep
getting stuck in Sink Valley. Anyway, that's not all—by entering dates for Week
1, look what you've won—the dates for all the weeks are automatically
calculated! Okay, it's about as exciting as watching the fungus grow in my sink,
but not everything in life's a Seinfeld episode.

 **Once the dates are entered, go ahead and key in your expenses. MILE-
AGE** is automatically calculated at the federal limit of 27.5 cents a mile.

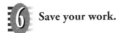 **Save your work.**

When you switch to
another **WORKSHEET**
file, repeat this process,
and select Default Sheet
to return to the 1-2-3
default icon bar.

If your company reim-
burses your **MILEAGE**
at a different rate, just
change the formulas.
Also, the formula rounds
the amount to the next
penny. Change the
formula if you want it to
round down, or to the
nearest penny.

342

DETAILS, DETAILS

Now, back to those icons. First, key in some entries as a test. Now, suppose you've just opened the TRIP template and you'd like to clear everything out so you can start a new month. Click on the icon with the big pink eraser (it's to the right of the File Save icon), and you'll wipe out old entries faster than Clearasil wipes out zits.

So what's the other icon for? Click on the blue **Printer** icon, and you'll print all four weekly worksheets and the monthly totals. If you want to print a single week, go to that worksheet and use the regular printer icon.

This icon clears out last month's expenses.

This icon prints all four worksheets and the monthly totals, too.

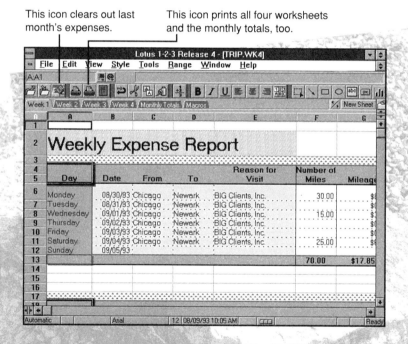

Look Ma, no hands!

BRIGHT IDEAS

Well, that's about it. Even though this worksheet was free, here are some additional ideas on how to really exploit it:

◇ Use the **Ctrl+D** macro to copy any values down the column (it's not just for dates anymore). For example, you could enter **$30** for lodging on Monday and copy it through the rest of the week.

◇ Print out a blank copy of Week 1, and take it on your trip (if you drive on the job, keep a copy in the glove compartment). Fill it in as you go, and key in the data at the end of the month. Couldn't be easier.

◇ Add a notes section at the bottom of each sheet for keeping track of things you learned on your trip, such as things to do for clients, and so on.

NAME THAT EMPLOYEE

5

PROJECT

With the help of this template, you won't ever have to dig through piles of files to find out how many employees have single medical coverage or which ones are up for a salary review. All of that information (and more!) can be yours at one low-low price (meaning "free"). And you don't have to use this template for employee tracking—use it for whatever you want, such as a client database, database for direct-reports, or even an address book of friends and family.

 Open the EEDATA.WK4 file from the \123R4W\HYPER directory.

 Choose File Save As, and save the file under a new file name, such as EEDATA1.WK4. This is for your protection. Anything you say can and will be used against you in a court of law.

 Like the previous project, this one also contains a customized SmartIcons bar, so select the EE Database icon bar. The employee database contains most of the basics: name, title, department, and so on. See suggestions at the end of this project for customizing this puppy to meet your exact needs.

Special bucket seats and icon bar   Custom menu

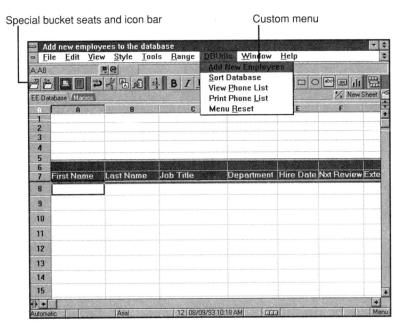

This baby's got four on the floor and it's ready to cruise!

ADDING EMPLOYEES

This project also contains a custom **MENU** (slick, eh?), called **DBUtils**. You'll find several cool commands there, such as adding employees, sorting the database, and even printing it. First, let's add an employee.

1 **Select Add New Employees from the DBUtils menu.** A-way we goooo!

2 **Enter information when prompted.** You don't have to enter a dollar sign with the **PAY RATE**; the cells in the database are already formatted for that (at least, the first fifty cells are—after that, you're on your own).

3 **After the pay rate, you'll see a customized dialog box for entering employee benefits.**

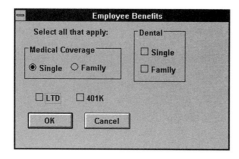

Entering our first employee—what a thrill!

 When you're done entering in employee info, you'll be prompted to update the employee to the database. If you click on **OK**, the employee will be added, and you'll be prompted to add another employee—it's as easy as that. If you have fumble-fingers like me, you can click on **Cancel** and make changes to the form, and then click on the **Copy Employee to Database** button to update the employee. If you don't want to add another employee, click on **OK** to update the current one, and then press **Enter** at the name prompt. You'll get a message asking you why you hired someone with no name, but just click on **OK**, and it's cool.

FEELING OUT OF SORTS

Now you've got this super list of names, and so on, but what do you do with it? Get it in order, dude! Use the **S**ort Database command on the **DBU**tils menu to sort the database any number of ways: by name, department, rate of pay, and so on.

Pick a sort, any sort.

347

If you encounter trouble **PRINTING**, check cell C127 on the Macro sheet. It points to the location of a printer setup file called EEDATA.AL3. Edit the path, if necessary. Also, you may want to print in portrait mode if your printer does not have a lot of memory. Use the Page Setup command, retrieve the named settings EEDATA.AL3, change it to portrait, and then save your changes.

You can use the **T**ools Data**b**ase **F**ind Records command to search for any group of employees. Under Find records in **d**atabase table, type **DBTBL**. Select the field to search in, and the value to look for. For example, you could select Last Name as a field, and Hoffa as a Value (good luck finding that one!). All the records that match your criteria are then highlighted.

To print a group of selected records, use the **N**ew Query command on the **T**ools Data**b**ase menu. Again, enter **DBTBL** under Select **d**atabase table to query. Choose the fields to include in the report, and select your criteria. Pick a nice big (blank) area of the worksheet (like maybe something beyond column AC) to place the results, and itza done! To print the query, click on it to select it, and then hit that **Printer** icon. For further hints, see the exposé on the phone listing in the next project.

Once you have the database the way you want it, you're ready for some great **PRINTING**! Click on the bright red **Printer** icon (it's next to the Save icon). This special icon is attached to a macro that prints just the employee database. Slick, eh?

BRIGHT IDEAS

There is a lot you can do with this worksheet to customize it for your own purposes. For example, you could add new fields (such as address) or even delete fields, but keep these things in mind:

◇   There are two database ranges: DBRANGE that starts at cell A:A8 and includes only the employee info. This range is used for sorting and printing purposes. The other range, DBTBL, includes the first row of headings, and it is used for query purposes. (By the way, keep your column headings in row 7 so queries can find selected data.) Reselect the proper ranges after you've made your changes, and everything should be copacetic.

◇   If you add new fields, you need to adjust the ENTRY macro to prompt you for the data. Go to the Macro worksheet, and move things around as necessary. Use {GET-LABEL} to prompt for text, and {GET-NUMBER} to prompt for numbers. Danger, Will Robinson: If you prompt for numbers, add an IF statement to test for nonentry in the field. (Look at cell B:B20 for clues.)

Here are some ideas for using this rather cool worksheet:

◇   Add a query to select employees with certain benefits or to produce an updated listing—paying for benefits on ex-employees costs you big-time money.

◇   Add addresses, and then link the database to a mailing labels program.

◇   Create a payroll worksheet, and link fields to it so it's automatically updated.

◇   Use the database to keep track of just about anything or anyone, such as clients, accounts, or direct-reports.

PHONE HOME

Never dial the wrong person again with this nifty template. Actually, the template itself should seem fairly familiar to you—it's the same one from the last project: EEDATA.WK4, complete with the same custom **MENU**, DBUtils. Follow the instructions from Project 5 to open the worksheet and get it set up.

When you're through with the EEDATA worksheet, be sure to select the Menu Reset command on the DBUtils menu. This will reset the **MENU** back to the Lotus standard. If you forget, no harm done; the menu doesn't work unless the EEDATA worksheet is active. If it bothers you, enter {MENU-RESET} into a cell, select it, and use Tools Macro Run to run the reset command.

Leave a message at the tone. . . .

The employee database (EEDATA.WK4) has a query already set up to print a phone listing consisting of employee's names, departments, and extension numbers (and anyone else in your calling circle). To use the phone listing, follow these E–Z steps:

 Enter the data in the database. Sorry to rain on your parade, but this project isn't going to work unless we have some employees (with phone extensions). If you need some help entering employees, see Project 5.

 Select the View Phone List command from DBUtils menu to view the resulting phone list. You need to always select **V**iew first, because it updates the query listing to reflect any new employees.

 Select the Print Phone List command to print out the PHONE LIST-ING. If you encounter trouble printing, check cell C121 on the Macro sheet. It points to the location of a printer setup file called EEDATA2.AL3. Edit the path, if necessary.

SORRY, WRONG NUMBER

The database query is set up to sort by employee name, but you can change that, if you want.

 First, click on the query to select it, and then use the Query menu to change the sort with the Sort command.

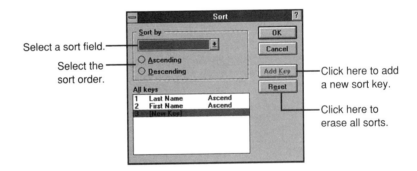

Select a sort field.

Select the sort order.

Click here to add a new sort key.

Click here to erase all sorts.

Easier than sorting socks.

 Click on Reset, select your sort key (such as extension or department number), and click on Add Key.

 **Repeat to add additional sort levels.** Click on **OK**, and away it goes!

Sidebar (HYPERTIP):

If for some reason you get blank lines in your **PHONE LISTING**, somehow the database range has gotten off. Use the Range Name command, and choose **DBTBL**. Reselect from cell A7 (the first label) to the end of the data, and click on **Add**. This will reset the query range. Now, run the command, and View Phone List again, which will refresh the query and display your employees.

The phone listing includes all employees (whether alive or dead), but you can, again, use the query commands to change the selection criteria. For example, select the query, and use the **Q**uery Set **C**riteria command. Now here's an interesting dialog box:

Click here to select a field.   Select an operator.   Select a value to compare to.

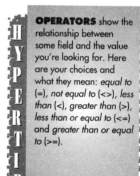

Believe me, this looks scarier than it is.

 **Click on the Field list box, and select a field, such as Department.**

 **Then click on the Operator list box, and select an operator. An OPERATOR** is a symbol that represents a relationship between a field and a value, such as *equal to* (=).

 **Next, select a Value, such as 445567.** Cha-ching! You've just told 1-2-3 to select all the employees in department 445567. If you want, click on **A**nd or **O**r, and repeat the process for more complex selections, such as "Include all employees in department 445567 who make more than $12.00 an hour," as shown in the figure here.

 **Choose OK.**

> **OPERATORS** show the relationship between some field and the value you're looking for. Here are your choices and what they mean: *equal to* (=), *not equal to* (<>), *less than* (<), *greater than* (>), *less than or equal to* (<=) *and greater than or equal to* (>=).

Since you're in a mood to change things, you could change the fields in the query by using the following steps:

Select any field to add to the phone query.

Choosy people choose their own query fields.

 Select the query by clicking on it.

 Use the Query Choose Fields command.

 Click on Add. Select any additional fields, and click on **OK**. To delete existing fields, select them, and then click on **C**lear.

 When you're done fine-tuning, click on OK.

BRIGHT IDEAS

Well, that's it! Here are some ideas for getting more mileage out of this one:

◇ If your company uses them, add a mail stop number to the database, and include it in the query.

◇ Use the database for family and friends, too, and create a separate query to select them.

◇ Add a field to the database that identifies your calling circle, and print those people on a separate list.

WHAT IT TAKES TO MAKE A BUCK

7

PROJECT

This worksheet will help you analyze your company's sales volume and cost so you can determine the break-even point—that mysterious point where you'll actually start making money. This project's worksheet is called BREAKEVN.WK4. Like many of the projects before it, it comes with a specialized icon bar.

1 Open the BREAKEVN.WK4 file from the \123R4W\HYPER directory.

2 Choose File Save As, and save the file under a new file name, such as BREAKEN1.WK4. This is for your protection. Should you make some changes to customize the worksheet and then hate them, you can go back to the beginning by using the original file.

3 Select the special icon bar, CVP Sheet (which translates to "cost-volume-profit" for us Earthlings).

Special icon bar just for you!   Classy menu

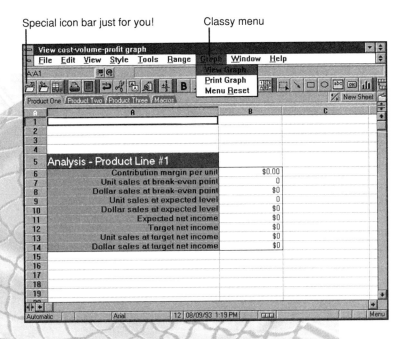

Just about everything you need to know about making money.

There are provisions in the template for up to three product lines. You can add more, if necessary. Notice also that this template contains a special menu like some of our previous templates (more on the Graph menu later).

ENTERING SOME BASIC DATA

To provide the detailed analysis for each product, the worksheet needs some basic data that you enter by clicking on the **CVP** icon (it's the one next to the File Save icon).

 Click on the CVP icon.

 Select a product line, and you'll see the Cadillac of dialog boxes:

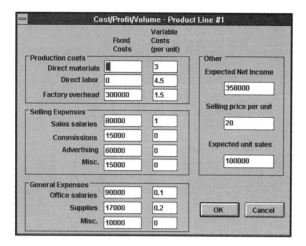

Just a few questions, Ma'am.

 To enter data, type a number (you don't need to enter stuff like commas and dollar signs). To move from field to field, press **Tab**. To move back to a previous field, press **Shift+Tab**.

 You'll need to be as complete as possible for the analysis to work. Some expenses, such as direct materials and direct labor, have no **FIXED COST** equivalents; others have both fixed and **VARIABLE COST** equivalents. Rule #521: *If a field doesn't apply, leave it blank or type 0.* In addition to fixed and variable costs, you'll need to enter expected net income, expected sales, and the selling price per unit. Once you're done, the macro returns you to the analysis area for your viewing enjoyment.

CHARTING YOUR COURSE

In case you've just suffered vapor lock from staring at all those numbers, cheer up! There's an easier way out of this. After entering the analysis data (see preceding instructions), open the customized **G**raph menu (how convenient!) to both view and print a graph for any of the three product lines.

FIXED COSTS are those that do not change as volume goes up. **VARIABLE COSTS** expand with volume, but note that you enter the *per unit* volume costs here, not totals.

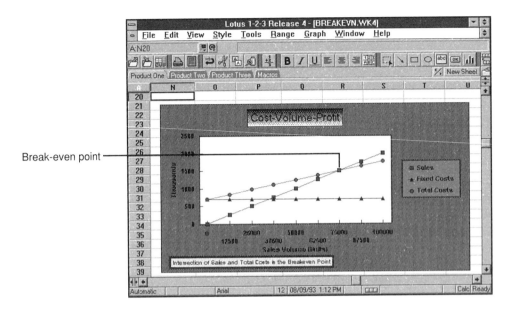

Break-even point

Now we're getting somewhere!

The graph charts the flow of different costs as sales volumes rise. The point where sales cost meets total cost is the elusive break-even point.

THESE OLD MENUS

When you're through with the Break-Even worksheet, be sure to select the Menu **R**eset command on the **G**raph menu. This will reset the menu back to the Lotus standard. If you forget, no harm done; the menu doesn't work unless the Break-Even worksheet is active. If it bothers you, enter {**MENU-RESET**} into a cell, select it, and use **T**ools **M**acro **R**un to run the reset command.

BRIGHT IDEAS

Here are some ways to adjust this template:

◊   The increments used in the graph are based on the sales volume. If sales are between 0 and 25,000 units, the increment is .20. When sales reach the 50,000 level, increments are .125. To change this factor, change the values stored in the cells T8..U10.

◊   Create a chart that compares the break-even point for all three product lines.

◊   Write a macro that prints the analysis for the product line you select. Use the print graph macros as guides.

BUSINESS BUDGET

PROJECT 8

Seems like everyone's on some type of budget these days, except that unlike the government, we've actually got to balance ours. Anyway, this little worksheet will make the process as painless as it's can be. It's called BUDGET.WK4, and it's the first in a "suite" of projects for small businesses. Beginning here with a budget based on projected sales, you can expand your accounting worksheets to include those found in later projects: cash flow projection, pro forma income statements and balance sheets, and a small-business plan. Best of all, some of these later projects are linked to the data you enter in this worksheet—this approach saves you lots of time in rekeying data, while providing a comprehensive overview of your business.

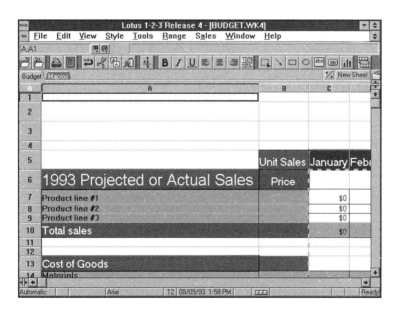

Happy! Happy! Joy! Joy! Budget time again.

When you're through with the BUDGET1 **FILE**, be sure to select the Menu Reset command on the Sales menu. This will reset the menu back to the Lotus standard. If you forget, no harm done; the menu doesn't work unless the BUDGET1 worksheet is active. If it bothers you, enter {MENU-RESET} into a cell, select it, and use **Tools Macro Run** to run the reset command.

After you input the **SALES FOR '92**, you can improve the accuracy of "Madam's predictions" by moving to AB11 and updating any actual sales for '93. Repeat the process for the other product lines at cells AB30 and AB50.

 Open the BUDGET.WK4 file from the \123R4W\HYPER directory.

 Choose File Save As, and save the file under a new file name, such as BUDGET1.WK4. This is for your protection. Should you make some changes to customize the worksheet and then hate them, you can go back to the beginning by using the original **FILE**.

 Open the Sales menu, and select Enter 1992 Sales, and then choose a product line. Previous entries display automatically, so you can also use this option to correct sales figures. Press **Tab** to move from field to field, and then click on OK, or press **Enter** when you're done. By entering actual **SALES FOR '92**, the worksheet will automatically project sales for '93, '94, and '95.

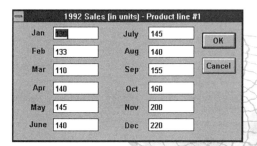

Ah, yes. I remember '92 now.

 Next, move to cells B7..B9, and enter the sales price for each product (like several previous worksheets, this one lets you input data on three different products).

 Enter the cost of materials, labor, and overhead in rows 14, 16, and 18. The percentages of total sales will automatically calculate.

 Before you're overwhelmed with budget boredom, enter operating expenses for sales and marketing in rows 30 to 37. Again, percentages of total sales will be calculated automatically at no charge to you. I know it's not much, but it's better than a stick in the eye!

 Enter general administrative expenses in rows 42 to 52.

 Now, enter an estimated tax percentage in cell B62. Remember to enter the percentage as a decimal—for example, 25% is entered as .25.

Enter interest paid on your business loan in row 61 by hand, or repaste the link from the CASHPROJ.WK4 template. You'll learn more about the Cash Projections worksheet in the next project. When you finish Project 9, return here to repaste the link to that file. To repaste the link, open CASHPROJ.WK4, copy the interest fields, and then switch back to the Budget file. Move to row 61, and then select the Edit Paste Link command to update the link.

 Oh, by the way, make sure you change the contents of cell C2 to something more specific than "Your Company Name."

When you're done, click on the **Printer** icon, and print this puppy. Then relax. Do lunch or watch "Luge Bowling." But above all, don't gross out over gross profit margins!

BRIGHT IDEAS

To customize this worksheet, here are some ideas:

◇ Add two worksheets, copy the contents of this one, and create a separate worksheet for each product line. Divide Cost of Goods and Operating Expenses for each of the three product lines to produce individual gross-profit margins.

◇ Add a worksheet for Actual Figures, then subtract the two to see how close to budget you are running.

◇ Graph the difference between actual expenses and budgeted expenses.

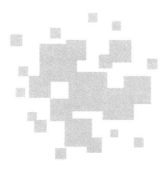

WHERE YOUR COMPANY'S MONEY GOES

PROJECT 9

I know where money comes from (cash machines), but who knows where money goes? If you have the unfortunate task in your company of trying to predict where money will be spent in the next year, this template can sure he'p.

 Open the CASHPROJ.WK4 worksheet from the \123R4W\HYPER directory.

 Choose File Save As, and save the file under a new file name, such as CASHPRJ1.WK4. This is for your protection. Should you make some changes to customize the worksheet and then you hate them, you can go back to the beginning by using the original file.

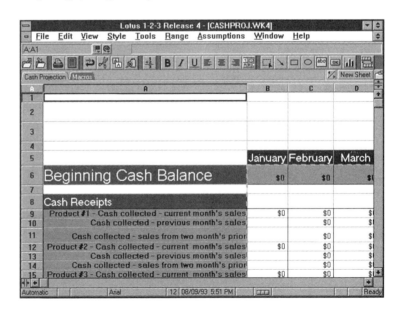

How low can cash flow?

Be sure to change the generic "Your Company Name" in cell A:B2 to something more meaningful.

A LINK TO THE PAST

Some cells in the Cash Projections worksheet are linked to the Budget worksheet, so you have two choices: You can manually enter the data from the Budget worksheet, or you can paste link it to the Cash Projections worksheet. When you paste link one worksheet to another, you create an active bond—in this case, after you link the two worksheets, if you make a change to the Budget worksheet, the Cash Projections worksheet will be automatically updated. If you decide to link the two worksheets, you'll have to repaste the links in the Cash Projections worksheet to reflect the directories on your PC (if you didn't do Project 8, the business budget project, do not pass Go and do not collect $200). To repaste the links:

 First, repaste the link to the sales price for each product. Open the Budget worksheet, and then select cells B7..B9. Copy them to the Clipboard before you switch back to the Cash Projections worksheet. Switch to the Cash Projections worksheet, move to cell AA6, and select Edit Paste Link.

 Repeat this process to link sales: Select cells B7..N9 in the Budget worksheet, and paste it to cells AE18..AO20 in the Cash Projections worksheet.

 Repeat this again to link projected sales: Select cells AB16..AB17, and paste them to cells AT18..AT19. Select cells AB35..AB36, and paste to cells AU18..AU19. Repeat by pasting cells AB55..AB56 to cells AV18..AV19.

The area of the worksheet beginning in cell AA6 projects sales for each of the three product lines based on incoming data from the Budget worksheet, and additional assumptions that you enter. If you opened the Budget worksheet to repaste links, save it and close it now. Also, if you opened that worksheet, its custom menu overrode the custom menu for the Cash Projections worksheet! (I guess customizing is not all it's cracked up to be.) No problem; simply save the Cash Projections worksheet and reopen it, or reactivate the menu with the Tools Macro Run command. When the dialog box asks you what you want to run, type **\0** and press **Enter**. Here comes the Assumptions menu out of hiding!

Open the Assumptions menu, and select Enter Sales Assumptions. Here, you'll enter the actual cost for each of the three products (the selling price is coming from the link to the Budget worksheet). Enter the amount of inventory you want on hand at the end of each month. This number is used in the Purchasing Budget that influences the cash flow projections (more on this later).

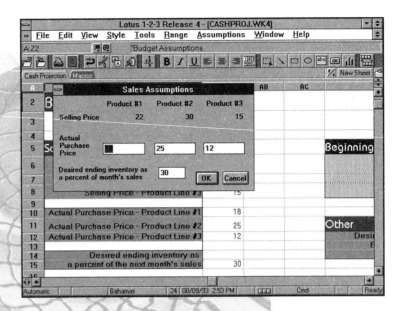

Entering sales projections.

Use the Enter **C**ash Assumptions command on the **A**ssumptions menu to enter an estimate (based on whatever credit procedures are in place) of the amount of sales that are paid for in cash, versus those that are paid for using some type of credit where the cash is received months later.

Use the Enter **O**ther Assumptions command on the **A**ssumptions menu to enter the opening inventory for each of the three products, the cash balance for January, the desired monthly ending cash balance, and the going interest rate.

Lastly (before your eyes glaze over), enter the rest of the data for the Cash Disbursements area (cells B22..M30).

Most of this data can be relinked to the Budget worksheet if you want: promotions, advertising, office rent, and equipment lease. Wages would be the total of sales salaries and administrative salaries coming from the Budget worksheet. *Interest on loans is computed automatically*; enter any other disbursements, and cha-ching! You're done!

Borrowing funds are computed from negative cash flow (gotta pay those bills somehow), and loan repayment is computed from positive cash flow. The net cash balance is the difference between the cash receipts and the cash disbursements, plus or minus any loan or loan repayment.

OUR STORE IS NOW CLOSING, PLEASE BRING YOUR PURCHASES TO THE FRONT

The Purchasing Budget, mentioned earlier, influences cash disbursements. Scope it out with the View Purchasing Budget command on the Assumptions menu. Part of the data you see here has already been relinked to the Budget worksheet; other parts are the result of assumptions you just input.

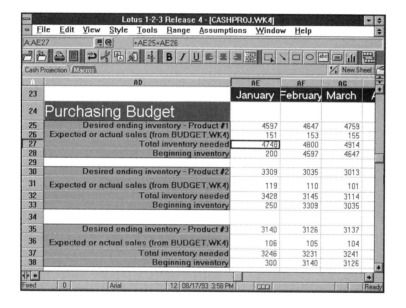

Keeping up with the Joneses.

Based on sales figures from the Budget worksheet, the Purchasing Budget calcs expected sales, subtracts that from the opening inventory, and adds the required ending inventory to arrive at the required purchase figure.

WRAP-UP

When you're through with the Cash Projections worksheet, save your hard work! Also, be sure to select the Menu Reset command on the Assumptions menu. This will reset the menu back to the Lotus standard. If you forget, no harm done; the menu doesn't work unless the Cash Projections worksheet is active. If it bothers you, enter {MENU-RESET} into a cell, select it, and use Tools Macro Run to run the reset command.

BRIGHT IDEAS

To customize this project, you can:

◇ Add menu options for printing the sales projections and the Purchasing Budget to act as support for the results found in the cash projection area.

◇ Change the formula used in computing loan repayment. For example, you may decide to use only half of a positive cash receipt total towards repayment in order to retain more operating capital.

◇ Create a graph to chart the flow of cash.

CHARTING YOUR COMPANY'S PRO-FORMANCE

A pro forma income and balance sheet may sound like accounting forms that are high in fiber and cholesterol-free, but they are really used to project results based on current estimates for sales and expenses.

 Open the PROFORMA.WK4 file from the \123R4W\HYPER directory. The file opens, and a new **MENU** is added to the menu bar.

 Choose File Save As, and save the file under a new file name, such as PROFORM1.WK4. This is for your protection. Should you make some changes to customize the worksheet and then hate them, you can go back to the beginning by using the original file.

 Like other worksheets in our "business suite," this worksheet can be linked to figures in the Budget worksheet. You can, of course, enter the budget data manually, but if you've already completed Project 7, why make the same tracks? After keying in the data for the Budget worksheet, save yourself some time by linking the following cells from the Budget worksheet:

Budget worksheet	Pro Forma worksheet
O10	B7
O20	B8
O56	B10
O61	B12
O62	B13

 If you linked the Budget worksheet to the Pro Forma worksheet instead of entering the data manually, the custom menu has reset itself. Don't worry; this is easy to fix. First, save the Budget worksheet and close it. Next, open the Tools menu and select Macro Run. Type **\0** and press **Enter**, and that ol' Financials menu will reappear.

HYPERTIP

Select the Menu Reset command on the Financials **MENU** to remove that menu when you're done with the file. This will reset the menu back to the Lotus standard. If you forget, no harm done; the menu doesn't work unless the Pro Forma worksheet is active. If it bothers you, enter {MENU-RESET} into a cell, select it, and use Tools Macro Run to run the reset command.

THE INCOME STATEMENT

The Pro Forma worksheet consists of two sections: a projected income statement and a projected balance sheet. To avoid brain-overload (always a good thing), we'll cover the income statement in this project, and the balance sheet in the next project.

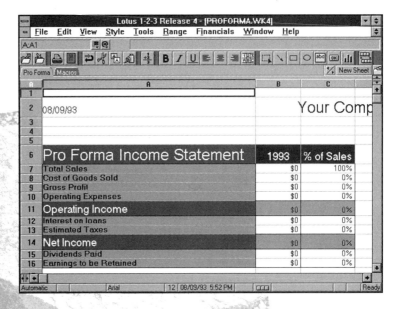

Incoming!

Most of the data for the 1993 section of the pro forma income statement comes from the Budget worksheet, which you either relinked or entered manually in the last section. The sales figures for '94 and '95 come from the projected sales area of the Budget worksheet, so get on over there (cells AR68 and AR70), and repaste the links to cells E7 and F7 in the Pro Forma worksheet (or enter the figures manually).

OH, THE JOYS OF OWNERSHIP

If your company is publicly held, then you'll need to enter the percentage of dividends that you intend to pay out. This amount is then subtracted from net income to calculate the amount of earnings to be retained. To enter dividend percentages, use the Financials Enter Dividends command.

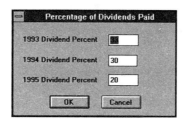

The figures for '93 influence '94 and '95.

After all the data is input for '93, the data for '94 and '95 (except for the sales figures) will be calculated based on the '93 ratio of that figure to '93 sales. For example, the figure for '94 cost of goods sold is calculated by using the ratio of '93 cost of goods sold to '93 sales.

To **PRINT** the income statement, use the Print Income Statement command on the Financials menu (duh-huh). For an explanation of the pro forma balance sheet, turn the page.

BRIGHT IDEA

Yup, there's only one:

◇ Use this worksheet file as a mini-evaluation of the profitability of new products you're contemplating.

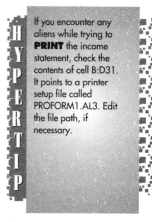

If you encounter any aliens while trying to **PRINT** the income statement, check the contents of cell B:D31. It points to a printer setup file called PROFORM1.AL3. Edit the file path, if necessary.

BALANCING ACT

As a reminder to our audience: When you're through with this worksheet file, be sure to select the Menu **R**eset command on the Financials menu. This will reset the menu back to the Lotus standard. If you forget, no harm done; the menu doesn't work unless the Pro Forma worksheet is active. If it bothers you, enter {**MENU-RESET**} into a cell, select it, and use Tools **M**acro **R**un to run the reset command.

Like the pro forma income statement, most of the '93 figures can be linked from the Cash Projections worksheet. Some, such as Property, Plant, and Equipment, can be linked from the Budget worksheet. As an option to linking, you can enter the data manually. If you've forgotten, here are the virtual steps for completing the links to this project:

 Open the Cash Projections worksheet, and move to one of the fields you want to link from (such as total cash).

 Use the Edit Copy command.

 Switch to the Pro Forma worksheet, and move to the cell you want to link to.

 Select Edit Paste Link. Who-ah! It's linked!

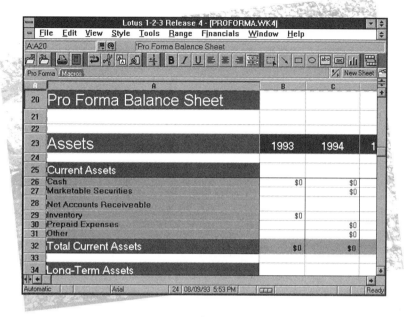

A reunion of sorts with old links.

For your linking and pasting convenience, here's a list of cells to link:

CASHPRJ1	PROFORM1
AE53	B26
AE56	B29
AE59	B35

If you linked cells from the Cash Projections and Budget worksheets, save them and close them now. Then reset the Financials menu by opening the Tools menu and selecting Macro Run. Type **/0** and press **Enter**, and here comes that ol' Financials menu again!

A LOOK AT YOUR COMPANY'S FINANCIAL FUTURE

To get a good look at these figures, use the View Financial Ratios command from the Financials menu, and you'll see something like this:

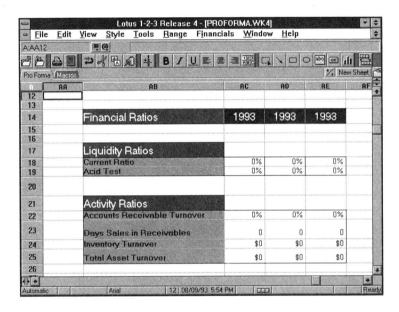

Getting the total picture.

To **PRINT** the balance sheet, use the Print Balance Sheet command from the Financials menu (talk about déjà vu!).

If you encounter any aliens while trying to **PRINT** the balance sheet, check the contents of cell B:D36. It points to a printer setup file called PROFORM1.AL3. Edit the file path, if necessary.

NEW KID ON THE BLOCK

12

If you're starting a new company, you already know the odds against success. But if you have a plan, you can meet the future with open eyes. (What a concept!) The Start Up worksheet's designed to help you open them.

 Open the STARTUP.WK4 file from the \123R4W\HYPER directory.

 Choose File Save As, and save the file under a new file name, such as STARTUP1.WK4. This is for your protection. Should you make some changes to customize the worksheet and then hate them, you can go back to the beginning by using the original file.

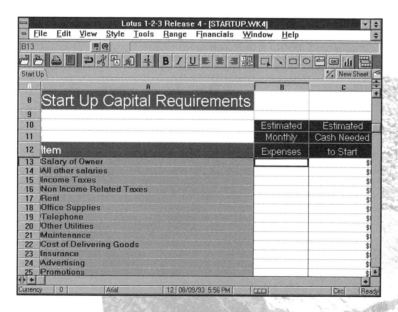

Open wide.

This project's relatively easy: Just plug in the numbers in the estimated monthly expenses (column B). Based on federal guidelines, the start-up costs for a single month are multiplied by two or three times. The total of these monthly costs are then added to one-time start-up costs to calculate a good estimate for the amount of cash you're going to need to start your business and keep it running.

Like the previous projects, be sure to change cell A:A5 to something more meaningful than "Your Company Name" (how about "My Company"?). To print your estimate, simply click on the **Printer** icon. Combine this estimate with the last four projects, and you can compile a complete business plan!

KEEPING TRACK OF STUFF

13
PROJECT

If tracking inventory is part of your personal hell, here's a worksheet to save you. Open the Inventory worksheet, and let's take a look around the warehouse.

There are several worksheets in this project, and we'll go over each one in turn.

 Open the INVENTRY.WK4 file from the \123R4W\HYPER directory.

 Choose File Save As, and save the file under a new file name, such as INVENT1.WK4. This is for your protection. Should you make some changes to customize the worksheet and then hate them, you can go back to the beginning by using the original file.

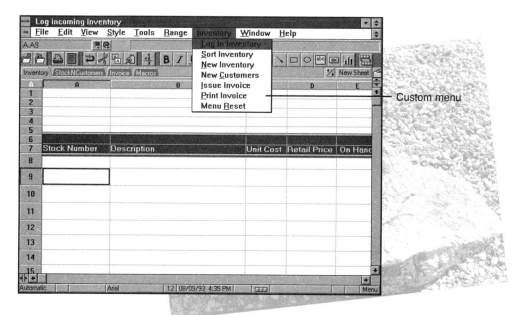

A tour of our little warehouse.

IN IT GOES, OUT IT GOES

With this worksheet, you can keep track of incoming and outgoing inventory:

 First, set up some inventory to keep track of; use the Inventory New Inventory command, and complete the required information: stock number, description, unit cost, and retail cost.

 To log in some stuff, use the Log In Inventory command. Select an item from the inventory, and then enter the amount of new stock. This will be automatically added to the amount already in stock. Play with this option as long as you like; add additional stock to items already logged in, or add new stock items. Click Cancel to quit.

 If you're feeling out of sorts, you can resort the inventory with the Sort Inventory command on the Inventory menu. You can sort the inventory database in any number of ways: by description, unit cost, retail cost, etc.!

CHARGE IT!

The real beauty of this project is that it keeps track not only of inventory, but of your customers, too. When some stock is sold, complete an invoice, and it'll be automatically deducted from inventory.

But first, you have to have some customers. Use the New Customers command on the Inventory menu to add some.

After you've added some customers, follow these steps to create an invoice:

 Use the Issue Invoice command on the Inventory menu.

 Enter an invoice number.

 Select a customer.

 Enter a ship date.

 Select a shipper, and a method of payment.

 Select the items sold.

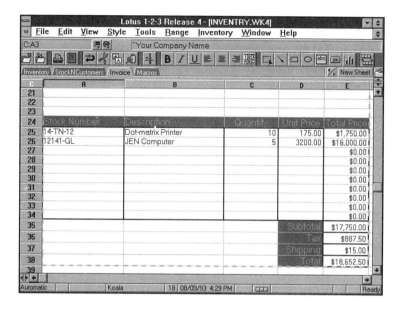

You break it, consider it sold.

A shipping cost is automatically added, based on the total and the shipper used. Cool, eh? To **PRINT**, use the Print Invoice command on the Inventory menu (again, make sure you change the cells C:A3..A5 to reflect your actual company name and address).

When you're through with the inventory file, be sure to select the Menu Reset command on the Inventory menu. This will reset the menu back to the Lotus standard. If you forget, no harm done; the menu doesn't work unless the Inventory worksheet is active. If it bothers you, enter {MENU-RESET} into a cell, select it, and use Tools Macro Run to run the reset command.

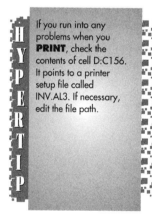

If you run into any problems when you **PRINT**, check the contents of cell D:C156. It points to a printer setup file called INV.AL3. If necessary, edit the file path.

BRIGHT IDEAS

There are many ways you can customize this worksheet:

◇ Change the shipping table to reflect actual costs in your area. The table is in cells D:N109..S117.

◇ Add information about each customer's home state, and add a table to calculate each state's amount. (Use the shipping table as an example.)

◇ Create a field for storing the invoice number, and then add one to it each time you print an invoice.

Checking your investments is easy with this project's worksheet. Before you dive in, you'll need some financial terms defined:

Annuity Any regular set of payments. For example, you may be socking $100 a month in an IRA, or receiving $100 a month as a kind of pension. Use the annuity part of the calculator to figure the value of your investment.

Amount Any flat sum. If you've invested $5,000, and you want to know how much it'll be worth in the future, or you want to know how much

you've got to invest now to get $5,000 some day, use the amount part of the calculator.

Goal Generally, some dollar amount you want to achieve. You can determine the investment required based on a particular interest rate, or a monthly amount to invest. Use the goal part of the calculator to help you with these calculations.

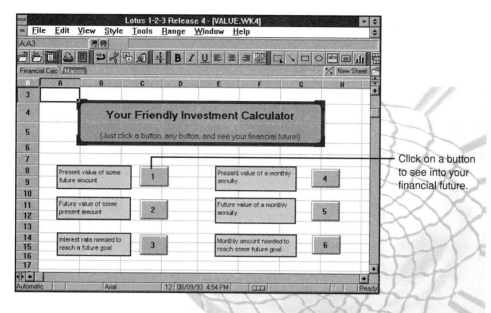

Click on a button to see into your financial future.

Makin' money.

1 Open the VALUE.WK4 file from the \123R4W\HYPER directory.

2 Choose File Save As, and save the file under a new file name, such as VALUE1.WK4. This is for your protection. Should you make some changes to customize the worksheet and then hate them, you can go back to the beginning by using the original file.

3 This worksheet has a special icon bar, so click on the SmartIcon icon at the bottom of the screen, and select Value sheet.

4 Using the calculator's easy: Just click on a button, fill in the required info, and you're outta here! You can **RETURN** to the calculator and perform additional calculations if you want.

To **RETURN** to the financial calculator, click on the **Return** icon (next to the File Save icon).

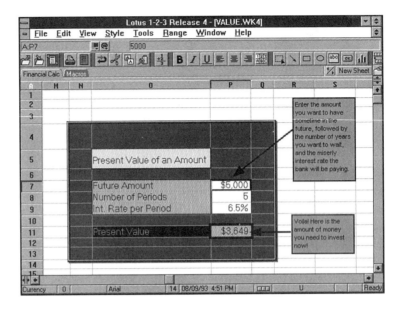

Figuring an investment.

BRIGHT IDEAS

To customize your financial calculator:

◇ Add a section where you plan your progress. Include the date, amount of payment, and current worth.

◇ Create a chart to keep track of your investment progress.

◇ Add a print macro to print each of the different financial analyses.

FORECASTING THE FUTURE (IN SALES)

PROJECT **15**

Whether you're planning a business—say, a lemonade stand in the front yard—or trying to take a look at how your employer's product may fare in the next few years or so, you'll find the FORECAST.WK4 template much more useful than a crystal ball.

This template lets you enter the preceding year's actual sales, and then lets you enter Worst Case, Most Likely Case, and Best Case growth percentage projections for the next eight years. It takes your data and plugs it into a preformatted graph, so you can look at the situation visually. Go to it!

PLUGGING IN THE NUMBERS

You get started by opening this template. From there, you choose a couple of menu options to help you enter data and take a look at results:

 Open the FORECAST.WK4 file from the \123R4W\HYPER directory. It opens and adds a new menu, **ASSUMPTIONS**, to the menu bar.

To remove the **ASSUMPTIONS** menu when you're done with this worksheet, choose Assumptions Menu Reset.

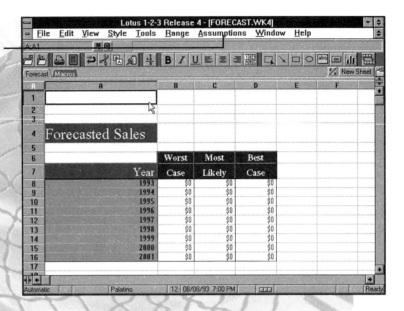

1-2-3 adds this handy-dandy menu for you.

---

2 Choose **File Save As**, and save the file under a new name, such as WIDGET.WK4.

3 Choose **Assumptions Prior Year Sales.** The Prior Year's Actual Sales dialog box appears.

4 Enter the total sales of the product for the last full year, and then click on OK. You don't need to enter any formatting like dollar signs or decimals.

5 Choose **Assumptions Growth Rate.** The first of three dialog boxes, Worst Case Percentages, appears.

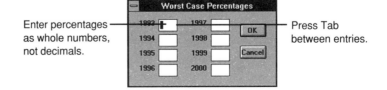

Enter percentages as whole numbers, not decimals.

Press Tab between entries.

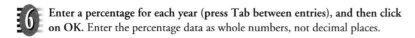

6 Enter a percentage for each year (press Tab between entries), and then click on OK. Enter the percentage data as whole numbers, not decimal places.

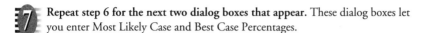

7 Repeat step 6 for the next two dialog boxes that appear. These dialog boxes let you enter Most Likely Case and Best Case Percentages.

8 Save the forecast. The data will remain intact until you **UPDATE** it.

When you **UPDATE** the data in this worksheet, press **F9** (CALC) to be sure all the values in the Forecasted Sales table are recalculated with the new percentages.

TAKING A LOOK AROUND

When you're done entering data, press **Home** to jump back to cell A1 and see the table of forecasted sales, in dollars. Conveniently, the worksheet also lets you jump to the graph it automatically creates for you. To see the graph, choose Assumptions View Sales Graph.

PRINTING OUT

Two named ranges help make printing out this worksheet easier. The range print1 prints the Forecasted Sales table and the Sales graph. Choose the range print2 to print out the Prior Year Sales dollar amount and the Growth Rate Assumptions (percentages you entered).

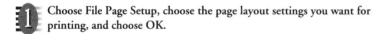

1 Choose File Page Setup, choose the page layout settings you want for printing, and choose OK.

2 Use the navigator or Edit Go To to choose the range name of the range you want to print.

3 Choose File Print, or click on the Print SmartIcon. The Print dialog box appears.

4 Change any print settings you want, and then click on OK.

BRIGHT IDEAS

If this template wasn't good enough or you want ideas for using it, here goes:

◇ Use the template to explore growth in product unit sales. When you enter the Prior Year's Sales, enter the amount in units. Enter all the percentages, and then reformat the output cells in the Forecasted Sales table with the Automatic style rather than the Currency style.

Make sure you add a label somewhere to remind yourself you're looking at sales "In Units."

◇ Use the template to set quotas for individual sales people or by regions. Add labels to explain what you're calculating.

381

GETTING PERSONAL (IN A BUDGET KIND OF WAY)

Spend a lot of time wondering at the end of each month where your money's flown off to? Feel like someone's been picking your pocket? Want to get a handle on your finances so you can save more? Well, here's a template for you.

This template lets you enter your expected income and expenses (and automate that entry). Then, month-by-month, when you enter your actual income and expenses, the template calculates the difference for you.

REVVING IT UP

You get started by entering the data for your budget. After you do so, the cells in rows 12, 31, and 33 automatically calculate the total amount you expect to

make, total budgeted expenses, and reveal the amount you should have left over for savings. Here's how to establish your budget:

 Open the file PERBUDGT.WK4 from the \123R4W\HYPER directory.

GETTING PERSONAL (IN A BUDGET KIND OF WAY)

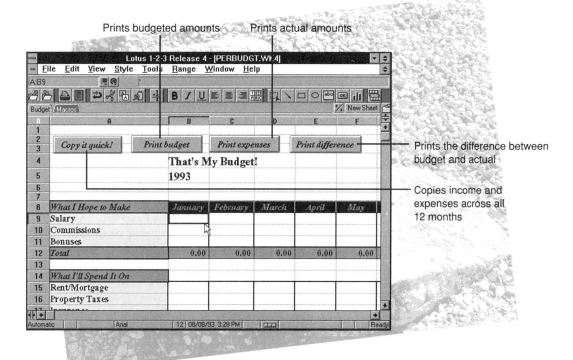

Prints budgeted amounts

Prints actual amounts

Prints the difference between budget and actual

Copies income and expenses across all 12 months

2 Choose File Save As, and save the file under a new name, such as 1993.WK4.

3 Enter your expected monthly salary, commissions, and expenses in cells A:B9..A:B11. Don't worry about entering these amounts across the columns.

4 Enter your expected monthly expenses in cells A:B15..A:B30. Again, you don't need to copy these amounts across by hand.

5 Press Home to go back to cell A1, and then click on the Copy It Quick! macro button.

6 Click to turn on the Salary and Expenses check boxes, and then click on OK. This copies the salary and expense amounts you entered across all 12 months.

 Go in and hand-adjust any entries you may need to. For example, you may want to increase your projected expense for Gas and Electric during the winter months.

 Save the budget.

THE MONTHLY UPDATE

This is where it gets ugly. Month-by-month, you need to open the template and enter your real earnings and expenses. After you do so, rows 50, 69, and 71 automatically total your actual income, actual expenses, and actual amount left to save, respectively. And, another **RANGE**, A:A102..A:N131, automatically calculates the budgeted and real income/expense amounts.

To go to the **RANGE** that calculates the differences between budgeted and actual amounts, click on the navigator, or choose **Edit Go** To and choose the range name **prtdiff**.

 Open the worksheet from the \123R4W\HYPER directory.

 Use the navigator or Edit Go to go to the range named prtexp.

 Use the arrow keys to move to the column for the month you need to enter expenses for.

 Make your entries down the column.

 Choose File Save, or click on the Save SmartIcon to save your work.

MAKING A PAPER TRAIL

Anytime you want, you can print your budget, real expenses, or the difference between the two. The template includes easy macro buttons that let you print each section in a neat landscape (horizontal) format. Note that if your printer doesn't let you print in landscape mode, you're on your own.

When the worksheet is open, press Home to go to cell A:A1.

 Click on the macro button that prints the section you want to see.

BRIGHT IDEAS

If you want to get really creative with this template:

◇ Change the fonts to make them jazzier.

◇ **CHANGE ROW NAMES** to meet your needs. For example, you may want to change "Clothing" to "Credit Cards."

◇ **ADD NEW ROWS** for other sources of income and expenses. For example, you might want to add an expense line for gifts. Just be sure to add the rows in between existing rows so your formulas are still accurate. You may need to add or adjust a formula here and there.

◇ Create a fake budget to show your significant other so you don't get in trouble.

> **HYPERTIP**
>
> When you **CHANGE ROW NAMES** or **ADD NEW ROWS** in one area of the worksheet, such as the Budget section, be sure you make exactly the same changes in the other sections, in this case the Expenses and Difference sections. Otherwise, the formula calculations in the Expenses and Difference sections will become completely meaningless.

LOVE YOUR CLUTTER

Have you ever really wondered exactly how much stuff you have filling up your house? You may not want to take on the monumental task of creating an inventory of your possessions, but you may need to do so for insurance purposes. And you'll be darn glad you did it if a meteor falls on your house and wipes out everything you have. Your insurance agent will already have proof that the insurance company owes you every bit of that $2.59.

This template automates the inventory procedure so that it's much less painful than it otherwise would be. Dialog boxes lead you through the task of entering items. You can sort the data, total the value of all of it or of specific types of items, print it, and more.

TAKING STOCK AND MAKING NAMES

Boom, baby! Here's how to enter items to your heart's content:

1 **Open the file HHINV.WK4 from the \123R4W\HYPER directory.** 1-2-3 adds the **INVENTORY** menu to the menu bar.

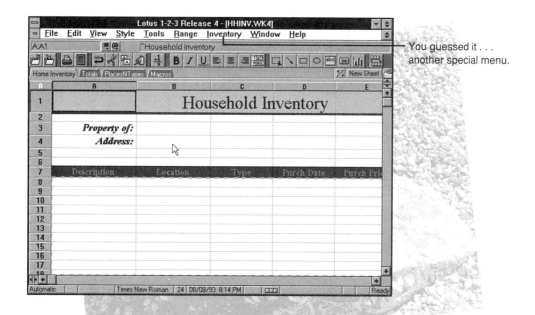

You guessed it . . .
another special menu.

 Choose File Save As and save the file under a new name, such as
HOUSE.WK4.

 Enter your name and address in cells B3 and B4.

 To start the database or add new entries, choose Inventory Log In Inventory.
The Description dialog box appears.

You can add more **ROOMS** and item **TYPES**. Choose Inventory New Places or Inventory New Types. Enter the name of a place or type. Then click the Home Inventory tab to return to the first worksheet in the file.

Respond to each dialog box that appears, making entries or selections, and clicking on OK when you're done. The dialog boxes are self-explanatory, but in case you need to hear the obvious, here's the lowdown on each:

Description—Enter a name for the item.

Now, where did I put that?—Double-click on the **ROOM** where the item is normally found.

What is it?—Double-click on an item **TYPE**.

When did I buy this?—Enter a purchase date.

I paid how much?—Enter a purchase price, no dollar signs.

So how much is this really worth?—Enter how much it would cost you to replace it, no dollar signs.

When the final dialog box asks if you want to update another item, click on OK to do so or Cancel to return to the worksheet.

Save the inventory.

SORTING IT ALL OUT

You may have reason to want to see how much junk you have in a particular room (thinking "garage sale," are you?) or you may need to sort it by Type, to look at the kinds of possessions that may need special insurance policy riders. You have the option of sorting the inventory or calculating a dollar total of items you search for. Here's how to do a sort:

Choose Inventory Sort Inventory. The Sorting the Inventory Database dialog box appears.

Click on the item you want to sort by, then click on OK. Your data is sorted.

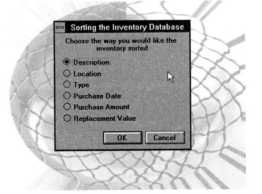

And, here's how to total selected items:

 Choose Inventory Inventory Totals. The Recap Criteria Selection dialog box appears.

 Click on the criteria (column name) you want to search by. You can turn on the check box for more than one criteria.

 As dialog boxes appear to ask you more specifics about the criteria you selected, respond to them, and click on OK. For example, if you choose Location in step 2, a dialog box appears and asks you to choose a room. After you **OK** this dialog box, 1-2-3 totals the items you specified and displays a total on the Totals worksheet.

IDIOT-PROOF PRINTING

It's pretty simple. Choose Inventory Print Inventory. It prints. Print one copy for your safety deposit box and one for your insurance agent.

BRIGHT IDEAS

You thought you'd hate this, but since it's so easy, you're looking for other ways to use this template. Here ya go:

◇ If you buy everything in bulk, use this template to inventory your stock. I always sleep better when I know how much toilet paper I have on hand.

◇ Use the inventory file to catalog your collections of things, like stamps or baseball cards. On the first sheet, you could change the location column header to "Country," then go to the PlacesNTypes worksheet, change "Location" to "Country," and replace the Location entries with country names.

◇ If you have business items to inventory, such as office supplies, you can use this worksheet.

A LOVE AFFAIR WITH YOUR CAR

18

PROJECT

For all but the truly anal-retentive, car care is usually handled on a need-to-do-it basis. That is, when you start getting a horrible smell or noise from the car, or a huge piece of it falls off in the middle of the road, you begin to care about the maintenance you need.

Keep your car from being found-on-the-road-dead. (My apologies to Ford owners.) This template not only provides a friendly table reminding you when regular maintenance should take place, but it also lets you enter when you actually do perform maintenance, and print your record automatically.

EASY DOES IT

Tracking auto maintenance is a matter of opening a file and plugging in what you've done:

 Open the file CAR.WK4 from the \123R4W\HYPER directory. 1-2-3 automatically displays the Auto SmartIcon set. The printer icon with the turquoise background is a special one created for printing this template with your data in it. A table of scheduled maintenance items runs down the left side of the worksheet. The different shades (columns) represent different mileage amounts when a particular type of maintenance should be due for the car. The mileage key is above and to the right.

The Auto SmartIcon set . . . with a special icon for printing.

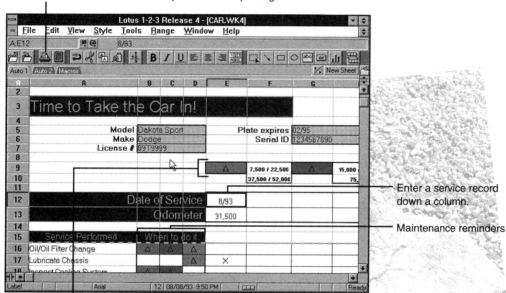

Enter a service record down a column.

Maintenance reminders

Key to maintenance reminders

2 Choose File Save As, and save the file under a new name, such as RIDES.WK4.

3 Enter the car Make, Model, License #, Plate Expires, and Serial ID in the appropriate cells.

4 To update the file to reflect having the car serviced, enter Date of Service and Odometer reading in the first available column to the right of those labels in the worksheet.

5 In the same column, type an X for each type of service received on that date. For example, putting an X beside Lubricate Chassis means you had the chassis lubricated on a particular service date.

 Click on the worksheet tab for Auto 2 to create a record for your other car.

 Save the maintenance file.

PUTTING IT DOWN ON PAPER

The Auto SmartIcon set includes a printer icon with a turquoise background. This icon simplifies printing, as follows:

 Click on the Printing SmartIcon. The Print Maintenance Record dialog box appears.

 Click on the button for Auto 1 or Auto 2, and then click on OK.

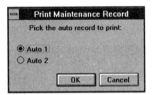

BRIGHT IDEAS

That's a good start, but you can do even more if you want to:

◇ Add more columns to the right as you need them. Start by formatting them with the same kind of borders and choosing the same number formats and alignments. Then, rename the ranges AUTO1 and AUTO2 to include the new columns you've added so the print macro works correctly.

◇ Convert it to a home maintenance worksheet by changing the maintenance items at the left.

TEAM TRACKER

Let's say, you (or your kid) are gearing up for a big season of softball, volleyball, soccer, or whatever. If you're really into it, you may want to track the teams and their scores. You may even have the horrible duty of being responsible for this.

Don't panic yet! This template can help. Enter scores, and you can calculate wins/losses, create a table ranking the teams, and show a chart tracking wins. Take this for a spin.

OPEN AND SHUT SCORES

This template has room for 20 teams and a 10-game season. Here's how to work it:

 Open the file SPORTS.WK4 from the \123R4W\HYPER directory. 1-2-3 automatically displays the Team SmartIcon set. The chart icon with the unique colors is a special one created for displaying a chart of team wins.

Click to chart the rankings.

Click to calculate wins and losses.

Click to create a ranking table.

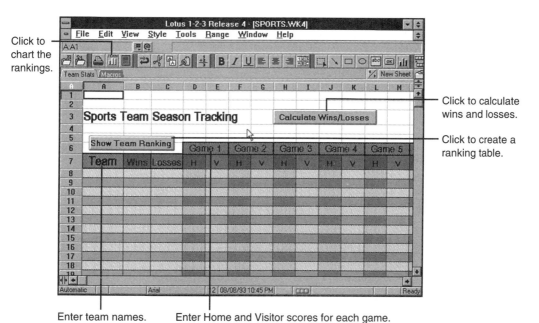

Enter team names.   Enter Home and Visitor scores for each game.

2   Choose File Save As, and save the file under a new name, such as SOCCER.WK4.

3   Enter the team names, as needed, in A8..A27 of the Team Stats worksheet.

4   To enter scores for a week, go to the column for that week and enter home team scores under H and visitor scores under V.

5   **Click on the Calculate Wins/Losses button.** The template calculates the wins and losses down columns B and C.

6   **Click on the Show Team Ranking button.** 1-2-3 jumps to a table that ranks the team by wins and losses.

7   **Click outside the team ranking table to deselect it.**

8   **Click on the SmartIcon for displaying a chart of the results.** You jump to the chart.

9   Save the file.

To put the Team SmartIcon set away, use the SmartIcon selector on the status bar to choose another set.

BRIGHT IDEAS

Feeling ambitious? Well, you can do a few more things:

◇   Print the scores and team rankings to distribute to others.

◇   If you have access to clip art, use sports graphics to spruce up the worksheets.

BE FIT OR DIE

You know how doctors who put you on diets always want you to write down what you eat in the hopes that public disclosure will embarrass you to keep you from eating. Well, you can use a similar (but more positive) kind of psychology to motivate yourself to stick with a fitness program.

As part of your motivational support system, we offer this fantastic, personal fitness tracker. So before you crack open that bag of potato chips, pump some iron and track it.

HUP, TWO, THREE, FOUR

This template lets you establish goals and track your progress for 13 weeks. Just do it!

1 **Open the file PERTRAIN.WK4 from the \123R4W\HYPER directory.**

2 **Choose File Save As, and save the file under a new name, such as START.WK4.**

3 **Choose Edit Go To, and choose the GOAL range.** Or you can use the navigator to go to that range.

4 **Enter your goals for Number of Reps and Body Stats.**

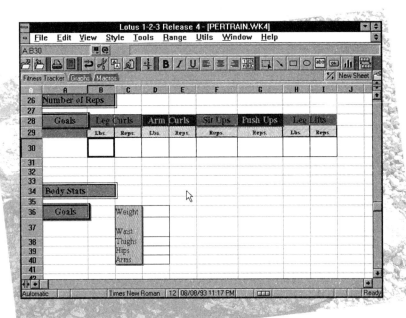

5 Press Home to go back to the top of the worksheet.

6 Enter your weight/reps from week to week.

7 Go to the range named body to enter the progress for your body measurements from week to week. Men can change the Hip Measurement label to Chest Measurement.

8 Save the file.

To remove the menu this template has **ADDED**, choose Utils Menu Reset.

PRETTY AS A PICTURE

You can get a graphical representation of your progress using the **U**tils menu, which is **ADDED** automatically to the menu bar when you open this file. Choose **U**tils Body **C**hart to take a look at your progress in meeting your target measurements, and **U**tils **E**xercise Chart for a peek at your strength and endurance improvements. The second command asks if you want to see the results by Reps or by Weight.

BRIGHT IDEAS

Can't get enough? Well:

◇ You can customize this worksheet for your exercise regimen. For example, if you're a runner, you can track Distance and Time instead of Weight and Reps. If you do stair climbing or step aerobics, you can track the Total Workout Time.

◇ Add a Reward section that tells you what you'll give yourself when you reach a particular goal. For example, anyone who reaches a goal weight clearly deserves a new Porsche—black, convertible.

◇ Create one for your kids. They'll love it.

PLACES TO SEE, PEOPLE TO DO

21

PROJECT

Keeping track of your time will be easy with this template, which stores up to five weeks of appointments, to-do lists, and what-have-yas.

 Open the file CALENDAR.WK4 from the \123R4W\HYPER directory.

 Choose File Save As and save the file under a new filename, such as CAL1.WK4. This is for your protection—the name is changed to protect the innocent.

 Select the Calendar SmartIcon bar. Click on the **SmartIcon** selector on the status bar and select **Calendar**.

 Enter a date in cell A:D6. As you sleep, that date is being used throughout the template to calculate all the other dates.

The top half of the worksheet is for tracking "to-dos," while the bottom half (which begins in cell A34) is for tracking appointments.

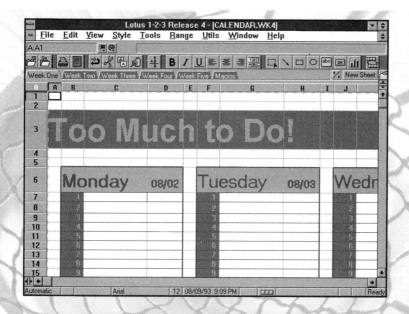

Just do it.

GIRLS (AND GUYS) JUST WANNA HAVE FUN

Now, we wouldn't give you a template as potentially boring as this without some surprises. Try this:

1 Move to cell A:C7 and enter something to do.

2 Press → to move to the next cell in the row.

3 Press Ctrl+F. Select the phrase that best fits your mood.

4 Press Enter or click OK, and an appropriate marker will appear!

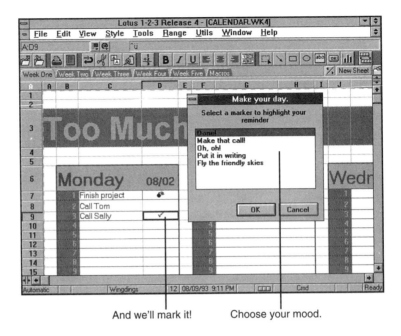

And we'll mark it!   Choose your mood.

Are we having fun yet?

I'M LATE! I'M LATE, FOR A VERY IMPORTANT DATE!

You can use the **CTRL+W** from any worksheet, not just the first one.

Now let's enter some appointments. Move on down to cell A:C37, and enter a fake appointment, such as a production meeting. Everything entered okay? Now, suppose that you have this meeting every week at the same time (darn). Instead of making the same entry over and over, just place the cursor in the cell you need to

copy, press **CTRL+W**, and a-way you goooo!

The macro copies the message to the same cell for all the weeks, cleverly skipping the Macro worksheet. Go ahead and click on another sheet and check it out.

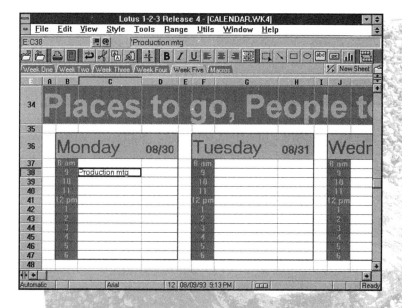

Copy cat!

KEEPING TRACK OF YOUR STUFF

The best way to keep track of the things you gotta do and the places you gotta be is to print them out after you've entered them.

 Press Ctrl+P

 Select a week to print, and it's done!

BRIGHT IDEAS

GE's not the only one with bright ideas. Here are a few:

✧   Add a macro to clear out old appointments. Use the eraser macro from Project 4 (see the range called CLEARALL) as a guide.

✧   Add more fun markers. From Program Manager, open the Accessories program group and click on **Character Map**. Select the Wingding font. Click on any

marker you want, then click on **C**opy. Switch to the Macros worksheet, cell F:O7. Paste. Format the cell you just pasted to as Wingding. After you add as many markers as you want, adjust the range FUNMARKER so it includes all the cells (both the descriptions and the markers).

INSTALLING 1-2-3 FOR WINDOWS

APPENDIX

When you install 1-2-3, you are copying program files from the 1-2-3 installation diskettes to your hard disk. 1-2-3 for Windows must be installed from Windows 3.0 or later by using the Program Manager.

 Insert the Install disk in the drive (A or B depending on the disk size and the configuration of your system).

 Click on the File menu, and then click on Run from the Windows Program Manager.

 In the Command Line text box type a:install if you inserted the install disk in drive A. Type b:install if the disk is in drive B.

 Choose OK. 1-2-3 displays the Welcome to Install window.

 Choose OK. 1-2-3 displays a series of dialog boxes to which you must respond to work your way through the installation program. Most of these dialog boxes are self-explanatory. However, if you need Help, use your mouse to click on the Help button contained in each dialog box, and 1-2-3 will display information about the options in the dialog box.

When you get to the Type of Installation dialog box, you will have to decide if you want the Default Install, Customized Install, or Install for Laptops.

DEFAULT INSTALL

If you choose **Default Install**, 1-2-3 will ask you to specify a disk drive and directory name for the 1-2-3 directory and then goes on to do the following:

- ◇ Copies files and features.
- ◇ Copies Help and sample files.
- ◇ Copies DataLens drivers.
- ◇ Adds icons to the Windows Program Manager.
- ◇ Sets 1-2-3 initial default settings.

The Default Install gives you a complete package, including the following additional features:

◇ Worksheet and File Audit capabilities.

◇ Backsolver, which finds values for one or more cells that make the result of a formula equal to a value you specify.

◇ Solver, which analyzes data in a worksheet and shows you a variety of possible answers to a problem.

◇ Lotus Dialog Editor, which lets you create custom dialog boxes.

◇ Macro Translator, which translates each {ALT} keystroke command in a 1-2-3 for Windows Release 1 macro to its 1-2-3 Release 4 equivalent.

◇ The Translate utility, which is a program that lets you convert data files to and from the 1-2-3 Release 4 file format.

◇ Spell Check, which checks for misspelled and repeated words in your worksheets.

CUSTOMIZED INSTALL

With **Customized Install**, you select which files and features you want. For example, if hard disk space is a concern, through Customized Install, you can specify not to copy Help and sample Files and features, such as the on-line tutorial and the animated tour of 1-2-3. Click on a **Select** button, click on the features you want to install to turn on the appropriate check box, and then click **OK**.

INSTALL FOR LAPTOPS

If you are installing 1-2-3 onto the hard drive of a laptop, choose **Install for Laptops**. This type of installation conserves hard disk space—often a precious commodity with laptops. Install for Laptops copies only the 1-2-3 program files to the 1-2-3 directory and does not transfer any additional features.

MORE SMARTICONS THAN YOU CAN SHAKE A STICK AT

APPENDIX

SmartIcons are those "clickable" pictures that make many 1-2-3 tasks quick and easy. A default set of SmartIcons is initially displayed at the top of the 1-2-3 worksheet window. You can use the **Tools SmartIcons** command to select one of several other specialized SmartIcon sets, to add your favorite SmartIcons to a set (by dragging them from the Available icons list to the list on the right), or to build your own customized sets. Here is a complete listing of the available SmartIcons and their descriptions.

Create a file
Open an existing file
Save the current file
Print the current selection
Preview the print selection
Close the active window
End the 1-2-3 session
Undo the last command or action
Cut to the Clipboard

Copy to the Clipboard
Paste Clipboard contents
Paste cell contents
Paste cell styles
Paste formulas as values
Paste a 1-2-3 file, DDE, or OLE link
Delete
Delete styles from a range
Sum values above or to the left
Complete a sequence in a selected range

Copy the topmost row to a range
Copy the leftmost column to a range
Copy the top left cell to a range
Fill a range with a sequence of values
Enter today's date
Find and replace characters
Select a range, drawn object, or query table
Go to the first cell in the next range
Go to the first cell in the previous range
Insert rows

Insert a range
Insert columns
Insert a worksheet
Delete selected rows
Delete a selected range
Delete selected columns
Delete selected worksheets
Embed data in the worksheet
Draw a chart using the selected range
Bold data

I	Italicize data
U	Underline data
U	Double-underline data
N	Remove bold, italics, and underline
	Change font and attributes
	Select a style template
	Copy a range's styles to another range
	Define or apply a named style
	Set color, pattern, border, and frame
	Add a range border and drop shadow

	Add a border to a range
	Align data to the left
	Center data
	Align data to the right
	Space data evenly
	Rotate data in a range
	Size columns to fit widest entries
$	Display values in Currency format
0,0	Display values in Comma format
%	Display values in Percent format

	Create and delete range names
	Work with versions and scenarios
	Transpose a range in place
	Sort in ascending order
	Sort in descending order
	Select several objects
	Draw a forward-pointing arrow
	Draw a double-headed arrow
	Draw a line
	Draw a segmented line

	Draw a polygon
	Draw a rectangle or square
	Draw a rounded rectangle or square
	Draw an ellipse or circle
	Draw an arc
	Draw freehand
abc	Draw a text block
OK	Draw a macro button
	Select all objects

	Increase the size of displayed cells
	Decrease the size of displayed cells
	Display cells in default size
	Show or hide parts of the 1-2-3 window
	Select the data to print
	Set rows as print titles
	Set columns as print titles
	Size data to printed page
	Size data by columns to printed page
	Size data by rows to printed page

	Insert a horizontal page break
	Insert a vertical page break
	Set orientation to portrait mode
	Set orientation to landscape mode
	Set the printed page layout
	Turn macro recording on or off
	Run a macro
	Select a macro command
	Turn Trace mode on or off

	Turn Step mode on or off
	Show or hide the Transcript window
	Create a query table
	Cross-tabulate values from a database table
?=	Find solutions that meet constraints
abc	Check spelling
	Send data by electronic mail
	Arrange open windows side by side
	Arrange open windows diagonally
	Go to top left cell

	Find bottom right corner of active area
	Find next cell up adjoining blank cell
	Find next cell down adjoining blank cell
	Find next cell right adjoining blank cell
	Find next cell left adjoining blank cell
	Go to the next worksheet
	Go to the previous worksheet
	Display contiguous worksheets
	Recalculate the worksheet
	Audit cells

	Find formulas
	Find cell dependents
	Find formula precedents
	Find DDE links
	Find links to 1-2-3 files
	Customize SmartIcons
	Select the next set of SmartIcons
	Start Ami Pro
	Start Lotus Dialog Editor
	Start Freelance Graphics

	Start Lotus Organizer
	Start Improv
	Start Lotus Notes
	Start cc:Mail
¥	Display values in Currency format
£	Display values in Currency format
	Start the Macro Translator
	Start File Manager
	Display the DOS prompt
	Start SmartPics

INDEX

INSTALLING THE DISK

The disk that comes with this book has some pre-fab worksheets and fun shareware programs all designed to make your day in 1-2-3 for Windows more enjoyable. Here's how to install the **DISK CONTENTS** to your hard drive, so you can begin working through Part 8 of this book, which features 21 neat projects:

1 Take the disk from the back of the book and place it in your floppy drive.

2 Go to the Windows Program Manager and double-click on the File Manager icon in the Main program group.

3 Use the File Create Directory command to create the following subdirectories on your hard drive:
\winpak
\noise
\hyper (create this subdirectory under the \123r4w directory, which is the main directory created when you install 1-2-3 for Windows, so that the total directory path is \123r4w\hyper)

4 Double-click on the drive icon for the floppy drive that's holding the disk for this book. You should now have two windows on-screen. To make things easier, you may want to choose the Window Tile command, then scroll down in the window for your hard drive until you see the directory you need.

5 Copy the following files from the floppy disk to the specified drive on your hard drive (you can drag to copy or use the File Copy command):

hyper.exe—Copy to the \123r4w\hyper directory
sheetico.exe—Copy to the \123r4w\programs\sheetico directory (this directory is created when you install 1-2-3 for Windows)
winpak#1.exe—Copy to the \winpak directory you created
noise.exe—Copy to the \noise directory you created

6 Still in the File Manager, double-click on each of the .exe files you just copied to your hard drive. Double-clicking the file extracts other files compressed in the .exe files. The extracted files are placed in the same directory as the .exe file that contained them.

7 To finish setting up the files you just extracted in the \winpak directory, go to Project 2; to install what you just put in the \noise directory, go to Project 3. The rest of the extracted files are ready to go. Check them out in Projects 4 through 21.

MORE THAN JUST A PRETTY BOOK

Sure, you could buy this book just because it has a cool cover and a lot of fun projects, but why? There's a much better reason: the cool free and shareware stuff on the disk in the back. On it, you'll get:

◇ WinPak#1, a superb collection of fun Windows icons, fonts, and screen savers (for Project 2).

◇ A speaker driver program that lets your PC speaker function as a sound card, if you're not lucky enough to have such a beast installed. You'll also get some WAV files (sound files) you can play in Windows (for Project 3).

◇ Preprogrammed spreadsheets that let you tackle these practical (well, okay, some of them are frivolous) projects:

Trip Planner: Project 4
Employee Database: Project 5
Company Phone List: Project 6
Breakeven Analysis: Project 7
Business Budget: Project 8
Cash Flow Projection: Project 9
Pro Forma (Income) Statement: Project 10
Balance Sheet: Project 11
Small-Business Plan: Project 12
Inventory: Project 13
Future Value of an Investment: Project 14
Sales Forecast: Project 15
Personal Budget: Project 16
Home Inventory: Project 17
Car Repair/Expense Tracker: Project 18
Sports Team Tracker: Project 19
Personal Fitness Tracker: Project 20
Business Calendar: Project 21

WinPak#1 is shareware, which means the authors are letting you try it for free in hopes that you will enjoy it. If you like a program and end up using it often, you are required to pay for the program (usually some small amount), and in return for your honesty, the author will send you an even better version. Registration information is bundled with the program.